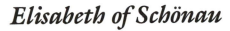

Elisabeth of Schönau

University of Pennsylvania Press
MIDDLE AGES SERIES
Edited by
EDWARD PETERS
Henry Charles Lea Professor
of Medieval History
University of Pennsylvania

A listing of the available books in the series appears at the back of this volume

Elisabeth of Schönau

A Twelfth-Century Visionary

Anne L. Clark

upp

University of Pennsylvania Press

Philadelphia

Library of Congress Cataloging-in-Publication Data
Clark, Anne L.
    Elisabeth of Schönau: a twelfth-century visionary / Anne L. Clark
    p.   cm.
    Includes bibliographical references and index.
    ISBN 0-8122-3123-6
    1. Elisabeth, of Schönau, Saint, 1129–1164.   2. Visions—History.
I. Title.
BX4700.E39C57   1992
282′.092—dc20
[B]   92-12937
                                                              CIP

BX
4700
.E39
C57
1992

For my mother and father

Contents

viii   Contents

Acknowledgments

QUITE A FEW YEARS HAVE ELAPSED since I first came upon the texts of Elisabeth of Schönau that are printed in the *Patrologia Latina*. At the time I was collecting material about individuals in the twelfth and thirteenth centuries who considered themselves or were considered by their contemporaries to be "prophets" or recipients of divine revelation. I was intrigued by the willingness of some medieval Christians to use the categories of prophecy or divine inspiration to interpret particular types of religious experience and particular types of oral or written discourse that were understood to be the product of these experiences. At the same time—those days of graduate school when one pursues more than one project at a time—I was also enrolled in Joan Ferrante's seminar, "Women in Medieval Life and Literature." It was my introduction to women's visionary literature, and I felt that a whole new world of medieval Christianity was opening to me.

The present book bears vestiges of these roots, whether it be in the discussion of twelfth-century prophetic models or in the comparison of Elisabeth's texts with those of other female visionaries. But in the meantime, much has also happened in the development of this book, and it is my joy to acknowledge the help I have received both from individuals and institutions in my research and writing. I am grateful to the following libraries for making available to me microfiche or microfilm copies of manuscripts: Stadtarchiv in Cologne, Hessische Landesbibliothek in Fulda, Universitäts- und Landesbibliothek in Halle (Saale), Bayerische Staatsbibliothek in Munich, the Bistumsarchiv and the Stadtbibliothek in Trier, Hessische Landesbibliothek in Wiesbaden, Hill Monastic Manuscript Library in Collegeville, and Centre National de la Recherche Scientifique in Paris. I would also like to thank the librarians and staff members at the Bodleian, the Stadtarchiv in Cologne, the Bayerische Staatsbibliothek, the Stadtbibliothek in Trier, and the Hessische Landesbibliothek in Wiesbaden for their help during my visits to their collections. I also gratefully acknowledge permission from the following libraries to quote from their manuscripts in this book: Österreichische Nationalbibliothek in Vienna,

Bibliothèque de la Sorbonne, and Bibliothèque Municipale of Avignon. I would also like to thank Seth Kasten, the head of User Services at the Burke Library of Union Theological Seminary in New York, for his interest and assistance in this project. The interlibrary loan staff of the Bailey-Howe Library at the University of Vermont has never flinched at the number or obscurity of my requests, and I offer them my thanks. The University of Vermont Committee on Research and Scholarship provided me with a generous summer stipend in 1989 to support my work on this project.

I have had the immense benefit of discussing my research with many people. The earliest stage of this research was facilitated by helpful letters from Kurt Köster and Ruth Dean. Conversations, sometimes in person, sometimes conducted via telephone, mail, or electronic mail, with Katherine Gill, Kathy Mooney, Brian Patrick McGuire, Timothy Reuter, and Sigrid Krämer have greatly contributed to my understanding of various aspects of medieval Christendom. Joan Ferrante, in addition to providing the setting for my first engagement with medieval women's writings, also read and responded to my dissertation with thoughtful attention. My adviser at Columbia, Robert Somerville, supported this project with his critical reading, his asking of difficult and important questions, and his suggestions of clues to begin answering them. I take great pleasure in thanking him for his valuable help and continued support. I would also like to thank Caroline Walker Bynum for her reading of this work, her many insightful suggestions, and her encouragement. The two reviewers for the University of Pennsylvania Press offered constructive and thorough responses to this book, from which I have benefitted. My colleagues at the University of Vermont have provided a stimulating context for ongoing conversation that has helped broaden my perspective on the material I study. This book is so much the richer for the insights and criticism I have received, though any of these colleagues, friends, and advisers may question what I've done with his or her offering. I dedicate this book in appreciation to my parents, who have also taught me many things. And finally, I would like to thank my husband, Kevin Trainor, for his unfailing support and his questions about the study of religion, both of which have contributed greatly to the completion of this project.

1. Introduction

Medieval Women and Modern Research

From the twelfth to the fifteenth century, many women revered for their holiness were women who claimed to have had an extraordinary type of religious experience: they saw visions.[1] These visions were understood to have a divine origin. Much of the religious writings attributed to women of this period are records of the revelations communicated in these visions. The following study of the twelfth-century nun, Elisabeth of Schönau, is an exploration of this aspect of medieval women's piety. It is a portrayal of the life of one woman whose interior experience, which she believed to be divinely inspired, led her to announce what she saw for the sake of the salvation of the world.

At the age of twenty-three, Elisabeth began to experience a series of visionary ecstasies which continued intermittently until her death thirteen years later. In a prologue to the collection of her visions, we are told by Elisabeth's brother Ekbert that he wrote down everything that was revealed to his sister by an angel of the Lord.[2] These writings consist of three series of chronologically arranged visions, a visionary work of moral exhortation entitled *Liber Viarum Dei*, a collection of revelations about the martyrdom of Saint Ursula and her eleven thousand companions, a series of visions about the bodily assumption of Mary, and several extant letters of Elisabeth, many of which also claim to offer divine revelation rather than mere human insight. The pages of these visionary records reflect a varied series of subjects ranging from a concern for spiritual guidance within the monastic life to a pervasive interest in the otherworld and its connection with this world.

Elisabeth spent almost all of her life within the walls of the convent at Schönau. Schönau, which belonged to the diocese of Trier and was located about ten kilometers east of the Rhine, was a Benedictine monastery with a women's and a men's community. Hildelin, the first abbot of the monastery, witnessed the entry of the young Elisabeth at age twelve and later encouraged her extraordinary career. About three years after Elisabeth's visions began, her brother Ekbert relinquished his promising career as a canon at St. Cassius in Bonn and retreated to Schönau to take up the life of a Benedictine monk. Among his various duties within the community, Ekbert served as Elisabeth's secretary, and he became abbot after Hildelin's death.

Despite Elisabeth's relative isolation in this rather obscure place, her reputation as a woman specially gifted by God soon spread beyond the walls of Schönau. The records of Elisabeth's visionary experiences circulated extensively: there are 145 known medieval manuscripts, forty-five of which transmit collections of these texts, while the remainder transmit individual works or fragments thereof.[3] By the end of the fifteenth century, Elisabeth's visions had been translated into Provençal, German, and Icelandic. The number of manuscripts of her visions as well as the mention made of her in contemporary chronicles demonstrate the appeal of this nun and her revelations.

Many factors complicate the picture of Elisabeth's experience and her popularity: the paucity of biographical information; the role of her brother Ekbert as secretary and editor of the visionary corpus; the association of Elisabeth with the dubious "discovery" and distribution of the relics of Saint Ursula and her eleven thousand virgin companions; the extreme physical and emotional torments that accompanied her visions. Some later readers have not only found these afflictions distasteful, but have also seen in them cause for questioning the "truth" of her visions. It is, of course, not the purpose of this study to judge the "truthfulness" of Elisabeth's visions. Rather, the aim is to present a comprehensive examination of the extant records of Elisabeth's experiences as well as other documents that illuminate the context of her career and subsequent reception and influence.

As a study of Elisabeth's life, this book takes its place within a rapidly expanding field. The religious life of medieval women in recent years has received considerable attention,[4] and there are obvious reasons why this should be the case. Feminist theory has inspired scholars of many disciplines to investigate aspects of women's experience that had been largely ignored or misunderstood. The results of such new research are seen in significant additions to and revisions of the historical record. For example, uncovering patriarchal structures in the medieval Christian church has been a major contribution of feminist historians of the Middle Ages.[5] The present study builds on this work, for one must recognize the pervasive misogyny in the worldview and the social organization of medieval Latin Christendom in order to understand the life and religious experience of a woman in this period. But the emphasis of this study is on the latter—the life and religious experience of Elisabeth of Schönau—rather than the former. Thus while the repressive circumstances of Elisabeth's world—for example, the enforced dependence of women's communities on men to provide spiritual and administrative services and the general ideology of women's subordinate nature—are highlighted in this study, my intention has been to draw a picture of *how* Elisabeth lived in this world. In pursuing an essentially biographical endeavor, I have looked at the symbols by which one individual struggled to interpret her own life and make it meaningful. And the symbols that she used were the symbols of her world, of Christian life and practice in a Benedictine monastery in the Rhineland in the mid-twelfth century. The present study is therefore an examination of the influence of religious and political environment on the life of Elisabeth, and of the way in which she adopted and at times transformed the symbols that she inherited to make sense of her own place within the world. Because this was my goal, I have devoted considerable attention to analyzing such questions as Elisabeth's commitment to the veneration of particular saints and her interest in the otherworldly fate of deceased acquaintances. These are not the types of subjects one sees greatly developed in much of the early feminist scholarship on medieval women, largely because these issues do not immediately correspond to modern feminist interests. But as one can see in some more recent scholarship, a substantially broadened scope of inquiry, balanced in a more nuanced, potentially less anachronistic theoretical framework, allows for a much richer interpretation of the complexity of women's religious lives in this distant period.[6]

A study of Elisabeth's life brings us into that disputed territory known as the twelfth century. While subject to the general criticism of all such arbitrary periodizations, the "twelfth century" nonetheless remains a very fruitful working construct for many medievalists.[7] There has been as yet no systematic attempt to survey the religious life of women in this period and to place it within the larger spiritual currents of the time.[8] For this reason, "twelfth-century female spirituality" has yet to be adequately characterized. Frequently, Elisabeth and Hildegard of Bingen, two of the most visible women in this period, are associated with the *mulieres sanctae* of the thirteenth century and beyond, despite at times profound differences between their religious lives and those of later women. This is not to suggest that there was a monolithic religious consciousness for all women of the twelfth century. In fact, the following pages make clear the distinctions between Elisabeth and Hildegard and suggest ways in which Elisabeth both corresponded to and diverged from her other contemporaries. Thus this analysis of Elisabeth's life is part of a larger effort to delineate the religious life of women in this crucial period of transition and vitality within Latin Christendom.

When I refer to Elisabeth's spirituality as "visionary," I refer to her claim of extraordinary sensory experience and the development of her religious life on the basis of that experience. I do not thereby intend to imply that visionary spirituality constitutes one particular type of religious experience with specific characteristics or phases.[9] Nor have I found any typology of "mystic versus the church" that adequately characterizes Elisabeth's life.[10] Such a model, often implicit in recent research on medieval women, fails to do justice to the complexity of Elisabeth's relationships with individual representatives of the ecclesiastical hierarchy and to her profound commitment to reform. Furthermore, Elisabeth's insights about herself and her world cannot be described as representing a feminist consciousness. This, of course, is not surprising since she was not a part of the historical culture in which the modern feminist movement has proposed various theoretical analyses of society.[11] Yet her awareness of her femaleness and its implications for her place in the world and her attempt to articulate her specifically female religious identity are crucial aspects of her spirituality. Thus Elisabeth's life and thought offer a rich possibility for viewing how a twelfth-century woman developed her self-understanding and stance toward her world and the world beyond.

While there has been no comprehensive examination of her life and visionary works until this study, Elisabeth has not been lost to the scholarly world. In fact, her name frequently appears in surveys of spirituality and mysticism, in histories of the Benedictine order, and sometimes even in general surveys of church history.[12] Often in such works, Elisabeth is compared to Hildegard of Bingen, her older and more celebrated contemporary. There are many reasons for this association: they were both Benedictine nuns from the Rhineland who claimed to receive divinely ordained visions as well as instruction to proclaim their newly gained revelation. Letters between these two extraordinary women are extant, and Elisabeth refers in her *Liber Viarum Dei* to having visited Hildegard. Furthermore,

Elisabeth was influenced by Hildegard, especially by her *Scivias*, which was completed in 1151, one year before Elisabeth's visions began.

Accounts of the association between Elisabeth and Hildegard date back almost to their own days. In the last quarter of the twelfth century, the annals of the Premonstratensian house at Pöhlde, an establishment with very close ties to Schönau (Ruotger, the brother of Elisabeth and Ekbert, was provost from 1156 until 1163), included the following notice at the year 1158: "In these days, God showed signs of his power in the weak sex in two of his handmaids, namely, Hildegard in Rupertsberg near Bingen and Elisabeth in Schönau, whom he filled with the spirit of prophecy, and he revealed many kinds of visions to them."[13] But unlike the *Annales Palidenses*, which, for obvious reasons, goes on to describe at length some of Elisabeth's visions, recent attention has focused more on Hildegard than Elisabeth. This is not surprising given Hildegard's more extensive and diversified corpus of writings. Beside Hildegard's highly evocative and, at times, idiosyncratic formulations of thought, Elisabeth's visions sometimes appear pedestrian. Thus, although Elisabeth has been included in numerous historical accounts, notice of her significance has often been limited to dismissive comparisons with Hildegard.[14] The modern preference for Hildegard stands in contrast to the apparent medieval preference for Elisabeth's works, witnessed by the substantially greater number of manuscripts transmitting them.[15] In the present study, Hildegard is examined in the context of her relationship with Elisabeth, but a comparison of the two visionaries is not here the primary basis for understanding the significance of Elisabeth's life.

Beyond the notice she has received in surveys, Elisabeth has also been examined in the context of research about the growth of the cult of Saint Ursula. Within the corpus of visionary records attributed to Elisabeth are found a series of visions and several letters concerned with identifying specific relics believed to be of the companions of Saint Ursula. Elisabeth's visions also provided hitherto unknown details about the martyrdom of the saintly company, including the presence of a certain Pope Cyriacus, whose name and existence had otherwise escaped the notice of all historians until Elisabeth's day! Two scholars have made significant contributions in piecing together the history behind these most imaginative visions of Elisabeth. Wilhelm Levison has disentangled the confusing stages of the growing legend about the martyred virgins and has described Elisabeth's role in this development.[16] Guy de Tervarent has shown the connection between the dispersal of the newly discovered Ursuline relics and the popularity of textual versions of the Ursuline legend such as that of Elisabeth's *Revelatio de sacro exercitu virginum Coloniensium* (hereafter, *Revelatio*).[17] These studies point to, without explicitly taking up, many interesting questions about Elisabeth herself, a subject beyond their immediate scope.

Another incident recorded in the visionary corpus has recently attracted comment and provided the focus for a number of discussions.[18] At one point Elisabeth describes a vision of a beautiful virgin sitting in the middle of the sun. When she asks her angelic interpreter what this signifies, she is told that the virgin is "the sacred humanity [*sacra humanitas*] of the Lord Jesus." At the urging of others, Elisabeth asks the angel why the humanity of Christ is represented by a female rather than a male form. At this, the angel offers an alternate explanation in which the virgin represents the holy virgin Mary.[19] This incident provides an interesting opportunity to study several aspects of Elisabeth's visionary experience: the process whereby Elisabeth has a vision and then arrives at an understanding of it, her nontraditional use of gender imagery, and the external pressures she confronted when proclaiming a message that deviated from a conventional articulation of the church's faith.

Alongside these interpretative studies of her specific visions stands the significant scholarly work that traces the diffusion of Elisabeth's visionary records. All the analyses of Elisabeth's visions done in the twentieth century have been based on the edition of the Schönau material produced by F. W. E. Roth in 1884.[20] While Roth printed more of the texts associated with Elisabeth than any of the previous editions (all of which were based to some degree on the 1513 edition of Jacques Lefèvre d'Etaples), this edition nonetheless has serious deficiencies. These problems have been demonstrated by Kurt Köster, who documented the chronological order in which the visionary records were produced, catalogued the manuscripts transmitting Elisabeth's visions, and noted the various redactions of the visionary texts.[21] My own examination of twenty-six manuscripts has allowed me to establish an outside control on Roth's edition, to revise Köster's theory of the transmission of Elisabeth's texts, and to feel confident that no major new discoveries of texts by Elisabeth will be made.[22]

A total reconstruction of what happened in the monastery of Schönau in the middle of the twelfth century is, of course, not possible. But a close investigation of the visionary records as well as other pertinent documents, including Ekbert's own compositions, does shed considerable light even on some of the more vexing questions surrounding the life of Elisabeth.

From this analysis emerges a portrait of a mid-twelfth-century woman who, though exceptional enough to leave us with a rich record of extraordinary religious experience, nevertheless also offers us rare insight into some of the more common hopes, beliefs, and frustrations of a pious woman of her day.

Reform and Religious Agenda in Mid-Twelfth-Century Germany

The brief career of Elisabeth of Schönau, occurring at the mid-point of the twelfth century, began after three decades of relative ecclesiastical peace in Germany. The signing of the Concordat of Worms in 1122 and the failure of the Salians to hold the throne in 1125 had led to a temporary respite in the bitter struggle between empire and papacy. Under Emperor Lothar III and his successor, King Conrad III, little resistance was offered to the party of ecclesiastical reform in Germany.[23] It was not until 1152, the same year in which Elisabeth proclaimed the onset of her visionary experience, that Frederick Barbarossa succeeded in securing the German throne and that the Empire was poised for another round of confrontations between *regnum* and *sacerdotium*. This intervening period, from roughly 1122 until the mid-1150s, has been called by one commentator "an interruption of Gregorianism," a period in which the elaboration of the papal monarchy as part of the papal reform program gave way to ideals less marked by political expediency and more concerned with enshrining an ascetic spirituality as a central part of ecclesiastical life.[24]

This interlude is perhaps best represented by the individual whose personality looms so large in it, that is, Bernard of Clairvaux. Bernard's influence, ranging from his role in convincing Lothar III to support Innocent II in the disputed papal election of 1130, to his ability to inspire the recruitment of hundreds of Cistercian monks, is well known. What is most important about Bernard for our purposes is his concern for the moral and spiritual state of the professional religious whose duty it was to guide members of Christendom to their salvation. *De consideratione*, his treatise of advice to his spiritual son Pope Eugene III completed in 1152 or 1153, is the most extended and best known of Bernard's reflections on the need for ecclesiastical leaders to adhere to their spiritual commitments while performing their often distracting and worldly duties.[25] In the midst of his own meditation upon the mystical union of the Bride and Bridegroom,

Bernard decries the present state of the church, whose worst enemies are no longer those who attack it from the outside but ecclesiastical leaders whose hypocrisy and avarice continually corrode the church's edifice from within:

> Today a stinking plague spreads throughout the whole body of the Church, and the more widespread it becomes—the more desperate! The more internal it becomes—the more dangerous! . . . They are ministers of Christ, yet they serve the Antichrist. They march along, honored with the possessions of the Lord, but they offer the Lord no honor. Thence this whorish splendor, this histrionic posture, this regal pomp which you see everyday. . . . For this, they wish to be and they *are* heads of churches, deans, archdeacons, bishops and archbishops.[26]

Absent from this critique is any direct condemnation of a specific political force or circumstance that would have led to these abuses. Bernard instead aims his accusations at the moral degeneracy of individuals who should be committed to a spiritual, even ascetic, life of the care of souls. It is this kind of concern for reform that marks much of the spirituality invigorating the church at this time. Thus a certain shift in spiritual priorities can be discerned. In the height of the Investiture Controversy, the so-called Gregorian party perceived the extirpation of lay intervention from the church as the necessary condition for any genuine reform within the church. Such an endeavor pitted pope against king and embroiled local ecclesiastical leaders in struggles to define their political relationships with their secular lords. But this dogged pursuit of ecclesiastical liberty from lay influence no longer claims the energy of many of the new and most visible spiritual leaders.[27]

The focus on regenerating the moral life of the clergy so that they can actively work for the salvation of all Christians provides the context for understanding the life of Elisabeth of Schönau.[28] In this setting, no simple dichotomy of papal versus imperial allegiance serves to illuminate fully the concerns of the people actively trying to shape the life of the church. Condemnation of clerical decadence and worldly ambition, for example, is not merely a propagandistic tool of imperial rhetoric, certainly not when it comes from someone like Bernard. Nor is it in the case of Elisabeth, even though, as noted above, her career coincides with a renewed tension between the German empire and the papacy. The difficulty of attributing polemical writings to either papal or imperial parties is evident, for example, in Elisabeth's pronouncements about the spread of the Cathar heresy. Her understanding of the spiritual renewal required for the church leads her to take up the issue of the increasing presence of the Cathars. Heresy, especially that of the Cathars, was likewise a major concern of the new reform party in the Curia.[29] But concern about the Cathars will also lead Elisabeth to a direct critique of the Roman papacy and even bring her to advocate the "emperor's choice" for pope, Victor IV, over Alexander III. We shall see that Elisabeth's visionary activity in general offers a very good case for examining how these spiritual concerns were articulated once it became evident that the issues of church liberty had not in fact been fully resolved.

Although the complex dynamics between papacy and empire and the agenda of internationally influential figures such as Bernard shape the broader context of Elisabeth's life, her life must also be seen within the fine web of relationships and concerns in her local sphere. The emergence of new religious orders, which were closely tied to the reform spirituality described above and which had several decades earlier caused controversy throughout western Europe, had made its mark on the Rhineland. Cistercian and Premonstratensian houses flourished here, and the Springiersbach reform of canonical life originated in the diocese of Trier. Elisabeth had familial as well as religious ties with these movements of apostolic spirituality. Yet for all her concern with the proper order of the church, there can be found in her visions little of the competitiveness, defensiveness, or criticism, or the catchwords of *vita apostolica* or poverty that characterized the emergence of these new groups.[30]

Elisabeth's indifference to these competitve concerns must be seen in contrast to the continuing attempts within these groups to define the proper mode of monastic spirituality, attempts of which she could not have been totally unaware. Her respected confidant, Hildegard of Bingen, received a searching letter of criticism from Abbess Tengswind of Andernach, the brother of Richard of Springiersbach. Andernach, a center of the women's Augustinian reform, was the home of three relatives of Elisabeth, one of whom was probably Tengswind's successor as abbess. Elisabeth corresponded with Hildegard as well as with her three relatives at Andernach on matters of great significance to her. But these matters did not include the debate on whether monastic life should be open to people of common as well as of noble birth, or any of the other issues on which Tengswind tactfully but unambiguously questioned Hildegard. This kind of polemical exchange finds no place in Elisabeth's thought. She evinces an implicit confidence in her Benedictine way of life,[31] and assumes a shared vocation of contemplation and virginity among all monastics. It is only when these traditional monastic concerns of contemplation and virginity are in question that she turns on her fellow monastics, such as the disreputable nuns in a convent in Bonn, with words of condemnation.

Elisabeth's own monastic environment was part of a movement that had its origins in an impetus for monastic reform. While little is known of the spiritual culture of Schönau apart from the activities of Elisabeth and her circle,[32] certain observations can still be made about the monastery's religious orientation. It was founded in 1114 as a Benedictine priory dependent on the abbey of Schaffhausen in Swabia. Schaffhausen itself was a center of the Hirsau movement, a movement which seems to have dominated the Benedictine scene in Germany from about 1080 to 1150.[33] Unlike Cluny, whose customary served as the basis for the Hirsau constitution, the monastic reform associated with Hirsau often included the establishment of nuns' cloisters in conjunction with those for monks.[34] Perhaps Elisabeth's confidence in her life as a Benedictine nun, unruffled by the appearance of other forms of life and spiritualities, was due in part to her experience from the age of twelve in an establishment that had a self-conscious commitment to reform of the church at large and to women's monastic life as part of that reform.

Furthermore, unlike the Cluniac movement, which stressed the *libertas* of monastery from lay as well as episcopal control, the Hirsau monasteries were aligned with both lay nobles and local bishops.[35] Thus Elisabeth's lack of concern with the freedom of church institutions from outside control might be seen not only as a result of the "interruption of Gregorianism," but also as related to her own specific monastic background. In fact, the connection between Hirsau monasteries and their bishops is exemplified in Elisabeth's letters to Archbishop Hillin of Trier, which reveal her view of the episcopal office as mouthpiece for her own pronouncements about the state of the universal church.[36] And the connection between Hirsau monasteries and lay nobles is exemplified in Elisabeth's relations with the family of Count Rupert of Laurenburg, the son of the founder of the Schönau priory and himself the patron responsible for converting Schönau into an independent monastery.

Elisabeth lived in an age that witnessed significant change in the possibilities of defining Christendom as a sovereign political entity and in defining the options for individual Christian lifestyles. Within these currents of change, she fused traditional elements of her monastic background with her sense of her interior experience to create a spiritual identity for herself and a vision for the life of the church.

2. The Life of Elisabeth

Despite his obvious interest in publicizing and promoting the experiences of his sister, and despite his obvious literary skills, Ekbert never wrote an extended, narrative account of Elisabeth's life. In fact, it appears that no medieval *Vita* of Elisabeth was ever produced.[1] What is known of Elisabeth's life and background is gleaned from autobiographical references within the visionary records, from Ekbert's brief introductory comments to the visions, and from his letter to his three kinswomen describing Elisabeth's death (*De Obitu Elisabeth* [hereafter, *De Obitu*]).

Elisabeth and Ekbert were not the only members of their family to have careers within the religious establishment. Their mother's paternal uncle Ekbert, whom Elisabeth saw in a vision enjoying his heavenly reward, was the bishop of Münster (1127 until his death in 1132), after having been a deacon at the Cologne cathedral and provost of St. Cassius in Bonn.[2] Both as deacon and as Bishop of Münster, Ekbert played an active role in supporting the reform movement. He emerged as a colleague of Rupert of Deutz and Abbot Rudolph of St. Trond in their opposition to the consecration of Alexander of Jülich to the episcopacy of Liège.[3] As bishop, Ekbert acted as an adviser to King Lothar III and, in this capacity, participated in the synod at Würzburg in 1130 in which Lothar decided to support Innocent II in his conflict with Anacletus II. Lothar sent Ekbert to Clermont to convey his recognition to Innocent, and after Lothar's meeting with Innocent at Liège in 1131, he sent Ekbert to Rome with a message of warning to Anacletus.[4]

But Bishop Ekbert of Münster is best remembered for his role in the events surrounding the conversion of the young Jewish moneylender from Cologne, Judas Levi. In his *Opusculum de conversione sua*, the baptized Hermann recounts his initial meeting with Ekbert at Mainz, where the visiting bishop found himself in need of the young moneylender's services. Judas, at the age of twenty, made the loan to Ekbert without requiring any security. Judas was later ordered by his elders to go to Münster and stay with Ekbert until the loan was repaid. The twenty-week stay at

Ekbert's court furnished Judas with his introduction to the Christian faith, including an opportunity to debate the merits of the faith with Rupert of Deutz, who was with Ekbert for a while. Judas also accompanied Ekbert on a visit to the Premonstratensian house at Cappenburg, and it was this establishment that he entered as a novice after his baptism. It appears that Hermann did not stay at Cappenburg, for there is documentary evidence for a "Herimannus Judaeus" at St. Cassius in Bonn from 1149 until 1153.[5] Not only was St. Cassius the place at which Ekbert had been provost before he became bishop at Münster, but it is also the establishment at which Ekbert's great-nephew Ekbert (of Schönau) was a canon. Hermann, the Jewish convert who referred to Bishop Ekbert as "that good shepherd [who] used to administer the nourishment of the word of God to the sheep entrusted to him,"[6] must later have known Bishop Ekbert's great-nephew and godson, Ekbert of Schönau.

From a vision similar to the one revealing Bishop Ekbert in the company of venerable deceased bishops, we learn the names of two other relatives of Elisabeth. However, unlike Bishop Ekbert, Helid, the maternal uncle of Elisabeth's father, and Theodericus, Elisabeth's maternal uncle, are still languishing in the pains of purgatory. Nothing but their names are given except for the fact that Helid is enduring punishment for his frequent jovial speech.[7]

Elisabeth's father Hartwig is also known only in name, and her mother's name has been lost. Emecho, Ekbert's successor as abbot of Schönau, wrote a life of Ekbert, but the first part of this document is no longer extant, so details of the family background are missing.[8] Other siblings include Ruotger, the prior of the Premonstratensian house of Pöhlde, and an unnamed sister who came "from afar" to Schönau for Elisabeth's funeral.[9] Another female relative—sister, cousin, or niece—is also among the nuns at Schönau.[10] Three other *cognatae* (cousins or nieces?) of Elisabeth and Ekbert are known. Guda, Hadewig, and Regelindis, the addressees of Ekbert's *De Obitu*, were members of the community of St. Thomas at Andernach.[11] Guda may have been the *magistra* at Andernach, although Ekbert's address to the three women does not distinguish her as such.[12] Simon, a later abbot of Schönau, was yet another relative, a nephew of Elisabeth and Ekbert.[13]

On the basis of their family connections, Elisabeth and Ekbert have been thought to be from a well-established family, perhaps of the minor nobility in the Rhineland.[14] It is also clear that their family came to have significant influence in, if not to dominate, the monastery at Schönau for at least two generations and it seems likely that there was some connection between Elisabeth's family and that of Count Rupert of Laurenburg, who had played an important role in establishing the house.[15] Elisabeth's vision about the deceased Count Rupert, her desire to inform his widow Beatrice of the prayers and alms needed to free him from purgatory,[16] and the presence of Beatrice at Elisabeth's funeral[17] suggest this relationship. A connection between Elisabeth's family and that of the Laurenburg counts would also be consistent with the fact that Elisabeth gained admission to the Benedictine convent at Schönau as a child.

The motivations for Elisabeth's entry at Schönau remain a mystery. Unlike Hildegard of Bingen, whose parents are said to have dedicated her, their tenth child, as a tithe to God at a hermitage at St. Disibod, and unlike numerous holy women of the thirteenth and fourteenth centuries whose entry into convents represents the fulfillment of a childhood desire to remain a virginal *sponsa Christi*, the absence of a biography of Elisabeth leaves the early years of her life without any of the standard hagiographical motifs, let alone factual information.[18]

In his earliest introduction to the visionary records, Ekbert sums up the pertinent information in two sentences. He tersely states that Elisabeth made her monastic profession at Schönau during the abbacy of Hildelin and that after eleven years in the monastery, at the age of twenty-three, in 1152, "she began to see visions."[19] Thus Elisabeth was born in 1128 or 1129 and was received into the Schönau monastery at the age of twelve. It appears that Elisabeth made her monastic profession as an adolescent, and Ekbert repeats this impression in *De Obitu*.[20]

Elisabeth's life as a Benedictine nun was not a time of serenity and well-being. Even before her visions began at the age of twenty-three, she perceived herself as tormented in an extraordinary way. At the beginning of the first book of visions, Elisabeth confesses that since the day she undertook her monastic profession, she has been continually besieged by the "arrows" of the Lord (cf. Psalm 37:3). She understands her various illnesses, as well as any tribulations of the sisters of her community, as the hand of the Lord upon her.

The beginning of Elisabeth's visionary experiences did not offer an end to her physical suffering, and her spiritual tribulation seems to have been aggravated. She describes herself as disoriented and increasingly overcome by sadness: "Nearly all my senses were topsy-turvy inside me."[21] This sadness led to tedium, food and drink had no appeal for her, and she soon tired of life. But she reports that God saved her from the final temptation of suicide, although even this did not spell the end of her suffering. Elisabeth's reflections on her time of melancholy exemplify what Urban Küsters has characterized as the revalorization of *tristicia* in the piety of this period. Traditionally condemned as a serious vice in monastic life, melancholy now became the medium of reflexive self-confrontation.[22]

In the first three years in which she received visions, Elisabeth was sometimes moved to tell the sisters of her community what she saw. She said that doing so relieved her of some of the torments she was enduring.[23] The *magistra* of the women's community, one of Elisabeth's confidants, seems to have sought the advice of Hildegard of Bingen about the younger woman's troubling episodes.[24] During this time, Elisabeth also confided her visions to Ekbert when he visited her. Although Ekbert as well as the other Schönau nuns began recording her visions, Elisabeth and Ekbert agreed not to publish them until after her death.[25]

Abbot Hildelin took a keen interest in what was happening to the young sister in his charge, and his active intervention led to an incident that left a severe impression on Elisabeth throughout the rest of her life. The background to this incident can be pieced together from a letter of Elisabeth to Hildegard and from the visionary records. One of the early collections of the visions includes the report of a vision which must have taken place some time before August of 1154.[26] Elisabeth reports that an angel appeared to her and conveyed a warning of future disaster in lurid apocalyptic terms. According to this prophecy, Satan would receive power from God for inciting violence on earth, the sun would be suffused in bloody red and covered by shadows, and Christians would cry out at the immense tribulation. Elisabeth's prediction of a calamitous punishment occurring in a year in which the Annunciation coincided with Good Friday, motivated in part, no doubt, by the anticipation of this occurrence in the year 1155, revived an apocalyptic expectation that had been popular since the end of the tenth century.[27]

Elisabeth kept this prophecy to herself until August 8, 1154, at which time she felt compelled by the angel to reveal it to Abbot Hildelin. According to her letter to Hildegard, Elisabeth then begged Hildelin not to publicize this particular vision. In response, he ordered her to pray for a sign indicating whether the prophecy should be revealed or kept secret. On the feast of Saint Barbara (December 4), Elisabeth had a vision in which an angel exhorted her to preach penance. Hildelin interpreted this as a divine message to proclaim the prediction of imminent destruction, which he did "in the presence of magistrates of the church and religious men." Not surprisingly, some of these venerable men did not receive the word of doom with reverence, and some even accused Elisabeth of being tricked by the deceiver transformed into an angel of light (cf. 2 Cor. 11:14).[28] Elisabeth was ordered to test the angel, a task she undertook only with great trepidation and only because she was bound by obedience to do so. Within the course of the next several months, her experiences were enough to convince at least Hildelin, who left the monastery for a public preaching tour. His penitential preaching, interwoven with the dire threats that were part of Elisabeth's vision, moved many to great acts of penance during Lent of 1155. But something went wrong. Some unknown but zealous believer sent letters in Hildelin's name to Cologne containing the terrible warnings of Elisabeth's prophecy, and apparently these letters were read there in some public forum.[29] Not only did Hildelin lose exclusive control of the preaching and the content of the message, but this also became the occasion for certain "foolish people" to mock Elisabeth. The mockery only increased when the predicted calamities never materialized.

Elisabeth's sensitivity to derision was extremely acute. The entire letter to Hildegard was written as an explanation of the events which Elisabeth felt were so damaging to her reputation. She wanted Hildegard to know the true story and to recognize her innocence, for she admitted that she could bear mockery by the vulgar crowds "if only those people who walk in the habit of religion would not also bitterly afflict my spirit."[30] Although Elisabeth could accept the derision as God's testing of her patience (in accordance with an explanation she received in another vision[31]), she nonetheless continued throughout her life to feel the tension between a divine command to make known God's will and the possibility that her words would be dismissed as *muliebria figmenta*.

The events surrounding the apocalyptic prophecy of Elisabeth, the preaching in Lent of 1155, and the reactions, both positive and negative, to Elisabeth as prophet show no trace of Ekbert's involvement. It was not until sometime after the spring of 1155 that Ekbert entered the Benedictine community at Schönau and began to serve as his sister's secretary.

Joining the Benedictine monastery at Schönau marked a divergence from the direction in which Ekbert's life was already moving. He had studied philosophy in Paris under a certain "Magister Adam."[32] Traveling to France for education beyond the cathedral school curriculum was a fairly uncommon course of action for German canons—one unnecessary for ordination to the higher clergy, but appealing to "noble families with episcopal aspirations."[33] During this time, Ekbert was acquainted with

Rainald of Dassel, who would later become the Archbishop of Cologne and the Chancellor of Emperor Frederick Barbarossa. In fact, Ekbert may even have known Rainald before this and may have accompanied him to Paris to undertake study there.[34] Rainald appears to have been in Paris between 1140 and 1146,[35] so Ekbert's time in the same city may have overlapped at least part of this interval. Ekbert's relationship with Rainald continued beyond their student days: one of Ekbert's major theological works, his *Sermones contra catharos*,[36] is dedicated to Rainald, and, in addition to the dedication letter, one other letter of Ekbert to Rainald is extant.[37]

After his time in Paris, Ekbert became a canon at Saint Cassius in Bonn, a rich and important establishment where Bishop Ekbert, his great-uncle, had once served as provost.[38] Ekbert would later look back on his time at Bonn as a period of prosperity and satisfaction: "The glory of the world sufficiently smiled upon me and with a full hand the heavenly provider sufficiently poured out an abundance of worldly advantages to me while I was still a canon in the church of Bonn."[39] Undoubtedly these "worldly advantages" included the likelihood of future advancement, especially given Ekbert's personal connections with two archbishops of Cologne, Arnold II of Wied and Rainald.[40] According to Ekbert's biographer, it was because of his status and future opportunities that his friends were so shocked when he announced his decision to enter the monastery. The expectations of Ekbert's fellow canons at Bonn were borne out when Ekbert was offered the care of "a great church" in the diocese of Utrecht, which he declined, having already taken up the abbatial staff at Schönau.[41]

Emecho, the author of the *Vita Eckeberti*, relishes the story of Ekbert's conversion and narrates it with all the pride of a good Benedictine chronicler. But in addition to the theme of Ekbert's movement from the world to the austere life of the cowl, Emecho also highlights Elisabeth's role in her brother's spiritual progress.

As a deacon at St. Cassius, Ekbert often visited Elisabeth at the Schönau convent, and during these meetings she would exhort him to pursue ordination to the priesthood. Ekbert objected: he cited fear of the difficulty of priesthood as his reason for remaining in the office of deacon. Elisabeth did not rest content with offering him her own words of encouragement and soon delivered to Ekbert a command from the Virgin Mary herself. Apparently he was persuaded, for he was ordained in 1155. By a similar process he was persuaded to join the order of St. Benedict, and, sometime after Penetecost of 1155, Ekbert made his profession at the monastery of Schönau.[42]

Ekbert's entry into the Schönau community was of vast significance for Elisabeth's life. Although, according to Emecho's account, Elisabeth was only concerned that her brother adopt the Benedictine life, it appears that in this case doing so was tantamount to taking up residence at Schönau. Elisabeth tells of her joy or, more precisely, her relief when Ekbert came to live with her. His decision, an answer to her prayers, allowed a great burden to be lifted from her.[43] For three years she had been receiving visions, as well as commands to reveal the accompanying divine messages. But she had already seen the results of indiscreet publication of her visions: disbelief and even derision. Elisabeth now had someone she could trust (someone perhaps a little more sophisticated and prudent than Abbot Hildelin), someone who could discern which of her visions were fit for public consumption and which were better reserved only for those who would understand.

New issues came to the fore in Elisabeth's visions after Ekbert's move to Schönau. In the diary entries that record events after Ekbert's permanent arrival at Schönau,[44] Elisabeth makes rather frequent reference to family members and to friends of Ekbert. Even more strikingly, she describes being urged by "a more learned one" to explore issues of a marked theological interest not noticeable in the earlier records. For example, she entertains questions about the accuracy of the work of Dionysius the Areopagite and the meaning of obscure passages in the letters of the Apostle Paul. Such questions seem to reflect an engagement in academic study, in contrast to the concerns of the earlier visions that seem to arise more directly from the liturgical life of the divine office and veneration of the saints.

Ekbert's presence at Schönau and his inevitable influence on Elisabeth led to another dramatic change in the visionary materials produced at this time: more than a change in subject matter or spiritual concerns, it can be called a change of genre. Before Ekbert came to reside at Schönau, Elisabeth's visions and utterances were recorded by other sisters in the convent and by Ekbert during his visits.[45] These notes were arranged in the order of occurrence, as a kind of visionary diary. With Ekbert's arrival, this process continued; the materials that form the second part of *Liber Visionum Secundus* and *Liber Visionum Tertius* date from the period of Ekbert's residence at Schönau. A simple quantitative comparison between the material of the two periods yields an interesting result. In the three years prior to Ekbert's arrival, ninety-four chapters of visions were recorded, but in the later period, at least three times as long as the earlier, only thirty chapters of visions in the diary were produced.[46] This diminished interest in the recording of Elisabeth's "routine" visionary experiences is paralleled by a new development. The period of Ekbert's continual presence at Schönau witnessed the composition of the three major visionary works: the *Liber Viarum Dei*, the series of revelations about Saint Ursula and her companions (*Revelatio*), and the visions about the bodily resurrection of the Virgin Mary (*Visio de resurrectione beate virginis Marie* [hereafter *De Resurrectione*]). These three works are unified compositions focused on specific topics. While the unifying thread of the visionary diaries had been Elisabeth herself and what she experienced, her later works reflect a new phase in her career in which she was encouraged to use her special relationship to God to address certain spiritual concerns more directly. Under Ekbert's influence, attention is shifted from herself to what Elisabeth perceived she could and should address "for the edification of the faithful."

The importance of Ekbert's decision to join his sister at Schönau and take an active role in her visionary career is obvious. What is not as obvious, however, is his reason for giving up his own promising career to serve as Elisabeth's secretary. Familial ties can account for his early visits to Elisabeth, but his rejection of his earlier intentions must have a deeper cause. Although a conclusive determination about Ekbert's motivations awaits a detailed study of his life, certain comments can be made at this point.

These events cannot simply be explained as Elisabeth successfully badgering her brother into joining her, as others have implied.[47] As a woman and as someone living a cloistered life, she wielded no authority over him. Ekbert's resolution to put aside his earlier achievements and prospects must have been based on some genuine attraction to what he saw as his new life. A letter to Rainald of Dassel, full of vivid detail of ecclesiastical decadence and exhortation to strive for a more spiritual life, gives some indication of his possible disillusionment with the worldly life of many of the church's officials.[48] His devotional works show a zeal for a personal, affective piety not dissimilar to that of Bernard of Clairvaux. Finally, there is his belief in the truth and importance of what was happening to his sister.

The fact that Ekbert took Elisabeth's experiences seriously is demonstrated by his repeated recourse to her as a source of truth. This is not to deny that he manipulated her to serve his own interests, but his manipulation was a manipulation of access: he believed that she had access to knowledge beyond that which he had gained in studies at Paris. He could use her as a conduit simply because he believed she was in fact a conduit. And not only could she offer him details that were otherwise out of his reach, but the proclamation of her visions made the details more persuasive to the faithful than any details he could quote from a book: "Through you heaven was opened to earth and the secrets of God hidden from the ages flowed forth to us through the instrument of your mouth, and your eloquence was more precious than gold, sweeter than honey [cf. Psalm 18:11]. . . . You made the glory of the citizens of heaven known to us and placed it as if before the eyes of our mind, and your blessed stories greatly inflamed our hearts with the desire for the homeland which we await."[49] In fact, Ekbert seems to have been so attracted to the experience of his sister that he had some desire to share in it himself. In an early collection of Elisabeth's revelations, Ekbert included a vision which he himself had had.[50] Later, in a very poignant scene from his description of Elisabeth's death, he describes one of the final conversations between them: "And I said: I do not now presume to be like a prophet; pray, that your spirit may be twofold in me, but if the Lord would wish to give your spirit only onefold to me, it would suffice. And she said: Dearest, may the will of the Lord be done in you."[51] Here Ekbert recalls the scene where the prophet Elijah, about to die, is asked by his successor Elisha for a twofold share of his spirit (cf. 4 Kings 2:9). This scene and his own occasional visions demonstrate his appreciation of and attraction to visionary spirituality.

It is only by ignoring the possibilities of Ekbert's own spiritual interests and by imposing an anachronistic critique on Elisabeth's experiences that one is left with the weak explanation that Elisabeth somehow prevailed upon her brother to join her. Rather, one must picture Ekbert choosing an alternative life for himself, a life whose potential disappointments he had not yet experienced and which offered him the possibility of participating in an extraordinary spiritual phenomenon from which he could personally benefit. Ekbert's decision accords well with a pattern of other medieval clerics who were attracted to holy women whose piety was manifested in visions and other extraordinary devotions.[52] Furthermore, Ekbert may have been influenced by his sister's exposure to public ridicule due to Hildelin's intemperate announcement of her visions. A desire to protect his family's name and more carefully manage Elisabeth's public image could also have strengthened his decision to join her at Schönau. This same desire may also have motivated the agreement between Elisabeth and Ekbert to keep her revelations secret until she died. Their agreement was, however, rendered moot by Hildelin's preaching.

In the decade between Ekbert's arrival at Schönau and Elisabeth's death, her visionary career blossomed despite, or perhaps even in conjunction with, her continued state of physical infirmity.[53] Her selection as *magistra* of the Schönau nuns, of which no details are given, seems to pale in significance beside the events more directly related to her experience of revelation. One of these events, Schönau's acquisition of new relics, served as the catalyst for the production of Elisabeth's most popular visionary text (*Revelatio*). An old graveyard outside the city walls of Cologne had been discovered, and the corpses, identified as the bodies of Saint Ursula and her eleven thousand virgin companion martyrs, were being taken to various local religious establishments, including the Benedictine abbey at Deutz.[54] Gerlach, the abbot of Deutz, "who burned with much pious devotion for collecting and honoring the bodies of that holy group," sent two bodies, one of which was identified as Saint Verena, to the monastery at Schönau.[55] Schönau's acquisition of these bones from the Cologne site is only one example of the proliferation of Ursuline relics throughout Germany and France from the twelfth to the fourteenth century.[56] But the delivery of the relics to Schönau was of momentous importance for the growing cult of Saint Ursula, for at Schönau the precious bones were greeted by a woman who saw them arrive escorted by an angel and who later reported a conversation with Saint Verena herself.[57]

The potential of Elisabeth's peculiar access to the departed martyrs whose bones were being excavated by the hundreds was not lost on Abbot Gerlach of Deutz, due, no doubt, to Ekbert's or Hildelin's intervention. She reports that Gerlach sent her some stones from the graves on which were inscribed the names of the buried, hoping that she would be able to reveal whether or not the inscriptions were authentic. She adds that he did this because he suspected a profit motive among those who had "discovered" the holy bodies.[58] Gerlach's doubts were not shared by Thioderic, a monk of his community who wrote a brief treatise on the relic discovery, emphasizing the authenticity of the inscriptions "which I dug out of the tombs with my own hands."[59]

The abbot of Deutz certainly had good reason to be suspicious. Bones of men, women, and children, as could be expected from any graveyard, were exhumed. However, the field outside Cologne was not believed to be just any graveyard, but the burial site of eleven thousand blessed women. Here the traditional legend of the slaughter of eleven thousand women and the new discovery of a cemetery with bones of men, women, and children confronted each other with potentially disastrous results for those who were interested in confirming the cemetery as the site of the legendary martyrdom. And here is where the words of a woman who spoke of knowing the secrets of heaven could have a decisive effect. With little choice left to her (she describes herself as forced),[60] Elisabeth turned her attention to the legendary martyrdom and produced one of her most creative and vivid visionary scenarios.

In this same period, Elisabeth also deepened her friendship with Hildegard of Bingen through letter writing as well as at least one personal visit. Her letter explaining the events surrounding the preaching of her apocalyptic vision elicited a response in which Hildegard assumed the voice she used in most of her other correspondence, a voice of spiritual authority dispensing guidance and consolation to those in need.[61] Addressing Elisabeth's complaint about the reckless preaching of her revelation and the public incredulity which ensued, the elder visionary acknowledges that whoever is inspired by God ("homines istos quos inspiratio dei ita imbuit") will be harassed by demonic suggestions, because God is testing them but will not let them perish.[62] This consolation is accompanied by an explanation of the true nature of the prophetic experience:

> Those who wish to do the works of God, let them always consider that they are earthen vessels [cf. 2 Cor. 4:7] because they are human beings, and they should always look to what they are and what they may become, and leave the celestial things to the one who is celestial, because they are exiles, ignorant of celestial things. They only sing the mysteries of God like a trumpet, which only makes a sound, but does not work unless someone else breathes into it so that it can give forth the sound.[63]

Hildegard's warning about avoiding celestial mysteries, interesting as it is coming from one who herself claimed knowledge of such secrets, makes most sense if it is understood to apply to Elisabeth's explicit prediction of certain future events. As Kathryn Kerby-Fulton and Dyan Elliot have suggested, a simple message preaching the need for penance would not raise the suspicions that a more elaborate prophecy of impending catastrophe would.[64]

Hildegard concludes by characterizing herself as a poor trumpet living in fear who occasionally brings forth a note from the living light.[65] In doing this, she identifies herself as sharing the role she described for Elisabeth, thereby offering herself as both a model and a fellow sufferer to her younger companion. The relationship evidenced in this correspondence continued to have an important place in Elisabeth's life. In 1156 she went to visit Hildegard at Rupertsberg and, having been inspired by Hildegard's *Scivias*, she began her own *Liber Viarum Dei*.[66] In this as well as the later visionary diaries, some of Elisabeth's visions are indeed reminiscent of images used by Hildegard. For example, Elisabeth's description of a triangular column representing the Trinity and her vision of the heavenly Jerusalem being constructed of stones representing souls that have been purged of their impurities, were probably suggested by her acquaintance with Hildegard's *Scivias*.[67] These visions, along with the opening chapters of the *Liber Viarum Dei*, are the most allegorical of Elisabeth's visions, and she appears to have been introduced to this style, which is generally not sustained throughout the visionary texts, by Hildegard. But even in these cases where the parallels are the strongest, the similarities are general and incidental to the overall integrity of each woman's work. It was not the content of Hildegard's work so much as her example as another woman visited with divine revelation that served as Elisabeth's inspiration.

Furthermore, the influence in this relationship may not have run only in one direction. Elisabeth's visions about the Cologne martyrdom, a subject of great interest to the Rupertsberg visionary, would have been known to Hildegard. Hildegard wrote six hymns commemorating the martyrdom of the eleven thousand virgins, but she did not share Elisabeth's concern to authenticate either the existing legend or the newly discovered relics. One of her antiphons does, however, address the issue of the presence of men among the crowd of female virgins and, in so doing, echoes Elisabeth's declarations about religious men accompanying and ministering to Ursula and her companions.[68]

With growing confidence, Elisabeth also turned her prophetic energy to what she perceived as a great threat to the faith of the church—the Cathar heresy. There were Cathars in the Rhineland at early as the 1140s,[69] and the tension caused by their presence came to a climax in the summer of 1163 when several were charged with heresy and executed outside the city of Cologne.[70] The Cathars had been a matter of great concern to Ekbert from the days before he joined his sister at Schönau,[71] and his interest probably fueled Elisabeth's.

But Elisabeth's condemnation was not aimed solely at those heretics who were seducing the faithful with ostentatious displays of rigid morality. Harsh words were directed to the clergy and learned teachers of the church who allowed the heresy to flourish by neglecting their pastoral duties. She shared this concern with Hildegard of Bingen, who publicly preached against clerical neglect of the spreading heresy.[72] In addition to her preaching, Hildegard wrote a short visionary treatise against the Cathars, a text known by Elisabeth.[73] Elisabeth responded to Hildegard with her own visionary condemnation of the Cathars and negligent clerics.[74] This shared concern over the plight of the church added another dimension to the relationship between the two women.

Both women focus on the basic doctrinal issues that the Cathars question: the creation of the universe by God and the incarnation of the Word of God.[75] Both women evoke the scene of Apocalypse 6:9-11, where the dead saints buried in the ground cry to God to be vindicated from the degradation they now suffer as the earth is filled with the offense of the Cathars.[76] There is evidence that Cathars in the twelfth century rejected the veneration of saints.[77] It is not clear, however, whether Hildegard and Elisabeth, each of whom composed texts celebrating the memorials of saints, are referring to such a practice or whether they have both simply incorporated this passage as they did so many other suggestive, apocalyptic scenes that vividly illuminate the danger of the church's present state.

It is particularly striking that both women chastise the leaders of the church for their desultory response to the Cathar threat. Hildegard berates the clergy for not fulfilling their responsibility to teach the people, for being distracted by their own desire and greed, and for claiming they do not have time for leading people.[78] Elisabeth's accusations are even more pointed:

> My pastors are weighed down as if in a heavy sleep, and how should I awaken them? . . . Indeed, the law passes away first from the priests and the elders of my people [Cf. Ezek. 7:26], because they seek to sell the sacrifices of my sacraments. Those who sell, sell judgment unto themselves, and those who buy, buy a double-edged sword. . . . There are some who do not enter my flock through the door, but they come up by a different way, like thieves and robbers [Cf. John 10:1]; thieves because of their avarice and robbers because they lose the souls committed to them. They cover their depraved deeds lest they be seen by the people. For that reason, they do not boldly speak out against every heresy because they are reprehensible in their own ways.[79]

Here Elisabeth refers not just to the personal defects of the clergy that Hildegard noted, but she links the current neglect of responsibility to the institutional abuse of church office—simony. The perversion of ecclesiastical office carries in its trail the spiritual downfall of the faithful.[80]

Hildegard and Elisabeth directly link the flourishing heretical movement to the inadequacy of ecclesiastical leadership, whether this is due to the basic moral weakness of the clergy or to the abuse of church office. Their critique of the clerical establishment is heightened by their perception of themselves as willing to shout to the world a message of repentence. They share a sense of their need to fill the vacuum the weak and depraved clergy have left. Elisabeth exhorts Hildegard's further efforts in reclaiming the faithful from the menace of heresy: "O lady Hildegard, bring to completion the work of the Lord just as you have worked on up till now, because the Lord has placed you as a worker in his vineyard."[81] And Elisabeth sums up her own contribution as the effort to awaken and invigorate the ecclesiastical hierarchy: "Blessed is the one who fears the Lord of all creation and therefore importunes the highest priest so that he will remove the opprobrium from his people [cf. Isaiah 25:8], and all of Israel will be saved."[82]

Their impatience with the negligence of the clergy and their stepping in to fill the vacuum of leadership led neither visionary to abandon hope in the structure of the church. Hildegard, speaking in the voice of God, exhorts the faithful to listen to the words of the priests "into whose ears my words will thunder and who will speak these words to you in my name."[83] Elisabeth offers advice to clergy as well as secular leaders to prepare themselves to confront the heretics: "You who are learned, examine the books of the New Testament and recall its words, you will discover such fruit. Be renewed in the Holy Spirit and revive your souls for the edification of the church."[84]

As Raoul Manselli has noted, the remonstrances of these two women had at least one effect. One cleric was moved to use his learning to compose a treatise to be used in the debate with and examination of Cathars.[85] In 1163 Ekbert of Schönau, sometime after the burning of the heretics at Cologne, began his *Sermones contra catharos*.[86] This treatise, addressed to Rainald of Dassel, the archbishop of Cologne, is intended as a handbook to be used by investigators of the heresy. It compiles the appropriate scriptural authorities for examining the Cathars who themselves have made an effective, selective use of Scripture in defending their beliefs. "For," as Ekbert confesses, "it is no small shame to us, who are learned, to be dumb and speechless in the presence of the heretics."[87] Here Ekbert appears to acknowledge the situation decried by Elisabeth and Hildegard: the failure of the learned clergy to confront the Cathars with a genuine defense of the orthodox faith.[88] Even after Elisabeth's death, Ekbert retained some connection with Hildegard in their common attention to this heresy. A young demon-possessed woman, who was brought to Hildegard to be cured from her affliction, was said to have revealed the whereabouts of certain Cathars. According to his biographer, Ekbert acted upon this information, went to Mainz to interrogate the accused, and succeeded in turning them aside from their heresy.[89]

In this case the friendship between Elisabeth and Hildegard, their shared pastoral concern about the danger of the Cathars, ultimately bore fruit beyond their own mutual support and fulfillment of spiritual needs. As women not directly identified with the ecclesiastical establishment, their distance allowed them to see the success of the heresy directly connected to the failure of the clergy. Their proclamation of their visionary critique could serve as a prick of conscience and a call to action to those who would harken to their words.

Elisabeth's reputation as a visionary soon spread beyond the walls of Schönau. In his introduction to her letter collection, Ekbert tells of a certain monk from an abbey in the diocese of Metz who was "very learned in sacred letters" and who came to investigate (*perscrutari*) what God was doing through Elisabeth. Having satisfied himself that Elisabeth was truly inspired by God, he nonetheless felt compelled to give her some advice of his own. He then returned to his home, but only after requesting Elisabeth to send some divinely inspired message of consolation or encouragement to his abbot and brothers.[90]

Another witness to Elisabeth's growing fame, dating from the period soon after Elisabeth's death, testifies to the spread of her reputation beyond the local Rhineland area. Roger, an English Cistercian monk from the abbey of Ford, learned of Elisabeth's visions while visiting William of Savigny (the sometime abbot of Savigny and later abbot of Cîteaux). Roger sent a copy of the visions to Baldwin, his abbot at Ford, and, describing the heavenly origin of *Liber Viarum Dei*, told him: "And indeed I do not know how this work will be appreciated where you are, but I do know that in these parts it is eagerly copied and read and heard not only by the unlearned but by bishops and our abbots."[91] Roger also suggested that Abbot Baldwin have one of his monks make another copy of Elisabeth's work to send to the community of religious women in which his mother lived. Thus Roger not only furnishes proof for the spread of Elisabeth's reputation into France but also served to introduce Elisabeth's works into England, where they were well received.[92]

Although Roger wrote his letter to Baldwin at least a decade after Elisabeth died, his letter shows no awareness of Elisabeth's death. He copied a manuscript that was based on a model produced in Schönau in the period immediately preceding her death. Unlike the version Roger copied, the visionary collections produced in Schönau after Elisabeth died included Ekbert's *De Obitu*, the letter to his kinswomen at Andernach describing his sister's death.

Despite the fact that Elisabeth's last days are the best documented part of her life, there remains some controversy over the date of her death. In *De Obitu*, Ekbert gives a number of important clues for determining it. Yet despite his ostensible clarity, the various clues he gives cannot be made to fit into a consistent picture of a single year. He states that Elisabeth died on Friday, June 18, at the age of thirty-six, in the thirteenth year of her visionary experience.[93] Although the date of her birth is not known, the thirteenth year of her visionary experience suggests that she died in 1164. However, in 1164, June 18th was a Thursday. On the other hand, in 1165, June 18 occurred on a Friday, and 1165 is thirteen years *after* Elisabeth's visionary experience began. Thus 1165 has also been suggested as the year of her death. While neither choice is without question, the later date, which allows the repeated references to a Friday death to stand, seems somewhat more likely.[94] Despite Ekbert's possible hagiographical intentions in making her death correspond to the day of the Lord's death, he still had to acknowledge that he was writing about an event that an entire community witnessed, and thus he was not free to manipulate basic events to fit a symbolic purpose.

The irreconcilable data about Elisabeth's death point up another curious aspect of her career. Even with a devoted secretary living with her, someone who knew well the details of her life, some of the most basic information about her experience eludes us. It is clear that Ekbert's primary interest, whatever his intimate devotion to his sister, was directed not to her personality or her involvements with the world around her, but to the revelations which he believed to come from God.

Elisabeth's death did not halt the spread of her reputation. Her visionary texts offered new material for theologians and historians,[95] information from her visions about the Cologne martyrdom was worked into chronicles, and occasionally her revelations about the bodily assumption of Mary were noted in the continuing debate about Mary's otherworldly state. Not surprisingly, Elisabeth's memory was kept alive at Schönau. Abbot Emecho, Ekbert's biographer and successor, wrote two brief texts, one in prose, one in verse, praising Elisabeth. He appears not to have known Elisabeth personally and includes few historical details. Yet his writing reflects a familiarity with her visions and a strong devotion to her as one who served as a medium of divine revelation:

> Hail full fount, small brook of divine knowledge, dripping mellifluous drops of sacred teaching.
> Hail blooming shrub in the forest of Schönau, surrounded by the boundless branches of your visions.[96]

Roth suggests that this poem may have been written for an office dedicated to Elisabeth.[97] As an addendum to *Visionen*, Roth printed the outline of a fifteenth-century office from Schönau dedicated to Elisabeth.
There is even some evidence that this office was celebrated beyond the
walls of Schönau, but there seems to have been no dispersion of her relics
during the Middle Ages.[98] Elisabeth was never canonized and no canonization process is extant. She was included in the *Martyrologium Romanum*
of 1584, but, as Köster notes, she is remembered only for her exemplary
monastic life; her visions remain unmentioned.[99]

   This neglect of the visions may not be accidental. At least two medieval authors warned that the Roman church did not approve Elisabeth's
visions. Writing during Elisabeth's lifetime, the Parisian theologian Jean
Beleth cited Elisabeth's revelations about the corporeal assumption of
Mary in his own discussion of the assumption. But after describing Elisabeth's assertion of Mary's corporeal assumption forty days after her death,
Beleth added that *De Resurrectione* "was not approved in the Roman
church."[100] Almost two centuries later, Nicholas Trevet wrote of Elisabeth
in his Anglo-Norman *Cronicles*, referring to her great sanctity and her
many visions. "Mes," he continued, "la court de Rome ne le voleit auto-
rizer ne confermer."[101] Trevet does not specify what was not approved,
although the context indicates that he may be referring to the visions
about the assumption. There is no extant "official" commentary on Elisabeth's visions; there was probably no condemnation per se of the visionary
texts. Yet there appears to have been some recognition among writers in
the twelfth through fourteenth centuries that some of Elisabeth's visions
were controversial and therefore suspect.

   Despite this eclipse of her reputation as a visionary in the martyrology, the overwhelming evidence of the dispersion of manuscripts indicates that Elisabeth's visions had a great appeal in the Middle Ages. With
or without any official endorsement, the visions were copied and read and
recommended to others. Nor did any lack of official approval dampen the
enthusiasm of the sixteenth-century humanist Jacques Lefèvre d'Etaples.
In 1513, Lefèvre published the first printed edition of Elisabeth's visions,
along with visions of Hildegard of Bingen and Mechtild of Hackeborn
(1241–99). In his dedicatory letter to this edition, Lefèvre declared that
the visionary books of Elisabeth "well express the energy of the Spirit
and make manifest angelic speech in the simplicity and sincerity of holy
visions."[102]

3. The Visionary Texts and Collections

The process by which Elisabeth's visions got from her mouth into the hands of such readers as Roger of Ford was complex. Words exclaimed in a spontaneous, often prayerful way were carefully reconstructed into full accounts of interior experiences, recorded by Ekbert and the nuns of Schönau, edited and arranged by Ekbert into chronological or thematic sequences, and copied into a growing collection of visionary books whose popularity carried them to cloisters throughout Germany, France, and England. This process and the texts that were its final products are the subject of the next two chapters.

First, a description of the visionary records is given, including the books directly ascribed to Elisabeth as well as related texts such as Ekbert's *De Obitu* and adaptations of Elisabeth's visions by other writers. In Chapter 4, these descriptions are used to formulate an assessment of Ekbert's role in the production of the visionary corpus. These two chapters thus provide a map through the visionary literature and a basis for the later analytic chapters.

The Visionary Texts

In the latest and most extensive collection of the Schönau literature, six books of Elisabeth's visions plus Ekbert's *De Obitu* are transmitted. The three visionary diaries (*Libri Visionum Primus, Secundus*, and *Tertius*), the *Liber Viarum Dei*, the revelations about Saint Ursula (*Revelatio*), and a collection of letters comprise the six books ascribed to Elisabeth. (The once independent series of visions about the assumption of Mary [*De Resurrectione*], was annexed to the end of *Liber Visionum Secundus*.) These texts, with the exception of the book of letters, roughly represent the chronological order of the events recounted in them.

Before turning to the individual texts, however, the question of Elisabeth's literacy and, more specifically, her proficiency in Latin, the lan-

guage of all surviving records of her experience, needs to be clarified.
Ekbert himself raises this issue in his expanded introduction to *Liber Visionum Primus*. Reporting that after her ecstasies Elisabeth spoke in Latin,
he describes those ecstasies by saying they occurred *non sine evidenti mi-
raculo*, and he clearly portrays Elisabeth's Latin recitations as miraculous.
In fact, Ekbert offers this to his readers as proof of the authenticity of
Elisabeth's revelations: the speeches must have a divine origin because
Elisabeth did not learn them from anyone else nor did she compose them
herself.[1] It must be noted that Ekbert's purpose in this passage is not to
make a statement about Elisabeth's education or literary skills, but rather
to emphasize the miraculous quality of her revelations and thus protect
them from any criticism aimed at their authorship by Elisabeth.

Ekbert makes a similar statement in a letter to Abbot Reinhard of
Reinhausen which was probably composed about the same time as his
introduction to *Liber Visionum Primus*. Again he emphasizes the miraculous nature of Elisabeth's experience, and then he goes on to describe her
utterances in a manner reminiscent of, though not identical to, the description in the *Liber Visionum Primus*. In this case, Ekbert insists that
Elisabeth does not know how to compose in Latin and that she never
learned it.[2] Ekbert's more explicit insistence on the impossibility of Elisabeth's authorship (and hence the divine origin of her revelations) may be
due to the immediate context of his statement. His point is to explain that
Elisabeth is engaged in composing letters of spiritual direction to specific
individuals and communities, and that these letters reveal the will of God.
His explanation to Reinhard is not theoretical: Reinhard himself is the
recipient of one of Elisabeth's letters of vigorous warning about the evil
of simony and other vices.[3]

Ekbert returns to the question of Elisabeth's Latinity once more, this
time in a prologue added as one of the finishing touches to his final version
of the collection. In this context he states that, of the revelations that Elisabeth received from an angel, "some he [i.e., the angel] pronounced totally
in Latin speech, others totally in German, but some he delivered partly in
Latin and partly in German." He adds that he wrote down the revelations
in such a way as to leave the Latin revelations unchanged, "but where they
were in German, I translated them into Latin as clearly as I could, adding
nothing from my own presumption, seeking nothing of human favor nor
earthly advantage, with God as my witness to whom all things are naked
and open" (cf. Heb. 4:13).[4]

Ekbert's assertion of Elisabeth's bilingual visions stands in contrast to his earlier descriptions of her pronouncements in Latin. It is curious that in his last shaping of the visionary collection Ekbert has decided to include this information when there is no evidence of translation within the texts themselves and when such an admission may appear to weaken his argument for the miraculous nature of Elisabeth's experiences. Perhaps he was moved to include this information in response to questions about Elisabeth's native speech.[5] Yet it is clear that at least one of Ekbert's purposes in this passage is to exonerate himself from any suspicions of having had an active role in composing the revelations attributed to Elisabeth. Therefore, although Ekbert may be responding to questions about Elisabeth's native tongue, it seems more likely that his statement was given in response to questions about himself, and his concluding oath of innocence confirms this impression. Such a formulaic oath is, of course, no indication of the truth of the sworn statement.[6]

All three of Ekbert's references to Elisabeth's Latin pronouncements are given in apologetic contexts in which he was not primarily concerned with describing Elisabeth's literary abilities. But recognizing the apologetic purpose of Ekbert's remarks about Elisabeth's Latin skills does not fully answer the question of her literacy. Considering that Elisabeth probably came from a well-established family and that she entered the convent at age twelve, it seems quite likely that she could have been educated in Latin.[7] Even though Ekbert wishes to diminish her Latin skills, nowhere in the entire corpus does he hint that Elisabeth had difficulty understanding Latin, and his description of Elisabeth as having "little or no skill in Latin speech" evinces a certain hesitance to assert complete ignorance.

Commenting on Elisabeth's literacy, Elisabeth Gössmann compares her to Hildegard of Bingen, who deliberately devalued her literary learning in order to enhance her role as unlearned prophetess.[8] This observation could certainly be extended to include not only the remarks attributed to Elisabeth but also the words of Ekbert describing Elisabeth. Gössmann points out that the assertion of ignorance must stand in contrast to repeated references to Elisabeth reading the psalms and the passion of Christ. For example, Elisabeth describes spiritual torments that made even her customary pleasures of devotional reading tedious: "When I had hardly finished reading one psalm, I threw far from me the psalter which had always been a pleasure for me. Again, thinking it over and wondering to myself at what had happened to me, I picked it up again [and] read."[9] Not only the explicit reference to reading, but also the image of throwing the book across the room and picking it up again emphasizes her act of reading, as opposed to hearing the psalter read by someone else.

Thus Ekbert's effort to devalue any originality on Elisabeth's part in the revelation of her visions seriously compromises the value of his remarks about her Latinity.[10] Her repeated references to reading make it plain that she knew Latin sufficiently well to read the Bible as well as the letters she received from her correspondents.[11] But on the other hand, his admission that he translated some of the visionary records must be taken into account when reading the visions. One must therefore hesitate before ascribing any particular turn of phrase to Elisabeth, recognizing that it may reflect Ekbert's rendering of an idea or image that Elisabeth may have expressed orally in German.

THE VISIONARY DIARIES

The phrase "visionary diary" (*das visionäre Tagebuch*) was used (and I believe coined) by Köster to refer to the three books of Elisabeth's earliest visions. The phrase is well chosen, for it captures significant characteristics of these books: their chronological arrangement, and the personal, even intimate feeling that results from the subjective orientation of the narrative. These books, especially *Liber Visionum Primus* and the first half of *Liber Visionum Secundus*, include some of the most direct reports of Elisabeth's words, and the emotions portrayed in these accounts, whether fear, enthusiasm, bewilderment, or joy, are often palpable.

The first two visionary diaries were each composed in two stages: an original early version and a later expansion. The original version of *Liber Visionum Primus*, found in Redaction B,[12] is comprised of records of events from around May 18 until August 29, 1152. In some manuscripts it bears the title *Liber eiusdem de temptationibus inimici, quas primo sustinit et de revelationibus divinis quas post modum vidit*. This text was later expanded to extend the narrative until the Assumption (August 15), 1154. In this version, fifty-three new chapters were added to the end of the original; the title *Liber eiusdem de temptationibus* no longer appears; Elisabeth's controversial prophecy about an impending calamity, which had been appended to the end of the original version, was dropped; and Ekbert's introduction was expanded. This is the version printed in Roth's edition.

Elisabeth's prologue, which follows Ekbert's introduction, is cast as a direct address to her brother after he has joined the community and taken on the responsibilities as her secretary, and as she is about to give him a sequential account of all the events that occurred as much as three years earlier. While this prologue serves its literary function as an introduction to the narrative that follows, it obscures the process that actually took place. The prologue implies that the narrative which follows is a direct transcription of Elisabeth's report to her brother after he came to live with her. However, the chapters which follow include clear evidence that the recording process began before this date, that not only Ekbert but also the nuns at Schönau recorded some of Elisabeth's visions, and that Ekbert himself recorded Elisabeth's visions before he came to live with her.[13]

In the final version of *Liber Visionum Primus*, over 125 different visionary episodes are reported, some by no more than one sentence in the context of describing other more significant visions. The more detailed narratives often follow a general pattern in which the day is specified according to its feast in the church calendar and the time is noted according to the hours of the divine office. Next comes a description of some kind of physical suffering (e.g., "infirmata sum"; "cor meum percussum est"; "in agone laboravi"; "me febris valida apprehendit") that precedes the vision. Then Elisabeth gives a description of the vision itself, which is often reported as occurring *in extasi* or *in excessu meo*. After the vision, she frequently bursts out in words of praise of God or explanation of what she just saw.

The second visionary diary (*Liber Visionum Secundus*) also begins with an introduction by Ekbert. Here, his defense of the possibility of divine revelation imparted to women may indicate some negative response to the first diary. He also defends the appearance of a second book of visions. The preceding book had ended with the angel's announcement that Elisabeth would not receive her accustomed visions until the time of her death, but clearly the present book (as well as all the other visionary texts) comes from the period after this announcement. Ekbert puzzled over this apparent contradiction, and offered his opinion that the angel must have referred to only one particular type of vision when he asserted the termination of Elisabeth's revelations.

The accounts of Elisabeth's visions, which comprise the first part of *Liber Visionum Secundus* and record events from May 14 till August 11, 1155,[14] are very similar in style to those found in *Liber Visionum Primus*. There are, however, some differences in content. For example, Abbot Hildelin is much more prominent in the events recorded in the later book where there is frequent reference to his priestly and liturgical role. He seems to have played a heightened role in Elisabeth's life after his preaching of her prophecy. Furthermore, the subjects of the chapters that are only found in the second, longer version of *Liber Visionum Secundus* immediately, though subtly, indicate the presence of Ekbert. Revelations about deceased relatives of Elisabeth and Ekbert, and friends of Ekbert,[15] extended attention to an incident in which an unnamed priest in the community (possibly Ekbert himself[16]) accidentally spills consecrated wine, and the initiation of the pattern in which Elisabeth is directed to ask a question in order to learn some otherwise unavailable theological information of a strikingly academic nature[17]—all subjects that suggest Ekbert's influence—comprise over half the chapters of the new material. Thus as a whole, *Liber Visionum Secundus* represents a continuation of the diary begun in *Liber Visionum Primus* but with two significant new circumstances in effect: Abbot Hildelin's increased involvement in Elisabeth's life, and Ekbert's influence on the subjects of Elisabeth's visions once he had come to live at Schönau.

Liber Visionum Tertius, the final visionary diary, resembles *Liber Visionum Secundus* in its obvious compilation of disparate materials, and it especially resembles the later part of *Liber Visionum Secundus* in the disappearance of chronological indications that allow conclusive dating. Of the thirty-one chapters that comprise *Liber Visionum Tertius*, only the first eighteen represent, strictly speaking, the diary-type entries found in the earlier journals, and even these chapters appeared in various combinations before they were given their definitive arrangement in this book.

A few of the visions in *Liber Visionum Tertius*, notably chapters 6, 7, 11, and 12, are reminiscent of the experiences described in the earlier books. In most of the material comprising the diary entries, however, there is a distinctive theological interest. Whereas in the earlier visions, Elisabeth described herself as passively seeing something that appeared to her, in these chapters she initiates conversations in which she repeats to the angel a question she has been given by Ekbert. Elisabeth describes herself as going into her ecstatic state armed with questions she is to pose to the angel, her source of divine information.

These chapters also differ from their earlier counterparts in that there is much less emphasis on the details of Elisabeth's experience. There is, for example, scant elaboration of her psychic state during her visions. In a similar vein, *Liber Visionum Tertius* includes only one reference to the physical discomfort so characteristic of the earlier dictated records. Another common feature of the early accounts, the reports of Elisabeth's spontaneous speech when she returned from ecstasy, is missing in *Liber Visionum Tertius*. In its place is a noticeable tendency to reassure the audience that Elisabeth's words are not her own, but are always the communications she learned in conversation with her angelic tutor.[18] The bulk of the visionary narrative itself is now devoted to recounting the angel's response to predetermined theological questions. In the last visionary diary, the emphasis is clearly on the content of Elisabeth's message as a divinely sanctioned revelation and not on Elisabeth herself as a person having an extraordinary experience.

LIBER VIARUM DEI

The popularity of the *Liber Viarum Dei* in monastic communities is attested in Roger of Ford's praise of it and in his declaration that many bishops and Cistercian abbots eagerly read it. Also, a marginal note in a thirteenth-century manuscript from the Cistercian abbey of St. Mary at Himmerod in the diocese of Trier indicates that the *Liber Viarum Dei* was selected to be read at collation in that monastery.[19] This popularity may be attributed to the fact that *Liber Viarum Dei*, displaying the tendency seen in the final stages of the visionary diaries, is a unified exposition of moral exhortation. The focus shifts away from Elisabeth's experiences per se to an interest in the spiritual information accessible from and communicated in those visions. Thus there is a certain utilitarian appeal in the *Liber Viarum Dei* as a handbook of spiritual guidance.

The visions recorded in the *Liber Viarum Dei* begin around Pentecost (June 3), 1156, and continue with some regularity until the final vision on August 22, 1157. Some insight into the origin of the *Liber Viarum Dei* is given in Elisabeth's description of a vision in which she saw a large pile of books stored in a tent. In this vision, the angel lifted one of those books, named it "The Book of God's Ways," and announced that Elisabeth would receive the revelation of this book after she had visited Hildegard of Bingen. Elisabeth then affirms that all these events were happening according to the angel's prediction, thus acknowledging her visit to Hildegard prior to the experiences recorded in the *Liber Viarum Dei*.[20]

This visit took place in 1156, five years after Hildegard completed her first major visionary composition, the *Scivias*.[21] Elisabeth seems to have had in mind the work of the older visionary as she reflected on the images that formed the core of her own work. The title *Scivias*, an abbreviated form of the exhortation *Scito vias domini*, suggested the subject of Elisabeth's *Liber Viarum Dei*—the various paths that lead to eternal beatitude. The influence continues beyond the title: both books begin with a vision of a high mountain, with its brightly illuminated peak occupied by a radiant figure representing Christ or God.[22]

Despite Hildegard's influence on Elisabeth's interest in this subject, the two visionary compositions remain fundamentally different in intent and effect. Hildegard's *Scivias* is nothing less than a compendium of Christian theology in which she paints, in her own complexly allegorical and highly idiosyncratic fashion, a vast canvas detailing both universal salvation history from creation and fall to apocalypse and the moral life of the individual human being. Elisabeth's *Liber Viarum Dei*, by contrast, is much less ambitious. Taking her cue from the image of the "ways of the Lord," she sets out to describe the paths by which faithful Christians ascend the mountain of earthly life to reach the realm of heavenly beatitude. The text is comprised of ten sermons, each being an exposition of one of the paths that she sees scoring the side of the mountain.

Thus, although both women share a fervent concern to outline the proper Christian life, the theological impetus to place this life in a larger context of Christian belief remains unique to Hildegard. Even the expression of moral perspective differs markedly between Elisabeth and Hildegard. Hildegard's extensive exposition of the Christian life takes the form of her description of personified *virtutes*, such as *patientia, abstentia, iustitia,* and *spes,* which are essentially divine graces working in the life of a person. In contrast, Elisabeth's moral scheme is based on the *ordo* of the individual believer within the Christian world. Thus she describes ten paths as the diverse ways of Christian life: contemplative life, active life, martyrdom, marriage, virginity, the way of the rulers (*rectores*), widowhood, the solitary life, the way of children, and that of adolescents.

Elisabeth's interest in articulating the diversity of authentic Christian modes of life is striking. While she does not go as far as did Honorius Augustodunensis in his *Speculum Ecclesie* or later Jacques de Vitry in his *ad status* sermons, both of whom articulated moral concerns corresponding to various secular livelihoods, she strives to formulate a universal picture comprehending the lives of all Christians.[23] This in itself illustrates a significant difference between her work and that of Hildegard. Hildegard focuses on what Barbara Newman describes as the salvific synergy between God's grace and human cooperation[24] and, in so doing, differentiates the multiplicity of divine graces at work in an apparently undifferentiated human life. When Hildegard distinguishes among various Christian lives, she turns to the traditional tripartite scheme of monastics, clerics, and people living in the world, although describing them with characteristic flair as the living odor (*vivens odor*), the perfumers (*pigmentarii*), and those living in the world (*saeculares*).[25] Elisabeth, on the other hand, focuses on the differentiation of human lives and expands the traditional scheme to represent more adequately the range of Christian vocations. Such a difference in perspective is not absolute—Hildegard certainly recognizes that there are different *viae* for different Christians, and Elisabeth certainly recognizes the role of various divinely aided virtues in living a God-fearing life. Nonetheless, this difference leads to the significantly distinct types of moral expression found in these two works despite occasional similarities of imagery and Elisabeth's recognition of Hildegard's influence on her own visionary life. Elisabeth's view of the Christian world comprised of these diverse groups reflects a strong contemporary concern to define society according to social and religious roles and to affirm the multiplicity of spiritual paths.[26] It is not surprising that the *Liber Viarum Dei* appears to have been a more popular text than the *Scivias*: there are twenty-nine known twelfth- and thirteenth-century manuscripts of the *Liber Viarum Dei* and eight of the complete *Scivias*.[27]

The content of the ten sermons consists largely of moral exhortation and, in some noteworthy cases, condemnation of contemporary decadence. Few of these sermons are presented as completely independent set pieces dropped into the framework of the *Liber Viarum Dei*. Rather than being just sermons that have been conveniently gathered into a book, most of the discourses involve Elisabeth's portrayal of conversations between herself and the angel that took place over the course of days or even weeks. The revelation of the sermons as portrayed by Elisabeth is always closely associated with the events in her life, and the circumstantial details of the delivery of the sermons are retained within the text.

The fact that these sermons retain this colloquial and circumstantial character suggests that neither Elisabeth nor Ekbert viewed the text as a collection of exemplary sermons to be used by other preachers, despite their applicability in many homiletic contexts. Elisabeth clearly conceived the *Liber Viarum Dei* in even greater terms than simply providing possible source material for other preachers. She sent copies of the book to the bishops of Trier, Cologne, and Mainz, accompanied by a letter in which she charged these prelates "to announce to the Roman church and all the people and the entire church of God the words which you will find in this present book."[28] Thus the words of the *Liber Viarum Dei* are to be proclaimed to the whole church, not just through the copying and recopying of Elisabeth's words, a task about which she was also concerned,[29] but through the preaching of these three chosen bishops. This sense of urgency in spreading her revelations coincides with a sense of Elisabeth's newly emerging confidence: in the *Liber Viarum Dei* there are no signs of Elisabeth's hesitance to proclaim her revelations. The change in genre from visionary diary to thematic collection of revelations represents a new stage in the development of Elisabeth as visionary persona and charismatic teacher.

REVELATIO DE SACRO EXERCITU VIRGINUM COLONIENSIUM

In turning to the book of visions about the martyrdom of Saint Ursula and her companions, we confront the text which, judging from the number of manuscripts transmitting it, was the most popular of Elisabeth's creations in medieval times. The seventy medieval manuscripts that transmit the *Revelatio* far exceed the copies of the two later twelfth-century compositions which continued the elaboration of the Ursuline legend.[30] Conversely, this same work has evoked the most negative response from critics ranging from Reformation polemicists to modern historians. Typical of this response is Wilhelm Oehl's characterization of the text as the most unpleasant fruit of old German mysticism, an adventurous, clumsy piece of work which nevertheless found countless readers and believers.[31]

With the visions and conversations narrated in this text, Elisabeth played a crucial role in the elaboration of the legend that had already grown to fantastic proportions. The cult of Saint Ursula and her eleven thousand companions is not easily untangled: its convolutions exercised the Bollandists for over two hundred pages in the *Acta Sanctorum*.[32] By the mid-twelfth century, two crucial events in the development of the cult had already taken place—the definitive expression of the legend in two Latin *passiones* and the discovery of an ancient Roman cemetery believed to be the burial site of the eleven thousand virgins.[33] The relic trade that resulted from this "discovery" is the immediate cause behind Elisabeth's new visionary document about the Cologne martyrs, and the weight of an existing literary tradition created the tension that Elisabeth addressed.

The two *passiones* that narrate the story of the Cologne martyrdom were preceded by numerous liturgical texts celebrating the observance of the Ursuline cult, but these *passiones* related the events in greater detail. The second and much more widely known of these *passiones*, *Regnante domino*, provides the standard version of the legend before Elisabeth's reworking of it.[34] According to this text Ursula, the young, beautiful, and very saintly daughter of a Christian king of Britain, sought to escape a marriage offer from a neighboring barbarian king and received a revelation of her impending martyrdom as a divinely ordained solution to the undesired proposal. She announced as her conditions for accepting the proposal that she be provided with eleven thousand, or more precisely,

10,999, virgins to accompany her for a respite of three years, as well as eleven ships to accommodate this company of young women.[35] When the three-year respite ended, God sent a strong wind that blew their ships far from Britain. Finding themselves sailing down the Rhine, the maidens disembarked at Cologne. They continued on to a quick pilgrimage to Rome, paying their respects to the tombs of the saints and spiritually pre- paring themselves for their ensuing ordeal. On their return to Cologne they were attacked by Huns, who had been besieging the city, and were slain when they resisted the barbarians' advances.

It is possible that Elisabeth knew *Regnante domino*, a popular text eventually transmitted in over seventy manuscripts.[36] Although she does not make use of two of the five proper names found in this text,[37] she does make several references to the accepted version of Ursula's story. Her lan- guage in these cases usually recalls scenes from *Regnante domino* without reproducing any direct quotation from it.[38]

Elisabeth's references to knowing another version of the legend also reveal her overwhelming awareness that she is involved in some question- able activity.[39] The potentially suspicious character of her revelations has everything to do with the two aspects of the Ursuline cult mentioned above—the existence of an authoritative literary tradition about the Co- logne martyrdom and the discovery of a burial ground outside the walls of Cologne. Elisabeth was aware that some of her assertions about the distant event contradicted the accepted version of that story. Rather than attempting to hide or diminish the significance of these discrepancies, Elis- abeth takes the opposite course and highlights the contradictions, giving greater scope for an imaginative re-creation.

The original impetus for developing an innovative scenario did not come from Elisabeth's reflection on the martyrdom, however imaginative or creative her new history was. It was Abbot Gerlach of Deutz's request for her to confirm the identity of the relics that led to her visionary reports. The inscriptions Elisabeth received from Gerlach, which can be found in the larger collection of *tituli* recorded by Thioderic of Deutz, formed the kernal of her revelations. Several of Thioderic's inscriptions appear to be from actual tombs that were excavated outside of Cologne, but many oth- ers bear the marks of twelfth-century fabrication. Someone, perhaps Thioderic, quickly "created" these epitaphs to accompany the newly ex- humed corpses.[40] After all, a bone without some kind of designation is merely a bone, and these were *relics*—some identification was needed. But whoever created these epitaphs frequently did not go beyond providing names and occasional descriptions of the status or origin of the martyrs. The larger task of fitting these names into the existing legend was left for Elisabeth.

Gerlach's desire to authenticate the relics and the text that Elisabeth produced in response reflect the dynamics of a period which Brian Stock has characterized as denoting the emergence of a literate culture. Not only were there more individuals who could read and write, but, more significantly, patterns of thought and behavior were shaped by an acknowledgment of the authority of texts.[41] Elisabeth here seems to stand at a time of major cultural transition. On the one hand, the concern for authenticating the physical remains of the purported saints is part of an increasingly literate society in which the sacred nature of physical objects is subject to scrutiny and in which textual proof for a sacred object is frequently sought.[42] On the other hand, the text that is produced purports to be a record of oral transactions, that is, the conversations between Elisabeth and the saints in question. Furthermore, the goal of authenticating the relics is achieved simply by providing witness to the inherently sacred nature of the objects rather than by a process of reasoned argumentation.

Elisabeth's self-consciousness about actively participating in literate culture is particularly obvious when she encountered the inscription that read *Sanctus Ciriacus papa Romanus*. How could she create a role for a Roman pope whose historical presence could be authenticated or disproven by consulting an authoritative text such as a list of Roman pontiffs? Her achievement was to create a scenario that allowed both her own text and the existing authoritative text to be true. In this scenario, Cyriacus becomes a native Briton,[43] who had been the nineteenth Roman pontiff for one year and eleven weeks when it was revealed to him by God that he was to leave the Roman See to join the virgins who were soon to arrive in Rome. When Ursula arrived, he resigned his office in the sight of the whole church "with everyone else protesting, especially the cardinals who judged it as madness that he would turn away as if after the folly of mere women."[44] But Cyriacus was still mindful of his responsibilities and would not leave Rome until, at his advice, Anterus was named as his successor. The fact that Cyriacus could not be found in any catalogue of Roman bishops is attributed to the indignation of the clergy who punished his abdication by excluding him from the records of Roman popes. Elisabeth's revision of the Ursuline legend made its impression on artists—very few medieval paintings of the Cologne martrydom omit the scene of Cyriacus's resignation in Rome—as well as on chroniclers.[45] For example, Alberic of

Trois Fontaines, writing in 1242, incorporated all this new and surprising data into his historical record and flatly stated that all historians and chronographers up to the time of Elisabeth were in error about the events of the Cologne martyrdom.[46]

VISIO DE RESURRECTIONE BEATE VIRGINIS MARIE

Like the revelations about Saint Ursula, Elisabeth's visions about the bodily assumption of Mary formed a very popular text. Despite concern that the text failed to meet certain standards of orthodoxy, it had a wide appeal, appearing in all the major collections of the visionary books as well as having a fairly extensive circulation independent of Elisabeth's other visions. *De Resurrectione* is the shortest of Elisabeth's complete texts, usually occupying only two folio pages. This brevity facilitated Ekbert's surprising incorporation of it into the conclusion of *Liber Visionum Secundus* when he created the final version of the collection. But even as the conclusion of the second visionary diary, *De Resurrectione* retained its original title and setting, which are not particularly congruous with the material directly preceding it.

The text is a series of six visions spanning the period from October 22, 1156, to March 25, 1159. Like other visions in the second and third visionary diaries, this series is focused on questions that Elisabeth had been directed to investigate in her ecstatic trances, and the subject was a point of theological dispute—the corporeal assumption of Mary.[47] Elisabeth reports that she eventually received the response to this and related questions. Her visions specifically affirm Mary's bodily resurrection and establish a new date for the Feast of the Assumption.

In this text, Elisabeth records her discomfort at announcing something that conflicted with tradition and her hesitation to publish something that would reveal her to be an *inventrix novitatum*.[48] Yet she also perceives that she had not received her revelations in vain. As she explains, Mary assured her that the visions were intended to be announced, not to the faithful at large, but to those people especially devoted to her. Despite Elisabeth's intended limitation of the audience for these revelations, this text was included in all the major versions of the visionary collections, a fact which suggests that Ekbert did not always heed Elisabeth's own concerns about the publication of her visions.

Ekbert's decision to publish the revelations about Mary's bodily assumption must be related to his own theological concerns, which prompted the inquiry in the first place. But given his general caution, Ekbert must have decided that this text would not bring disrepute to his sister and his monastery. Only several decades earlier, Peter Abelard had defended Mary's corporeal assumption by asserting the possibility of continued divine revelation—what was unknown to the early fathers could have been revealed to later generations.[49] The possibility that Abelard envisioned is exactly the reality that Ekbert prompted. The popularity of *De Resurrectione* indicates that Ekbert appears to have correctly judged the contemporary milieu and its receptivity to the new revelations about Mary's assumption.[50]

Another indication that Ekbert correctly judged the reception that Elisabeth's *De Resurrectione* would receive is the fact that before the end of the century a versified abridgment of the text appeared. Somebody adapted the material in this text, shifting from a first- to a third-person narration to create the new text, *De secunda [festivitate] assumptionis beate Mariae virginis*.[51]

The new text is not a slavish abridgment of Elisabeth's visions. It diverges in certain aspects and uses materials other than those contained in Elisabeth's text, including, it would appear, a ninth-century treatise on the Assumption attributed to Saint Jerome.[52] This later abridgment makes no mention of Elisabeth's fear of the potential scandal resulting from her introduction of new doctrine and liturgical practice, although it shares the original concern for establishing the correct observation of the newly revealed feast and even gives directions about the liturgical office to be used. No apology, hesitance, self-defense, or rationalization accompanies this implication that the church had hitherto erred in its celebration of Mary's assumption. Yet, despite the confident tone of the later abridgment, *De secunda assumptionis* never gained the popularity of the original, autobiographical version of Elisabeth's *De Resurrectione* witnessed by its wide circulation and the Anglo-Norman and Icelandic translations made of it.[53]

Letters

Twenty-two letters ascribed to Elisabeth of Schönau are known. The earliest collections of the visionary materials included several letters that are related in subject matter to particular books in the collections, and Ekbert later collected these and others into a separate book. Several letters were never part of Ekbert's collections but were added to the visionary material outside of Schönau.[54] The letters include little evidence about the time of their composition; only one can be assigned a precise date of composition and several others can be roughly dated.[55] There is some evidence that suggests that Elisabeth's composition of letters directed to specific communities and individuals outside of Schönau was part of her practice before Ekbert came to live with her and take charge of her visionary career.[56]

When Ekbert collected the letters into a separate book, he wrote an introduction describing the circumstances of Elisabeth's "announcement" of the letters. According to this introduction, a learned monk from the abbey of Busendorf came to Schönau to investigate Elisabeth's claims of miraculous revelations.[57] After he met with Elisabeth and decided her revelations were genuine, he requested "that sometime he may be worthy to receive from her a letter of the same grace as [found in] the other things which had been announced by her in the spirit."[58] He likewise requested some edifying words to be sent to his abbot and brothers. Ekbert reports that on that same night Elisabeth "suddenly and unexpectedly pronounced" the first letter, and three nights later she likewise announced the letter to the abbot of Busendorf. Ekbert summarily concludes the introduction by stating that from that point Elisabeth had the grace of announcing letters.[59]

Most of Elisabeth's addressees are named, although three remain uncertain.[60] The circle of correspondents is generally limited to the area of Trier and the neighboring dioceses of Cologne, Mainz, Metz, and Speyer. Sometimes Elisabeth refers to receiving letters from her correspondents, but only in the case of Hildegard of Bingen is anything resembling a mutual correspondence extant.

Except for two cases—a letter directed to the bishops of Trier, Cologne, and Mainz and a letter addressed to Hillin, the archbishop of Trier—Elisabeth's letters are addressed to monastic audiences. Both of these letters exhort the addressees to preach the word of God revealed to her in the *Liber Viarum Dei*. In two other letters, Elisabeth identifies still more relics of the Cologne martyrs, but most of the letters focus on pastoral concerns. Whether she is ordering German archbishops to preach penance to the Roman church, exhorting abbots or abbesses to wield their pastoral staves with diligence and discretion, prescribing the appropriate penance for an accidental profanation of the Eucharist, counseling monks not to long to go on pilgrimage to Jerusalem, condemning simony, or criticizing ecclesiastical leaders for neglecting the threat of the Cathars, Elisabeth's primary concern is to offer guidance for the smooth maintenance of righteous, devout, and peaceful community life. And she announces these words with the confidence that, when she speaks, a much greater voice is sounding through her.

EKBERT'S *DE OBITU ELISABETH*

Circulating with the records of Elisabeth's visionary experiences is a relatively short text composed by Ekbert. *De Obitu Elisabeth* is Ekbert's narrative description of the final days of Elisabeth's life. This text is the only extended biographical account of Elisabeth that Ekbert has given, albeit of only her last two weeks.[61]

Two versions of this text are extant—a shorter, apparently original version and an expanded account.[62] There are two main differences between them. First, the long version includes a passage concerning the appointment of Elisabeth's succesor as *magistra* of the Schönau nuns and the possible eclipse of Elisabeth's reputation after her death.[63] This passage is recorded as Elisabeth's own words. But its appearance in only the longer version indicates a passage of time during which the first matter may have been settled and the second (the demise of Elisabeth's reputation) may have been weighing heavily on Ekbert's mind.

The second difference is that, in large portions of the longer text, every third or fourth sentence is not found in the original. It is possible that the Vienna *De Obitu* represents a consistent abridgment, but it seems more likely that the other manuscripts represent a later version expanded by Ekbert himself working from an earlier, shorter version. This is entirely consistent with other examples of Ekbert's expansions of previously published works, and he would be especially free to do so in this case, where he was clearly the author and not just recorder of the work. It appears that Ekbert composed the original version of *De Obitu* very soon after the death of his sister and sometime later, perhaps within the year,[64] made additions to the text which reflect the later situation of the monastery and his own later concerns.

De Obitu begins with an introduction addressed to Ekbert's three kinswomen Guda, Hadewig, and Regelindis at the convent of Andernach. He expresses his grief at Elisabeth's death although he hastens to assure his readers that this is not due merely to the loss of his sister, but for the loss of one who provided such palpable spiritual advantages to himself and others. He does not portray Elisabeth simply as a passive medium of communication, but emphasizes her role as mediator, as one who has "effectively negotiated between God and humans."[65] Unlike contemporary imagery used to describe Mary as *mediatrix*,[66] there is no intercessory quality to Elisabeth's negotiation. This is particularly noteworthy because Ekbert is writing here of a deceased person, one who could have some intercessory power as a saint in heaven. However, Ekbert is not concerned with Elisabeth's presence in heaven, but rather with what she did while she was alive, with her unique contribution to the salvation of those who believed in her visionary gifts.

In the second and much longer part of the text, Ekbert gives a day-by-day description of the end of Elisabeth's life, from Pentecost until June 20, the day of her burial. Despite the difficulty in correlating the information given in this text with external data about the date of Elisabeth's death, and even though at two different points he admits he cannot remember everything Elisabeth said and did in her final days, he nonetheless provides an orderly outline of the major events.

Several themes prominent in the earlier visionary records recur here in Ekbert's text. Elisabeth's concern for her reputation, her reaction to criticism, and her fear that her life (and now her death) may be misunderstood by others are major motifs in *De Obitu*. Related to the question of Elisabeth's reputation are Ekbert's repeated attempts to underscore the marvelous nature of her final days. He describes how those who gathered to witness marveled at her continued survival and at the discretion of her sermons despite the weakness of her body and her inability to eat. This wonder at her continued soundness of mind despite her physical torment is of particular value to Ekbert. He comments on how Elisabeth's mental clarity is accompanied by a kind of emotional detachment, so unlike the rest of her earlier, emotionally volatile life.[67]

Because *De Obitu* is unlike all the other texts in the Schönau corpus in that it is not primarily a record of Elisabeth's visionary experience, a somewhat different image of Elisabeth emerges. Her visions are still preserved, and she is certainly remembered as one who received divine revelations, yet a substantial portion of *De Obitu* reflects an image of Elisabeth as *magistra* and spiritual leader of the Schönau community. The nuns' attachment to and dependence on Elisabeth is poignantly conveyed in Ekbert's description of Elisabeth sitting up in bed, leaning against the breast of one of the sisters. This sister confides to Elisabeth that the nuns have always depended on her to indicate to them when one of their dying sisters was to be taken out of bed and placed on the shroud. Now with Elisabeth herself dying, the sisters will not know when to do this unless she indicates the moment. Later in the text, the last thing Elisabeth does before she dies is extend her hand and signal three times that she is to be moved onto the shroud.

Ekbert reports that in her final days Elisabeth spent much time delivering sermons to the community about their continued commitment to the life they have chosen. He mentions that she did not hesitate to exhort priests and deacons and that she also addressed the lay people that gathered round her during those last days. Ekbert uses this deathbed setting to confirm his overall portrayal of Elisabeth as a spiritual authority, even if in this immediate context she makes no startling revelations but confines herself to moral exhortation. He is also careful to illustrate that as a spiritual authority she is not led to forget her place in the hierarchy of the monastic community. Preparing to die, Elisabeth extends her hands to the abbot, affirms her past obedience to him, and reminds him of his responsibility to her, recalling the words of the Rule of Saint Benedict that on the day of judgment the abbot must make account to God of all souls charged to his care.[68]

Elisabeth's relationship to her community is, of course, not simply one of a nun to her convent. Ekbert includes two references to the glory of Schönau due to the extraordinary experiences of Elisabeth,[69] remarks that would certainly please the monks and nuns at Schönau and that reflect his own interest in maintaining Schönau's claim to honor. In this same context, the question of Ekbert's own relationship to Schönau is also raised. In the later version of the text, Ekbert reports that Elisabeth exhorted him never to leave Schönau even if he is called to a more prestigious or wealthier place.

Thus in *De Obitu*, Ekbert fills out the image of Elisabeth as visionary by including many details about her role as nun, *magistra*, and spiritual adviser within her community, as well as preacher to both clergy and lay people beyond the walls of her monastery. Ekbert's portrait is, of course, unabashedly flattering to Elisabeth and commendatory of Schönau. Yet despite the rhetoric of praise, it is still possible to gain insight into Elisabeth during the last period of her life and to detect traces of Ekbert's concerns in composing the text after her death.

The Development and Dissemination of the Visionary Corpus

While a complete explanation of the development of the visionary corpus must await a critical edition of the texts, some observations can be made at this point.[70] Because the three texts that form the core of the visionary collection (*Liber Viarum Dei, De Resurrectione, Revelatio*) all record events that transpired after Ekbert's move to Schönau, it can be noted that no compilation of texts predates Ekbert's arrival. In fact, although Elisabeth's visions began in 1152 and the nuns of Schönau wrote down her descriptions of her experience, there is no evidence of a formal collection of visionary texts published outside the walls of Schönau until at least 1159.[71]

It is also the case that Ekbert was willing to expand texts that had already been published. The first collection of the early autobiographical materials (*Liber Visionum Primus*) was later expanded, and the second diary as well circulated in both early and later, longer versions. Within Elisabeth's own lifetime it is possible that two different collections of her works were in circulation: a "core collection" of the three major thematic texts and a collection in which this core was preceded by the original version of the first visionary diary. After her death, Ekbert continued to add to the collection by including his own composition about Elisabeth's final days and by organizing the later, hitherto unpublished "miscellaneous" records into the final visionary diaries.

In addition to Ekbert's steady enlargement of the visionary canon, the manuscripts also reveal Ekbert refining the collection by occasional suppression and revision of old material.[72] Elisabeth's prophecy, which spurred the blazing if indiscreet preaching of Hildelin, appears at the end of the original version of *Liber Visionum Primus*, but when that text was expanded to its full length, the prophecy disappeared. A brief vision in the Ursuline revelations suffered a similar fate due—it seems likely—to the desire to suppress the implied accusations of impiety directed at the Premonstratensian cloister at Ilbenstadt contained in the passage.[73] Third, a brief adjuration to future scribes copying the *Liber Viarum Dei* is omitted in the final version of the collection.[74]

Two brief compositions of Ekbert found in some of the early versions of the collection were also dropped. A prayer that comes at the end of the complete *Liber Visionum Primus* or at the beginning of *Liber Visionum Secundus* is found in Redactions C and D but was expurged in the final collection.[75] His description of a vision which he himself had at the abbey church of Deutz that originally formed a brief appendix to the Ursuline materials was also dropped.[76] These two compositions, which did not have the same controversial edge as the apocalyptic prophecy or the vision about Ilbenstadt, were probably dropped as part of Ekbert's effort to produce a clean collection of Elisabeth's visions stripped of extraneous materials. Similarly, a vision of Hildegard of Bingen about the Cathars, which sets the context for Elisabeth's own revelations about the Cathars, dropped out of the final collection, probably as a result of this same effort to produce an uncluttered "canon" of genuine, if expurgated, visionary material. In the final redaction Ekbert also added one final writing of his own, a letter to Prior Ulrich of the Premonstratensian cloister of Steinfeld which contained revelations announced by Elisabeth and was thereby appropriate for inclusion in an "official" collection of her visionary material.[77]

There are also other visionary records that were never part of the collection. The text about the Cologne martyrs had a very broad dissemination independent of its circulation in the various collections of Elisabeth's visions. Many of these manuscripts include one or two revelations that cannot be found in manuscripts transmitting collections of texts, thus suggesting that even as it appears in the earliest redaction of the collections, the revelations about Ursula may have already been subject to the censoring activity of Ekbert.[78] Other occasional unique and "noncanonical" episodes are also found in manuscripts from monasteries that had special connections to Schönau.[79]

In addition to suppressions, minor editorial revisions also characterize the difference between earlier and later versions of the collection. Many are largely stylistic, yet sometimes even relatively minor changes shift the weight of a passage to create a slightly different nuance. For example, for Elisabeth's introductory remarks in *Liber Visionum Primus* addressed to Ekbert, the manuscripts of Redaction B offer a consistent pattern of minor variants which represents the original version of the text. A comparison of the two versions reveals that Ekbert tended to make changes in the references to himself, whether he is omitting Elisabeth's addresses of intimacy ("mi dilecte"; "frater") or subtly revising the picture of his role in the production of the visionary corpus. Most strikingly, Ekbert wrote himself out of one sentence. The original rendering of Elisabeth's words ("it was pleasing *to you* and the lord abbot that *you commit* my words to writing") is changed so that Ekbert's role is hidden ("it was pleasing to the lord abbot that my words be committed to writing").[80] As Giles Constable has noted, there are infinite shadings between correction, revision, imitation, and falsification in the drafting of medieval documents.[81] These modifications in the introduction to *Liber Visionum Primus* illustrate Ekbert's willingness to change the records of Elisabeth's words, even after they had already been published, and to change them in such a way as to alter slightly their original spirit.

Ekbert made these changes when he added chapters 26 to 79 to the original visionary diary, that is, at the time he produced the texts that comprise Redaction C. This is the same point at which Elisabeth's infamous prophecy was dropped from the collection, and it marks as well the first appearance of *De Obitu*, thus suggesting that the revisions took place after Elisabeth's death. After the modifications made at this point, very few verbal revisions appear in the later redactions. New visions, of course, were still added, material deemed inappropriate was still dropped, and texts were rearranged, but the original version of *Liber Visionum Primus* remains the only text where rewriting can be seen. It is not surprising that the original visionary diary is the only text in which Ekbert's "polishing" went beyond a purely stylistic function. The other texts either were produced under his direction and thus presumably required less revision or else were first published after Elisabeth's death, only appearing in the collection when Ekbert was satisfied with them.

And yet the case for Ekbert's textual revisions must not be overstated. Within *Liber Visionum Primus*, only a few other passages beyond those given above are reworked. A perhaps unorthodox, or at least impolite, ranking of Saint Paul above Saint Peter is changed to a neutral quotation of a Pauline verse;[82] a series of saintly apparitions is rewritten so that the order of their appearances conforms to the calendar order of their feasts;[83] a general reference to Elisabeth's sufferings is recast to include a specific reference to the limited possessions of Schönau.[84] These reworkings of brief passages, along with the suppressions, rearrangements, and additions of new materials, suggest that Ekbert gained greater editorial freedom after Elisabeth's death. Despite his control over the publication of his sister's revelations, remarkably little internal change can be traced. From this we can conclude his own satisfaction with the collection as it stood.

These details help to fill out the picture of how Elisabeth's words were carried beyond her community to the world outside the walls of Schönau. One final aspect of the publication of Elisabeth's visions remains: the dispersion of manuscripts. It has been argued that the popularity of Elisabeth's writings, witnessed in the numerous manuscripts transmitting her texts, can be attributed to a rather simple cause. The dispersion of relics of the eleven thousand virgins from the reputed site of the Cologne martyrdom to monasteries throughout Germany and France and the Low Countries, either by sales or gifts, created a demand for texts that furnished information about these saints.[85]

It does appear that a pattern can be traced in which the acquisition of relics from Cologne generated an interest in Elisabeth's visions and contributed to the dispersion of her works. For example, in 1270–72, the Benedictine abbey at St. Trond received numerous heads from the mar-

tyred companions of Saint Ursula. Not surprisingly, Elisabeth's revelations
about the Cologne martyrdom as well as the earlier *passio, Regnante
domino*, are found in the fourteenth-century *Legendarium S. Trudonis*, indicating the monastery's interest in having textual support for the value of
its relics.[86]

Yet, of the 145 known manuscripts transmitting any text of Elisabeth,
fewer than a dozen of these codices contain the Ursuline revelations and
are also associated with establishments that had already acquired relics
from the Cologne cache.[87] Although it appears that the proliferation of
the relics of the eleven thousand Cologne martyrs enhanced the popularity
of Elisabeth's revelations about Ursula and her companions, the development of the Ursuline cult alone cannot adequately explain the possession
of Elisabeth's visionary works—as one mid-thirteenth-century writer put
it—in many monasteries in France as well as Germany.[88] In fact, Elisabeth's visions were often copied and appreciated for reasons quite different
from their potential role in the Ursuline cult. For example, we have already
noted Roger of Ford's recommendation that the *Liber Viarum Dei* be copied and read, as well as his testimony to its popularity. The whole British
transmission of Elisabeth's works which stems from Roger's copy is not at
all related to the spread of the Cologne relics, a cult that was never significant in medieval England.[89] Moreover, collections of Elisabeth's visionary
texts are usually found in manuscripts that transmit other devotional and
theological works by writers such as Hugh of Saint Victor and Bernard of
Clairvaux, thus providing further evidence for the way in which her works
were viewed. A now lost manuscript of the Carthusian house of Salvator-
berg in the diocese of Erfurt transmitted the visions of Elisabeth along
with the revelations of Mechtild of Magdeburg and the life and revelations of a certain virgin named Margaret. This is one of several books
comprised primarily of women's revelations, another of which in the same
series was entitled *Collectorium ex libris devotarum feminarum*.[90] A similar
appreciation for Elisabeth's works can be seen in the inclusion of her
visions in a collection of early Cistercian exemplum material begun at
Clairvaux within a decade of her death. *Liber Visionum Primus* and *Liber
Viarum Dei* comprise the single largest component of this "thoughtful
compilation meant for internal use in the monastery" that provides some
of the earliest evidence for a "dawning Cistercian fascination with the content of female visions."[91] It is clear that in these contexts Elisabeth's visions
were collected for what they claimed to be: divine revelations made to a
pious woman.

4. Ekbert and the Visionary Books

Scribe, translator, editor, censor, interrogator, publicist, and publisher—Ekbert of Schönau played all these roles in the process of transforming Elisabeth's oral proclamations into written records available for public reading.[1] Even a cursory perusal of the visionary collection reveals Ekbert's presence. But the exact outlines of these roles are much more difficult to determine, and tracing these roles must serve as the basis for assessing his influence on the experience of his sister and on the books that record it. Because all the material passed through the filter of Ekbert's editorial activity, it is only when the limits of his contributions to the finished literary product have been determined that one can confidently say anything about Elisabeth herself.[2]

Everything presented thus far in this study, that is, the outlines of Elisabeth's and Ekbert's lives, the descriptions of the visionary texts, the analysis of the divergent manuscript transmissions of the texts, raises the question of Ekbert's role and offers some basis for answering it. Ekbert's own writings also serve as a basis for comparison with the material he attributes to Elisabeth. This comparison aids not only in considering his possible theological influences on Elisabeth, but also in differentiating the style and language of the material associated with Elisabeth from that of Ekbert's theological writings.

Ekbert reflected on his own role and wrote about it at several points. In the expanded introduction to *Liber Visionum Primus*, he gives a general description of Elisabeth's experiences, and then continues:

> Since therefore all the things which took place around her appeared to pertain to the glory of God and the edification of the faithful, they were for the most part transcribed in writing in the present little book according to her narration in which she expounded each thing to one of her brothers from the order of clerics whom she knew better than the others. Although she had hidden many things from questioners because she was very timid and most humble in spirit, she was forced by the order of the abbot and for the sake of love and kinship to explain intimately in detail all things to that one who was diligently investigating everything and desirous of handing it all down to posterity.[3]

Here Ekbert portrays a scenario in which Elisabeth feared to reveal her visions to people who questioned her, but was forced by obedience to her abbot and ties of kinship to confide in one cleric with whom she had a special relationship.

This cleric, whom Ekbert does not explicitly identify as himself, was not a passive amanuensis, but instead actively investigated the details of her accounts. This impression of Ekbert closely questioning Elisabeth is explicitly confirmed in an episode in *Liber Visionum Tertius* where Elisabeth describes receiving understanding about a technical, theological issue and is then assured by the angel that he will aid her in recounting this information in her interrogation.[4] Indeed, part of Ekbert's investigation of Elisabeth's revelations may have involved his resorting to research in order to understand, verify, or explain what she said. This process is visible in *Revelatio* where there is a well-known tradition that Elisabeth's visions respond to and comment on. In general, however, the visionary records do not include transcripts of a question-and-answer-type investigation of Elisabeth's experiences or of a comparison of her words to authoritative sources. Rather, the descriptions of visions are presented as uninterrupted narrative expositions of the events.[5] Thus there is some discrepancy between what Ekbert says happened (diligent investigation) and what is preserved in the records themselves (uninterrupted narration). Ekbert emphasizes that what has been written down was done so according to Elisabeth's narration, but the narration presented in the records may reflect what Elisabeth said in response to a series of questions that would have prompted her elaboration of her experience.[6]

Ekbert's description of investigating and recording Elisabeth's words, like Elisabeth's prefatory remarks that follow it, somewhat distorts the process that actually took place. As was mentioned above, the recording of Elisabeth's words began before Ekbert came to Schönau to work with her. The nuns at Schönau wrote down the words of the ecstatic sister in their midst, both before and after Ekbert joined the community, and Ekbert himself recorded her visions during visits to Schönau before he moved there permanently. Ekbert does not explicitly refer to the use of previously written records, but his use of a passive construction to describe the literary process ("in presenti libello . . . conscripta sunt"), does not preclude the possibility that he gathered together existing written records. His terse description of the literary process found in his introduction to *Liber Visionum Secundus* is worth noting: "Those things, which the Lord deigned to work in his handmaid after the end of the first book, have been added to the earlier ones according to her own words."[7] Again a passive, impersonal construction is used. It is not until the prologue to the visionary collection found only in the last redaction that he identifies himself by name and describes himself actively writing down Elisabeth's dictation:

> I, Ekbert, brother of the handmaid of God, drawn by the wonder of God from Bonn to the monastery at Schönau, and at first a monk, and then called by the grace of God to the abbacy, have written down all these things and others which are gathered from her revelations in such a way that where the words of the angel were Latin I left them unchanged, but where they were German, I translated them into Latin, as clearly as I could, adding nothing from my own presumption, seeking nothing of human favor nor earthly advantage, with God as my witness to whom all things are exposed and open [cf. Heb. 4:13].[8]

Here in the midst of Ekbert's most explicit identification of himself as scribe (and translator), he also refers to "other [things] which are gathered from her revelations," obliquely indicating his inclusion of other written materials.

Ekbert's declaration that some of the visionary records reflect his translation indicates that there was probably some extended process involved in creating literary records from Elisabeth's oral descriptions. This accords with the impression created by an examination of the chronology of the later redactions of the visionary corpus. Redactions C, D, and E all include *De Obitu* and thus were compiled sometime after Elisabeth died. If the published texts were only verbatim records of Elisabeth's narrations, all of the visionary material could have been included in Redaction C, which appears to stem from the period in which Elisabeth died. But since the records needed further work such as translation, reorganization, literary polishing, and even revision, it is not surprising that some of the material did not appear until after Elisabeth's death.

As noted earlier, Ekbert's suppression of certain potentially damaging or questionable visions is another aspect of his work on the literary records of Elisabeth's experience. Of course, Ekbert never discusses these suppressions as part of his editorial activity, but he does refer to a similar type of censorship. In his letter to Reinhard of Reinhausen, Ekbert admits that he has not recorded all the marvelous things that have happened to his sister, and he offers three reasons for the incomplete records: the requirements of his other claustral duties, the scarcity of parchment, and the negative reactions of some people who have heard about Elisabeth. He does not say that he is concealing some of Elisabeth's experiences in order to avoid criticism but rather that the "malice of detractors" afflicts him with "tedium and inactivity."[9] In his *Vita Eckeberti*, Emecho describes Ekbert's discrimination as part of his achievement: "Diligently investigating all the marvels which our Lord worked with her, he put into writing those things that he saw to be appropriate for the use of the faithful, but those things that he knew would not profit the readers, he totally concealed."[10] Thus the records as they are preserved do not offer a complete picture of Elisabeth's experiences. Their inclusion in the collection indicates that they were judged by Ekbert to be appropriate for public reading.

It is not clear from the visionary records that Elisabeth had any part in the production of the texts other than narrating her experiences. While it has been suggested that Elisabeth apparently wrote down many things herself,[11] the evidence for this is questionable. Elisabeth's reference in *Liber Visionum Primus* to keeping a collection of written documents hidden under her bed[12] does not in fact indicate that she wrote the documents. Rather, this refers to the inchoate version of *Liber Visionum Primus* that Ekbert had already begun compiling from her narratives before his permanent move to Schönau. Moreover, Elisabeth never describes herself as writing; instead, she refers to her visions being committed to writing.[13]

Furthermore, there is no reference to Elisabeth examining the texts that came from Ekbert's hand or listening to his renderings of her words. Ekbert reports in *Liber Visionum Primus* that Elisabeth welcomed his role as editor and left "editorial" decisions to him.[14] Yet the fact that Ekbert attributes these words to Elisabeth in her opening speech of *Liber Visionum Primus* must be compared with two passages in the same book in which Elisabeth explicitly retains some discretionary privilege. In one case, Elisabeth asserted that she was not ready to announce a revelation she had received from the Virgin Mary[15]; whether she ever announced this particular message is not clear. In the other, she declared that because of potential disbelief she would refrain from reporting certain unusual experiences.[16] Thus Elisabeth is portrayed as not complying fully with the abbot's earlier order that she tell all her revelations to her brother. Consequently, she appears to retain some control over the publication of her visions. Yet even this does not indicate that Elisabeth had any active role in supervising the process of compilation or approving the finished literary product.

Although it appears that Ekbert was responsible for creating the literary documents that survive as records of Elisabeth's descriptions, this observation is not a reason to conclude that Elisabeth had no interest in the authenticity or correctness of the documents that circulated under her name. In a letter to Hildegard of Bingen, Elisabeth expressed her concern about being associated with written records that do not accurately reflect her genuine experiences.[17] This concern with the accurate transmission of her experiences also underlies the exhortation at the end of the *Liber Viarum Dei* in which scribes are urged to proofread carefully the copies they make of the text.[18]

The picture that emerges from this evidence is the following: Elisabeth began to have some type of extraordinary experience. She was afraid to discuss it with certain people who questioned her, but she did describe her visions to some of the sisters in her community, who wrote down what she told them. During Ekbert's visits to Schönau, and perhaps through news of Hildelin's preaching, he learned about his sister's pronouncements. His interest in Elisabeth's experience eventually led him to join her at Schönau and take up the task of compiling and publishing her visions. To do this, Ekbert gathered the material already written (some letters and the records that he incorporated into the visionary diaries), questioned Elisabeth about what she saw and heard, provided the impetus for new visionary experiences by presenting questions for her to bring to her heavenly informants, and recorded her descriptions of these experiences. He then worked over these records, translating, polishing, revising, until he had a text that satisfied his judgment about what was appropriate to be published. Elisabeth did not tell Ekbert everything she experienced, nor did Ekbert publish everything she told him.

This bare outline of events only raises more questions, not all of which can be answered from the evidence available. For example, the nature of the working relationship between Ekbert and Elisabeth remains mysterious. Tantalizing hints are given. Ekbert tells one correspondent that he can judge Elisabeth's experiences better than anyone else because of his closeness to her. But in emphasizing his access to Elisabeth ("cottidie cuncta comperio, que accidunt in ea"), he seems to suggest that he has a daily source of information about her, rather than direct personal contact with her.[19] At least once, Ekbert admitted the use of intermediaries.[20] Many of the visionary records, however, retain the words of Elisabeth's direct address to her brother and a familiar, conversational tone. Hildelin's insistence that Elisabeth reveal her visions to Ekbert, as well as the sibling relationship between Ekbert and Elisabeth, must have removed potential obstacles to their meetings, meetings that may otherwise have been suspicious and difficult to arrange in the life of a cloistered nun. In regard to the nature of their relationship, it is also interesting to note that there is no evidence Ekbert ever acted as Elisabeth's confessor. This role was reserved for Hildelin.[21]

The working relationship between Ekbert and Elisabeth comes to be understood by them as part of the same divinely ordained plan that made Elisabeth the recipient of God's revelations.[22] But once this relationship between Elisabeth and Ekbert was consolidated with Ekbert's move to Schönau, the character of the visionary records changed. There is a shift of emphasis from the kinds of experiences recorded in *Liber Visionum Primus* and the original *Liber Visionum Secundus*, such as Elisabeth's reports of being tormented by demons and her descriptions of the otherworld, to the more theological subjects of the later records. This does not mean that all of Elisabeth's experiences after the time of Ekbert's move were exclusively of one type; it just means that the selection of preserved material appears to reflect Ekbert's interests. Nor does it mean that once Ekbert came to live at Schönau he more freely changed Elisabeth's words. None of the texts was published before his move to Schönau, so if he had been involved in a massive changing of Elisabeth's words, there is no reason why it should have occurred only in the descriptions of events following his move.

It appears much more likely that, after he joined the Schönau community, Ekbert exercised more direct influence over the nature of the experiences themselves. This influence is so obvious because neither Ekbert nor Elisabeth felt any need to hide it. The visions of the later diaries and of the three theological cycles that postdate Ekbert's arrival all retain the words of his questions, the words which directed Elisabeth's attention to subjects she may otherwise never have considered. Ekbert was not alone in his belief that special graces such as Elisabeth's could be tapped to obtain otherworldly information to help solve puzzling questions. In 1148 or 1149, Master Odo of Paris wrote to Hildegard of Bingen requesting a solution to a controversy about the theological language of Gilbert de la Porrée. Odo expected Hildegard to arrive at a judgment based on her visions.[23] In Hildegard's case, however, there was no intimate relationship between visionary and investigator as there was in Elisabeth's case. Therefore, Hildegard's visions display an independence of perspective that cannot be found in the records of Elisabeth's visionary career once Ekbert became such an important presence in her life. With Elisabeth's more continuous association with her brother and with his active interest in pursuing theological questions through the medium of her visions, it is not surprising that the character of her visions changed. It appears that even if Ekbert had a certain agenda, theological or otherwise, in publishing the records of his sister's revelations, he was able to introduce his perspective to Elisabeth in such a way that it, to some degree, became her own, and thus he was able to eliminate the need to "rewrite" the records.

The fact that Ekbert allowed the evidence of his influence to remain so overt in the records he published reveals something of his own understanding of what was going on. Since he repeatedly stressed the divine origin of Elisabeth's revelations, he would not have allowed anything to remain in the texts that in any way compromised that claim. Therefore, his retention of his own questions in the visionary texts suggests that he did not think his direction of Elisabeth's attention to certain subjects would be understood by her readers as an action that invalidated the answers she received. Because Ekbert was working within a framework based on the divine reality of Elisabeth's experiences, he did not understand her answers to be simply the result of his own questions. Rather, the vision that she sees has an objective reality that is not affected by whether or not she asks to see it. If she learns something in her vision, it is true.

Ekbert's understanding of Elisabeth's visionary experience is comparable to the work of many twelfth-century biblical commentators who paid little attention to the historical careers or personalities of biblical authors since they believed the scriptural texts to be products of divine inspiration. In both cases, the activity of God rather than the circumstances of the prophet's literary activity is seen as the source and authority of the text.[24] This view of inspiration accounts for the ease with which biblical commentators could ignore the ostensibly human erotic context of the Song of Songs and the freedom with which Ekbert could leave evidence of his own role so obvious in the written records of Elisabeth's visions.

But if the questions came from Ekbert, where did the answers come from? When a question is posed for Elisabeth's visionary conversations with a heavenly personality, particularly a question in which she may have had no previous interest, how much of the answer must also be attributed to Ekbert? This is perhaps the thorniest of problems vexing the analysis of the visionary texts, and there is no simple solution. The different circumstances described in the various texts require examination of several different episodes.

Although the texts portray a certain divine tolerance for these questions from mortals, this tolerance has its limits: Elisabeth occasionally reports that the questions are inappropriate and thus they are left unanswered. For example, Elisabeth was tutored by Ekbert to ask the Virgin Mary whether Origen, the great teacher whom the church condemned as heretical and yet who so wonderfully sang the praises of Mary, could be saved from final damnation. Mary's response vindicates Origen of any malicious intent—his error was due solely to his excessive fervor for exploring the secrets of Scripture. But Elisabeth repeats that Mary would not tell her the state of his eternal fate. This is a secret that God does not want revealed.[25]

Here Ekbert perceives a set of conflicting circumstances, that is, the church's condemnation of Origen on the one hand and, on the other hand, his popularity as a biblical expositor. With no conclusive means of judging between them, Ekbert seeks the answer directly from heaven via Elisabeth's visionary conversations with Mary. Elisabeth refuses to be the medium of either an implicit criticism of the church's condemnation or of a criticism of the contemporary attraction to Origen. There is no reason to see this response as the suggestion of Ekbert: there would be no reason for him to pose a question for which he could only suggest such an inconclusive answer. This incident is more reasonably explained as Ekbert testing the limits of Elisabeth's access to privileged information. And the answer is Elisabeth's way of sidestepping a decision she does not want to make, with the subtle reminder of the danger of excessive fervor in exploring divine secrets. That, after all, was the cause of Origen's error.

This response recalls Elisabeth's reaction to another query. In the sermon on the life of ecclesiastical leaders in the *Liber Viarum Dei*, Elisabeth reports the following:

> While the angel was speaking those words about the pastors of the church to me, to certain people it appeared opportune for me to inquire about those things in which some doubting people took occasion for their error. Therefore, not as one hesitating in faith but as one desiring our faith to be confirmed by angelic authority, I inquired and said: "Lord, do the offices of those bishops who entered their episcopacy wrongly and not according to God, and of those bishops whose entrance was good, have equal power in ecclesiastical sacraments?" He responded saying: "Many, while they investigate such profound matters are more corrupted than corrected. The Lord would reveal such things if those people to whom they pertain would not more freely sin for it." Having said these things, he was immediately withdrawn from my eyes.[26]

Later Elisabeth receives the orthodox response to this question, but there are several points here worth noting. The apology for her question, while it seems well within her personality to offer an apology, nevertheless has a ring of Ekbert's style to it. The phrase *ex angelica auctoritate firmari* sounds more like the words of a student of theology than one of Elisabeth's customary turns of phrase. Although throughout her visionary experiences Elisabeth is concerned with questions of authority, the word *auctoritas* occurs only here, and, despite her numerous references to the angel, she never uses the adjective "angelic." Elisabeth appears to have accepted someone else's rationale for posing such questions to her informer. Second, despite resigning herself to the role of interrogator, she still allows her uneasiness to be manifested in her not-so-subtle hint that those people pushing her to such investigations may be guilty themselves of the sins they are examining.

These episodes in which no direct answers are immediately forthcoming to the externally motivated questions appear to reflect genuine interchanges between Elisabeth and Ekbert. Ekbert's question certainly influences Elisabeth's experience by turning her attention to new subjects, but in handing the question over to her, he has relinquished control over the response. In her response, we see Elisabeth's style of handling both these questions and those who would use her in this way.

The questions that go unanswered constitute only a minor fraction of the visionary experiences motivated by the participation of Ekbert and others. Much more frequently, Elisabeth is portrayed as directly responding to the queries with information gained from her conversations with angels and saints. In fact, whole texts are sometimes comprised of such circumstances. The revelations about the Cologne martyrdom, for example, are in essence a series of visionary records in which Elisabeth is presented with some data (i.e., the *tituli* from the Cologne tombs), and she in turn asks her heavenly interlocutors to comment on or reveal further information about each case. Here again, the external influence upon Elisabeth and her experience is undeniable—the questions motivate her toward certain action. There is no reason, however, to see the visionary announcements as anything but Elisabeth's response to an admittedly difficult situation. Her self-consciousness about what she is doing is patent in the text, as is her rationalization for the novelty of her revelations.

Furthermore, a spirituality redolent with a commitment to virginity and an impassioned devotion to the saints in heaven, the two primary religious aspects of these revelations, is exactly the religious perspective that characterizes her earliest experiences recorded in *Liber Visionum Primus*, those experiences least subject to external influence. In fact, the case of *Revelatio* is somewhat different than the questions about Origen's fate or simoniacal bishops, because here the externally conceived questions coincide with something that is already an area of genuine interest for Elisabeth. The text itself indicates this: Elisabeth describes her initial reaction to the arrival of Saint Verena's body at Schönau, and it is only after Elisabeth had already begun having visions about the martyrs that Abbot Gerlach of Deutz presented Elisabeth with the *tituli* for further identification and authentication. Thus, as in the case of the unanswered questions, the presence of externally provided questions in the visionary records does not mean the visionary response to the question should be attributed to Ekbert.

Like the revelations about the Ursuline martyrs, *De Resurrectione* is a text originating from a question which Elisabeth was instructed to carry into her ecstatic state. This time the question had distinct theological implications and, in fact, represented a controversial point in the development of Marian doctrine and piety. Again the question is externally motivated, and again one must ask, how much of the answer is Elisabeth's? First, it can be seen that in this case, presenting the question to Elisabeth appears to have involved instructing her, to some degree, about the controversy behind the question: Elisabeth reports that she asked Mary about her assumption because she had been told there was uncertainty on this subject in the writings of the Fathers.[27] The explanation of the doubtful patristic positions must have set the outside limits of what Elisabeth could expect to learn in her vision. This kind of preparation then necessarily influenced her experience. In addition, the way she was briefed could also reveal the inclinations or predispositions of Ekbert on this particular question. Elisabeth's uneasiness with this situation is revealed in her first report of Mary's response: "What you seek, you cannot yet know; nevertheless it will be that this will be revealed through you."[28]

Elisabeth reports that it is not until one year later that she receives a vision that her angel interprets to her as representing the bodily assumption of Mary. The preparation Elisabeth received regarding the background of the question and the distance between the original question and the received revelation leave much room for Elisabeth to absorb the views of others on this question, to reflect on them, and to respond to them. Her vision of Mary's bodily resurrection is consistent with her other expressions of Mary's regal nature and her fervent veneration of Mary. Consequently, Elisabeth's assertion of Mary's assumption should not be seen as a foreign belief foisted upon her by theologians who wanted supernatural confirmation of their opinions. Instead, we see Elisabeth treading lightly when she senses she is being led onto unfamiliar and controversial ground, biding her time to avoid any proclamation made in the name of Mary, and finally reaching the point where she sees, literally sees, the bodily assumption of Mary as a divinely revealed truth. Elisabeth's visions remained sufficiently independent of the control of any questioner that, in the course of her ecstatic reflection on the assumption, she ventured a revision of the traditional ecclesiastical observance of the feast. The true Feast of the Assumption was to be celebrated on September 23, which was to be made known only among Mary's special devotees.[29] Here was a development unprecedented in the earlier discussions of Mary's death and afterlife and not likely to have been a part of any preparation Elisabeth received regarding the doubts found in patristic writings.

The foregoing cases highlight Ekbert's influence through his proposing questions to Elisabeth, while at the same time they suggest that the answers to the questions remain essentially Elisabeth's. This pattern, however, cannot be traced in a series of episodes found in *Liber Visionum Tertius*, where the most technical theological questions are found, often focused on the interpretation of obscure scriptural passages or on the minutiae of angelology. In these episodes, Elisabeth announces long answers to often detailed questions, distinguishing the three heavens referred to by Saint Paul,[30] describing the precise events in the fall of the proud angels,[31] explaining the meaning of a passage from Dionysius the Areopagite so that it does not conflict with a verse from the prophet Isaiah,[32] and other such matters. The questions, once again, obviously come from Ekbert and demonstrate his direction of Elisabeth's visionary attention. Here, however, the answers also bear the mark of Ekbert's extensive influence. In addition to the way in which these visions differ in subject matter from the other records in the collection, these chapters also differ to some degree in style. In these episodes there is much less emphasis on the personal experience of Elisabeth, much more emphasis on the content of her revelations. And the announcement of the revelation sometimes takes on a rhetorical style that is not found in the other parts of the visionary canon. For example, Elisabeth's report of the angel's distinction between the three heavens takes the form of a systematic lecture in which the angel introduces each point with a rhetorical question.[33]

The difference between these records and the other parts of the corpus that also contain visionary answers to Ekbert's questions is due in some measure to the kinds of questions found here. First, they are much more removed from Elisabeth's own devotional concerns than the questions that stimulated the visions of *Revelatio* or *De Resurrectione*. Second, they are often so technical that they require a fairly detailed response. It is in these episodes that the fullest process of Ekbert's "investigation" must have taken place, his interrogation with leading questions that suggested the answers Elisabeth gave back to him. It is not surprising that in these chapters there is a preoccupation with confirming that what is recorded as Elisabeth's words is in fact the revelation proclaimed to her by the angel.[34]

Also linked with Ekbert's influence is another new style that emerges in *Liber Visionum Tertius* and can be seen likewise in the *Liber Viarum Dei*. In these texts, Elisabeth describes certain visions in minute detail, and the visual details are then given an allegorical interpretation. The allegory is attributed to her heavenly guide, usually the angel, but occasionally someone else such as Saint John the Baptist. The allegory is woven into the description of the vision and is not presented as later, rational reflection upon the vision. Some of the visions are even repeated, and, in the later occurrences, more allegorical details are furnished. Peter Dinzelbacher has appropriately characterized this development of allegoresis in Elisabeth's visionary canon as the interplay between her perceived images and exegetical knowledge. He proposes that this exegetical knowledge was mediated by preaching and Ekbert's suggestive questions, with the narrative being subject to some systematizing when Ekbert put it into final written form.[35] I would only add to this picture that Elisabeth's exegetical knowledge need not be limited to what she heard in sermons preached, but could also include what basic spiritual reading she would have been exposed to in the course of her monastic life, such as the writings of John Cassian and Gregory the Great. Moreover, Ekbert's suggestive questions and his systematization of her responses is not the only impetus for the new appearance of allegorical elaboration and interpretation of the visions; Elisabeth was also introduced to this style of visionary proclamation by Hildegard of Bingen.

But noting the emergence of allegorical elaboration of the visions and the presence of questions posed by Ekbert[36] does not fully explain Ekbert's role in the *Liber Viarum Dei*. The examination of his influence must be extended beyond these passages that so clearly mark his presence. At least since the time of F. W. E. Roth's edition of the visionary corpus in 1884, the *Liber Viarum Dei* has generally been seen as reflecting much more of Ekbert than Elisabeth. Köster accepts Roth's judgment that it bears the mark of a farsighted man of the world who had firsthand experience of the various ways of life described in the book, not of a woman who has spent most of her life within the walls of a cloistered convent.[37] For example, Roth suggests that the harsh condemnation of the sex lives of married people is not likely to have come from Elisabeth's mouth. But this example is open to question. Elisabeth's life in a convent did not necessarily reduce her to ignorance about other ways of life such as marriage. Married and widowed women were often found within the walls of Benedictine convents, women from whom unmarried nuns could learn about marriage. [38] Elisabeth also appears to have had contact with married women who visited her.[39] Furthermore, there is nothing in the sermon on marriage that requires much detailed knowledge about sexual practices, nor do the condemnations of particular sexual practices diverge sharply from the stock of common themes found in contemporary sermons about marriage.[40] Ekbert himself was uneasy with Elisabeth's treatment of this subject, and the sermon ends with a question he posed to her. He asks why fornication has been included in this sermon about marriage, since fornication is a sin that is not relevant to married people.[41] His concern that Elisabeth has confused the categories of adultery and fornication hardly seems likely if he himself had been responsible for composing the questionable part.

One issue in the *Liber Viarum Dei* sermon on married people is also treated in a later work by Ekbert, that is, the current Cathar restriction of legitimate marriage to people who are virgins. This Cathar belief is specifically addressed in Ekbert's *Sermones contra catharos*, in which he methodically demolishes the Cathar position. First he argues on scriptural grounds that the remarriage of widows is permitted, even counseled, by Saint Paul. This means that virginity is not a requirement for marriage, and therefore people who are not virgins before marriage can contract a licit and just marriage.[42] Then Ekbert counters the Cathar assertion of John Chrysostom's rejection of remarriage of widows with testimony from Augustine and Jerome. On this matter, Ekbert charges, the golden mouth of John Chrysostom did not taste heresy, but his words have been misused by the Cathars.[43]

In contrast to this polemical debate of the issue, the comment on this question in the *Liber Viarum Dei* is brief. Elisabeth raises the Cathar point that only marriage contracted among virgins is legitimate. Here the issue is taken head on, not through a discussion of the remarriage of widows, which was not the primary focus of the belief in any case. Elisabeth voices the angel's response to the heterodox conviction: "When such a marriage is possible, it is pleasing to the Lord." This response is qualified by a wry observation: "But it is very rare for such a thing to happen." And a final pragmatic point succinctly concludes the argument: "Besides, the number of the people of God would be excessively diminished."[44]

The difference in style and message is apparent in the two discussions of the same question. Ekbert's more learned approach certainly befits the purpose of his text, but just as Elisabeth incorporated his more technical theological distinctions on other occasions, so could she have done in this case. Instead, however, we see in the *Liber Viarum Dei* a more pastoral concern. The sermon is addressed to married people, people living in a state that is now being criticized by certain sectarians claiming a greater moral purity. Elisabeth's concern is to reassure them that their lives are acceptable in God's eyes, and thus her interest in the question is from a very different perspective than Ekbert's, whose attention is directed to the refutation of heresy. Although Ekbert may have been influential in introducing Elisabeth to certain issues—and he does seem to have sparked her concern about the Cathars—Elisabeth's sermon on marriage takes a different direction from Ekbert's writing on the subject.

In emphasizing Ekbert's contribution to the *Liber Viarum Dei*, Roth and Köster point to his letter to Rainald of Dassel as a close parallel to the ideas found in this visionary text.[45] A comparison between these documents does in fact reveal parallels, as both share a tone of outrage at the current depravity within the church. For example, the neglect of pastoral care due to clerical avarice and self-indulgence is one of the major offenses described in the sermon on prelates and Ekbert's letter. In the sermon, Elisabeth reports the angel's words from God: "Their foot is swift, and they run about in anxiety, so that they can tear out and devour the flesh of my people whose spiritual needs they do not serve, they who are slow to move a finger to rescue from iniquity my souls for whom I have tasted death."[46] The sentence is packed with images of contrasts: speed of foot/ slowness of finger; *carnalia/spiritalia*; the bestial devouring of flesh/ Christ's tasting of death. This condensed series of images serves to communicate the gravity, even the disgusting character, of the offense. Consider a comparable passage of Ekbert: "There is no one who would sweat to purge from iniquity their subjects' souls, which Christ purchased by his soul, but they are all intent to purge of profit their subjects' pockets."[47] Again the single sentence turns on contrasts: no one/everyone; purging souls of iniquity/purging pockets of profit. Both sentences emphasize that the neglect of pastoral care is due to avarice and, in both, the gravity of the neglect is due to the fact that the pastor is responsible for souls whose salvation has already been paid for, dearly, by Christ.

Thus there is an undeniable commonality of concern in the words attributed to Elisabeth and those written by Ekbert. But what is the weight that can be attached to this shared concern, a concern which is not uncommon in the reform-minded literature of this period?[48] More significant than the shared ideas in these passages is the similar crafting of the sentences. In both passages the message is communicated by the graphic contrasts between the good and bad pastors, and the crucial reference to Christ in each case is expressed with an image (*tasting* death or *buying* souls) that contrasts to the activity of the bad pastors (*devouring* flesh; *making* profits). There seems to be a single literary hand at work behind the composition of these two sentences. In the course of framing Elisabeth's exposition of her revelations, Ekbert's literary and editorial inclinations were apparently at work. His literary inclinations are manifest in the casting of the prose and, of course, his editorial impulse filtered Elisabeth's proclamations so that nothing inappropriate or too easily misunderstood by her readers would be left in the text.

The effects of Ekbert's literary shaping of the *Liber Viarum Dei* should not be exaggerated. The sermon on prelates has not been organized into a systematic exposition of the dangers or failures of the episcopacy. Unlike Ekbert's letter to Rainald, where a logical movement from one subject to another can be traced, the *Liber Viarum Dei* sermon remains a collection of discrete announcements that are not presented to build an argument or delineate a comprehensive portrait of the episcopacy. The urbanity of Ekbert's letter—his play with conventions of address and purpose of writing, his occasional classical allusions, the carefully structured parallelism in his sentences—is not generally evident in the *Liber Viarum Dei* text. Thus it appears that Ekbert did not give free reign to his own literary sensibilities in preparing the written record of Elisabeth's proclamations.

Despite Ekbert's role in crafting the prose of the extant text, there is still something fundamentally different between these two passages. The difference lies in the type of images used. What can it mean that a prelate "devours the flesh" of the members of his flock? The image, while graphic and powerful, does not describe any particular activity. On the other hand, slipping small profits out of someone's pocket refers to an all-too-recognizable offense. The sermon from the *Liber Viarum Dei* is full of biting invective against clerical corruption, but the offenses must be deciphered from the condemnations. There is rage: "Behold, you have made your sanctification stink in the sight of my people and it has been turned into an abomination to me." The pastors are condemned: "Their mouth is open and their tongue is versatile and sharp for harvesting my vineyard in which they did not labor." They are exhorted: "Be watchful and keep the night vigil over my flock, like emulators of the good [cf. 1 Peter 3:13], lest by chance a flock of goats come upon them, because there are evil spirits by whom the flocks of my sheep are dispersed."[49]

These suggestive images convey a powerful sense of the corruption and danger within the church due to the sin of the ecclesiastical *rectores*. But despite their vigor, these images remain very distant from the mundane activities of the people addressed. Instead, the language reflects a profound sensitivity to the degree of disturbance within the church, but the disturbance is understood and communicated in images reminiscent of Old Testament prophecy and apocalyptic expectation.

This visionary imagery is very different from the critique offered by Ekbert in his letter. He condemns prelates who would build stone tombs for themselves rather than contribute to the construction of the supernal city. And when Ekbert condemns building stone tombs, he means building stone tombs—"structures of stone in grottos or on estates chosen for leisure, buildings of little utility, desirable designs curiously worked with engravings and paintings."[50] His condemnation of simony is as clearly expressed: in order to maintain a significant advantage for their treasurers, prelates sell the gifts of the Holy Spirit. Schism within the church and unjust judgments made for monetary gain are also explicitly described and chastised. Ekbert's voice is full of concern for the degradation of the clergy, but it rarely speaks in the haunting yet enigmatic language of the *Liber Viarum Dei*.

Further distinctions between the texts are apparent. Ekbert advises Rainald that if he cannot bend his soul to the rule of the poor, he should at least observe the rule of the rich (cf. 1 Tim. 6:17–19). Thus Rainald should follow the example of Abraham, "the powerful patriarch, whom neither earthly opulence nor divine address made negligent of his condition."[51] In contrast, the sermon exhorts bishops to recall their predecessors who labored in need of basic necessities.[52] The rigor of the prophetic moralism in the *Liber Viarum Dei* has no room for such a model of opulence as Ekbert envisioned, nor is there anything in the *Liber Viarum Dei* comparable to Ekbert's sense of the exaltation of the episcopal office. Ekbert informs Rainald that as bishop he has been made a partner (*consors*) of God's name and thus could be thought of as being among the gods.

There is, of course, a huge responsibility incumbent upon anyone who shares God's name, so he urges Rainald to let the name of God stimulate him to imitating God.[53]

While it appears that the same hand may have crafted the prose of the *Liber Viarum Dei* sermon about prelates and Ekbert's letter to Rainald, nonetheless the ideas and the images point to a significant difference in the original conceptions that lie behind the shape of the words committed to writing. The sermon on the life of prelates can be recognized as representing Elisabeth's own reflection on the morality of the church, a reflection no doubt influenced by Ekbert's opinions. He was, after all, one of her main links with the world outside her convent. His presence is in the foreground in Elisabeth's description of her inquiry to the angel about the sacraments of simoniacal bishops. As in the case of the visions about Mary's corporeal resurrection and in the case of the rejection of Cathar beliefs, Ekbert introduced certain concerns to Elisabeth, but in her reflection upon them, she seems to have absorbed them into her own visionary perspective. When she expresses her concern about the morality of the church, it is transformed by her sense of having learned the divine view of these mortal activities. Elisabeth's view cannot then be reduced to a mere rehearsal of the opinions she may have learned from others around her. Like an artist who looks at the same scene as everyone else but whose representation of it is affected by her own personal experience and her medium of communication, Elisabeth's expression is a creation that reflects much more of herself than simply the fact that she heard certain opinions from her brother. And this sermon, like the records in the other visionary books, is a record of these creations.

There is, however, variation within the *Liber Viarum Dei*, and not all of the ten sermons share the visionary characteristics of the sermon on ecclesiastical *rectores* or the pithy yet compassionate pastoral concern of the response to Cathar marriage. Much more prosaic, for example, are the sermons directed to adolescents and children.[54] The straightforward style of these sermons may be due in part to the audiences to which they were directed, and their non-visionary character may indicate that these subjects did not move Elisabeth to the same kind of fervent reflection as did other subjects such as virginity, contemplation, and clerical morality. The relative brevity of these sermons corroborates this impression. Elisabeth's description of the ten paths in the beginning of the *Liber Viarum Dei* meant that ten sermons were required to complete the book, even if not all ten ways of life equally interested her. It seems likely that Ekbert's influence was more marked in these sermons, that he may have have been obliged to fill in these sections where Elisabeth's visionary proclamations were not so readily forthcoming. As in the technical discussions of *Liber Visionum Tertius*, Ekbert's greater role is suggested in the concern to verify that the words of the sermons are in fact the words Elisabeth learned from the angel in her visionary ecstasy: "When [the angel] had presented himself to me again, I spoke to him saying: 'My lord, can we safely affirm that all these words have come from you?' I said this because some of the words he had pronounced in such a way that I could not see his face, and others were pronounced in spirit by my mouth. So he, looking at me with great severity, said, 'Believe with your whole heart that these words which were transcribed have come from my mouth.'"[55] Perhaps Elisabeth was wary of the elaboration of some of her visions. This elaboration could either have been provided by Ekbert or elicited from her by his questions. In either case, Elisabeth appears to recognize that in the *Liber Viarum Dei*, more than her initial, immediate descriptions of her experience are being transcribed into the written record of her revelations.

Drawing together all the evidence presented above, we can assess the immense role that Ekbert had in the production of the canon of texts that record the visionary experience of his sister Elisabeth. If Ekbert had not committed himself to publishing her visions, it is doubtful how much would be known of Elisabeth today. As the one who presented Elisabeth to the world, Ekbert was also responsible for shaping and limiting what could be known about her. Given, however, the limitations that Ekbert imposed by his editorial decisions, his translation, and even his revision, one can still talk meaningfully, although always very carefully, about the visionary experience of Elisabeth and the spirituality reflected in her descriptions of her visions.

5. The Visionary Experience of Elisabeth

Prophecy and Tradition

The phenomena of Christian visionary experience and prophetic utterance did not begin with Elisabeth. She stands within a tradition of visions and prophecy that formed part of the intellectual environment of her day. Two aspects of this tradition are particularly important: the contemporary views about such extraordinary experience and the well-known examples of visionary literature. We turn first to an examination of the contemporary beliefs about visions and prophecy, for these beliefs set the parameters for what was considered possible as well as desirable.

The mid-twelfth century was heir to a tradition of conceptualization about divine revelation imparted to select individuals who were then commissioned to announce it publicly. The primary examples of this phenomenon were the prophets of Israel, whose revelations were included in the Old Testament, and the ecstatic preachers among the New Testament communities.[1] Although these prophets flourished in the distant past, there was nonetheless a consensus, at least in theory, that the possibility of such revelation continued into the present day. Even in the second to fourth centuries, as an orthodox position emerged from the confrontation with the Montanists (a group primarily rejected for their "ecstatic excesses"), there is no extant example of an anti-Montanist polemic that rejected the possibility of continued ecstatic prophecy. As James Ash has demonstrated, "The Church simply did not respond to Montanism by limiting the charisma of prophecy to a bygone apostolic age." To some degree, this consensus appears to rest on an interpretation of 1 Cor. 13:9–10, in which Paul is understood to indicate that prophecy is a gift given to last until the coming of the Parousia.[2]

Paul's directives about prophecy and speaking in tongues in 1 Cor. 12–14 also determined yet another important aspect of the traditional understanding of prophecy. A criterion of the social utility of prophecy was established: "For one who speaks in tongues, does not speak to humans, but to God; for no one hears that one, for that one speaks mysteries in the spirit. But the one who prophesies, speaks to humans for edification, exhortation and consolation. The one who speaks in tongues, edifies oneself; however, the one who prophesies, edifies the Church of God" (1 Cor. 14:2–4). Unlike speaking in tongues, which is incomprehensible to its hearers, prophecy must not only be lucid but must also serve the function of edifying the faithful. Paul Alphandéry has shown how this criterion of pedagogical utility accounts for the virtual disappearance of glossolalic prophecy in medieval Christianity as well as the development of the conception of rational prophecy often identified with the interpretation of Scripture.[3] For example, Peter Abelard defined the gift of prophecy as "the grace of interpreting, that is, of expounding the divine word."[4] It is interesting to note that as scholarly theologians wrote their commentaries on the Bible, they increasingly came to define prophecy as the activity of explaining the word of God. This equation of prophecy and exegesis is most striking when the exegesis is done in an apocalyptic mode.[5] Joachim of Fiore represents an interesting case in this regard: he claimed not to have *spiritus prophetiae* but only *spiritualis intellectus*, and wrote his great prophetic works as scriptural commentaries. Yet it was as a prophet that Joachim was widely regarded.[6]

In the twelfth century, however, prophecy was not exclusively identified with the rather learned activity of explicating Scripture. Numerous anonymous and pseudonymous written prophecies that were not biblical commentaries circulated during this period.[7] In addition, certain individuals were noted by hagiographers and chroniclers for their prophetic power.[8] Bernard of Clairvaux, who should never be overlooked in a discussion of twelfth-century charismatics, provides a good example of someone understood, both by himself and others, as a prophet. Otto of Freising, describing the preparations for the Second Crusade, characterizes Bernard's peculiar charismatic appeal:

> There was at that time in France a certain abbot of the monastery of Clairvaux named Bernard, venerable in life and character, conspicuous in his religious order, endowed with wisdom and a knowledge of letters, renowned for signs and wonders [*signis et miraculis clarus*]. The princes decided to have him summoned and to ask of him, as of a divine oracle [*tanquam a divino oraculo*], what ought to be done with reference to this matter. . . . [Pope Eugene III] granted to the abbot previously named, who was looked upon by all the

peoples of France and Germany as a prophet and an apostle [*ut propheta vel apostolus*], the authority to preach and to move the hearts of all thereto.[9]

Despite Otto's emphasis on the success of Bernard's preaching, he makes it clear that successful preaching is not the exclusive criterion of such prophetic activity.[10] Immediately after describing Bernard's eloquent and convincing preaching at Vezeley, he recounts the story of the monk Ralph, yet another successful crusade preacher "who inflamed many thousands of the inhabitants of Cologne, Mainz, Worms, Speyer, Strasburg, and other neighboring cities, towns and villages to accept the cross."[11] As part of his campaign, Ralph foolishly urged the people to slay the Jews living in their country. The ignorance that underlies such a program was hinted at in Otto's distinction between Ralph who "was only moderately imbued with a knowledge of letters," and Bernard who was "endowed with wisdom and a knowledge of letters."[12] Thus an intellectual quality, which is the hallmark of prophecy when it is identified with scriptural interpretation, marks even the view of prophecy that is not equated with exegesis.

But even Bernard, whose sanctity and wisdom passed almost without question, stumbled in the complexities of this mammoth event which he heralded in God's name. With the disastrous end of the Second Crusade, Bernard was compelled to defend his role in this endeavor. His rationale is striking. In his *De consideratione* addressed to Eugene III, he recalls Moses, the great prophet of Israel, who led the people out of Egypt, promising them a better land, yet failing to deliver them to the safety and bounty anticipated: "And this sad and unexpected outcome cannot be blamed on the foolhardiness of the leader. He did everything at the Lord's command and with his help, and with the Lord confirming his word afterward with signs."[13] Here Bernard diverges from Otto's emphasis on the intellectual character of his activity—for him it is not a question of foolishness or brilliance. The question is whether or not one has truly been inspired with God's message, and in this respect, Bernard sees himself as justified. Just as Moses received God's command to lead the Hebrew people into the desert in expectation of the land flowing with milk and honey, so Bernard himself, "at God's command," promised good news to those who undertook the cross. Bernard in fact defends himself from any accusation of being the foolish prophet described in Ezekiel 13 by recalling Ezekiel's condemnation and then explaining how he could have announced peace when there was no peace. For Bernard, the failure of the crusaders can only be referred to the same two observations to which one has recourse in studying the plight of the Moses in the desert: the abyss of God's judgments and the stiff-necked and defiant people whom he was called upon to lead.[14]

Otto of Freising echoes this explanation but also suggests another possible reason, one which Bernard himself would never have publicly admitted: "It is also true that the spirit of the prophets does not always accompany the prophets."[15] This idea of prophecy as a spirit or gift bestowed upon an individual that does not inherently change that person's nature (i.e., does not make the prophet infallible) is well in keeping with the traditional understanding of prophecy. Otto's words recall the teaching of Gregory the Great, who warned, "Sometimes the spirit of prophecy fails the prophets, and is not at all times present to their minds."[16] In fact, the notion of prophecy as a divine gift rather than an ontological characteristic of the prophet was so intrinsic to the traditional conception that room had to be reserved for wicked people who uttered true prophecy or for God to use a sinner to reveal a truth. In his *Decretum*, Gratian admitted the possibility of wicked people having the spirit of prophecy,[17] thus at least theoretically questioning the presumed connection between sanctity and the gift of prophecy.[18]

Bernard's sense of himself as one divinely ordained to reveal God's plan and to urge his fellow Christians to act according to his vision of the Christian life had led to his confrontation with Ralph, who had similar ideas about himself. The confrontation ended in Bernard's repression of Ralph's prophetic mission, almost at the cost of a popular insurrection in Ralph's defense.[19] But Bernard was also capable of recognizing in others a divinely given grace akin to what he perceived to be his own relationship with God. Most notably, he recognized and even sought official acknowledgment of the prophetic gift of Hildegard of Bingen.

In 1146 or 1147, Hildegard wrote to Bernard describing her visionary experience. She portrays herself being taught by the Holy Spirit through the medium of visions. And although she does not use the word *prophetia* to describe her revelations, she understands her revelations in terms of *expositio* of the books of the Bible, which, as was noted above, was an increasingly popular conception of prophecy. Characteristically, however, Hildegard distinguishes the *intellectus* she receives from purely academic knowledge about Scripture, and emphasizes that her own familiarity with the Bible is not one of scholastic hairsplitting.

Hildegard goes on to tell Bernard that she has kept these revelations to herself because there are already so many divisions (*scismata*) among

Christians. She has, however, shared her revelations with one monk of upright life who has comforted her in these fearful events.[20] Bernard's response, although somewhat aloof, acknowledges Hildegard's special grace,[21] but his real enthusiasm for her revelations would be demonstrated at a slightly later date.

Volmar, the monk in whom Hildegard had confided her visions, eventually told Abbot Kuno of St. Disibod, the superior in charge of the hermitage where Hildegard lived, about her extraordinary charism. Kuno in turn relayed this information to Heinrich, the archbishop of Mainz.[22] This news caused a stir: "Everyone said that these things were from God and from the prophecy which in the past the prophets had prophesied."[23]

According to Hildegard, the occurrences which the people gathered at Mainz believed to be prophetic were her visions in which she came to understand "without any human instruction" the Bible and "works of other holy people and those of certain philosophers"; her expounding of "certain things" based on these texts, though she scarcely had any literary knowledge; and her utterance of songs with their melody even though she "had never learned either musical notation or any kind of singing."[24] This is yet another example of the belief in the possibility of ongoing prophecy, of the continuation of God's direct intervention in human affairs via the inspiration of certain individuals with divinely imparted knowledge.

It is significant that in Hildegard's description there is no reference to any predictions of the future, nor is there any implication that the people in Mainz recognized her revelations as forecasting things to come. A notion of prophecy that is much broader than mere prediction of the future was quite traditional, again reaching back to the influential commentary of Gregory the Great on the book of the prophet Ezekiel. As Gregory points out, prophecy is the bringing forth or making known of secrets (*prodit occulta*), and these secrets can be of the past, present, or future.[25] Thus the essence of prophecy is not reference to the future, but the act of revealing things otherwise concealed.[26]

The discussion of Hildegard's spirit of prophecy did not end with the Mainz meeting. Archbishop Heinrich and others among the Mainz clergy decided to refer these wonders to Pope Eugene III, who was staying in Trier at the invitation of Archbishop Adalbero.[27] In response, Eugene sent a team of investigators to St. Disibod to question Hildegard and, when they returned to Trier, they repeated to the eager hearers all that Hildegard had revealed to them. Eugene himself then began to read to the assembly from the first part of Hildegard's *Scivias*. The testimony of the investigators and the reading of the *Scivias* were said to move the assembly to the praise of God. So might this edifying scene have ended, had not Bernard of Clairvaux intervened. He urged Eugene not to allow this manifestation of divine grace to be hidden, and Eugene was said to have sent letters to Hildegard and the monks at St. Disibod encouraging Hildegard to continue to preserve her revelations in writing.[28]

Peter Dronke has noted the significance for twelfth-century intellectual history of Eugene's approval of such a profoundly original work as the *Scivias*, especially in contrast to the condemnation of works of Abelard, William of Conches, and Gilbert de la Porrée, all of whose condemnations had been actively pursued by Bernard.[29] Eugene's action is also significant for religious history. In it we see an official, papal recognition of a woman's claim to receive divine revelation. This claim should be understood in a tradition of continuing divine revelation, but it also, at least implicitly, stood outside the conventional channels for the reception of grace and for the proclamation of God's word because the sacramental and teaching offices were largely the preserve of the ordained priesthood. We can also see in this scene the potential manipulation of a prophetic claim: Eugene was moved to recognize the marvelous grace God made manifest during *his* pontificate. Obviously though, this is a much less exploitative type of manipulation than Elisabeth of Schönau experienced when she was directed by Ekbert and others to seek specific information in her visions. And as a papal move, it anticipates the efforts half a century later of Innocent III, who tried to shepherd the burgeoning new spiritual, often charismatically led, movements of his day within the boundaries of ecclesiastical orthodoxy.

Within a year of this scene at Trier, Eugene would be faced with yet another person with an unconventional claim to a special relationship with God. Eugene responded to the charismatic and admittedly extravagant declarations of Eudo de Stella (Eon de l'Étoile) by sentencing him to the strict custody of Abbot Suger of St. Denis, in whose care he soon died.[30] Thus Eugene's acknowledgment of Hildegard's gift was neither matter-of-fact nor insignificant, and it again, like the acclamation of the Mainz assembly, illustrates the contemporary notion of the possibility of continuing prophecy.[31]

The revelations of Hildegard of Bingen and Elisabeth of Schönau brought into relief much about the belief in prophecy that was long present in the tradition. Despite the fact that the major literary prophet who would follow them, Joachim of Fiore, was a man, prophecy would be increasingly associated with holy women. According to André Vauchez, women came to be seen as having easier access to sanctity. Their spiritual perfection was defined by a total abandonment to God's will, which was then recompensed by the granting of exceptional graces such as the spirit of prophecy.[32] For example, the prophetic spirit is one of the spiritual gifts of Mary of Oignies that Jacques de Vitry praises in his *Vita* of this holy woman. The *Vita* was addressed to Bishop Fulk of Toulouse, who himself had encountered these women while traveling in Liège and had requested Jacques to provide him with written accounts of their lives that he could use in his ongoing crusade against the Cathars in Toulouse. In his introduction, Jacques elaborates on the piety of the numerous holy women in the area of Liège and bemoans their detractors who "scorn prophecies because they disdain spiritual people as insane or idiots and reckon the prophecies or revelations of holy people as phantasms or the illusions of dreams."[33] The Aristotelian legacy, in which women had a deficient rational faculty in the soul, made them particularly vulnerable to such accusations of idiocy or susceptability to the influence of dreams.[34] Yet this "scientific" view of women's deficient nature could not lead to a rejection of the possibility of women's prophecy. For example, even when rejecting the possibility of ordaining women by explicitly invoking their inferiority, both Thomas Aquinas and Bonaventure refer to the fact in their favor that women have been prophets.[35]

This tradition about continuing prophecy, which formed the intellectual environment of Elisabeth and her contemporaries, frequently intersected with, though never fully encompassed, several genres of visionary literature. The visionary and apocalyptic books of the Vulgate (Ezekiel, Daniel, 4 Esdras, Apocalypse) exerted a strong influence on the development of this literature in the early Christian centuries as well as in the Middle Ages. In each of these books, a seer glimpses a symbol or event that is not seen by other people, and in the latter three, an angel serves as interpreter for the human seer who is bewildered or frightened by the vision. These books provided images to be exegeted by future apocalyptic and prophetic commentators, as well as certain topoi of visionary experience.

Elisabeth picks up both experiential motifs and particular images from these books. Among the motifs of visionary experience, Elisabeth's description of looking *per ostium apertum in celo* is reminiscent of the opening verse of Ezekiel in which the seer declares "aperti sunt caeli, et vidi visiones Dei," and it directly echoes the words of Apocalypse 4:1.[36] Similarly, her sense of the hand of the Lord being upon her finds its precedent in Ezekiel 1:3, 3:22, and 33:22. Her references to being lifted up and carried away are parallel to Ezekiel 37:1, 40:1–2, and Apocalypse 21:10; and her sense of being *in spiritu* recalls the state described in Apocalypse 1:10, 4:2, and 21:10. Her elaboration of the role of the angel who serves as the interpreter of her visions is drawn from the similar motif found in Daniel 8:17–18, 4 Esdras 10:29–32, and Apocalypse 1:17. Elisabeth's familiarity with at least one of these biblical passages (the similarity with the passage from Ezekiel is closest) informed her perception of her own experience. Whether consciously or not, here she adopts what had become, at least by the end of the first century C.E.,[37] a convention of visionary experience. But the convention does not dominate the experience. None of Elisabeth's descriptions of her experience exactly mirrors biblical passages; the texts show her absorption of the visionary convention without dogmatic adherence to it.

The influence of the biblical visions included not just the conventions of visionary experience, but also extended to some of the visions described. Elisabeth had visions of the crowd of celestial inhabitants gathered around the throne of God that are reminiscent of 4 Esdras 2:42ff and Apocalypse 4:1ff and 7:9ff.[38] Her minutely detailed vision of the celestial Jerusalem is clearly dependent on Apocalypse 21:10ff.[39] Elisabeth knew that her vision of four four-faced creatures and a great shining wheel was from the prophet Ezekiel,[40] and that her images of the four evangelists corresponded to the forms "that sacred Scripture attributes to them."[41] Her vision of Christ at the beginning of *Liber Viarum Dei* drew details from the vision of the Son of Man in the Apocalypse (1:13ff.) and Daniel's interpretation of Nebuchadnezzar's dream (Dan. 2:31–35) was the basis of yet another vision.[42]

Again, none of Elisabeth's versions of these visions exactly replicates the original narratives. Details are changed, new points are added, and no vision of Elisabeth includes every aspect of a particular biblical image. The loose way in which these images surface in Elisabeth's descriptions suggests that she is not intending to demonstrate her ability to see exactly the same visions as the biblical visionaries did. In fact, her apparent freedom with these images is striking. A slavish reproduction of the canonical visions could easily be worked into an apologetic for the authenticity of her experience. While Elisabeth clearly seems to identify her own experience with that of the biblical visionaries, she has allowed their visions to inspire her and has allowed herself not to be constrained by their models.

Thus these scriptural passages offered vivid symbols which Elisabeth could then transform with her own visionary imagination into images that have meaning for her. How much of this process was conscious and how much unconscious is impossible to determine, but as discussed below, the mental and physical states that Elisabeth called ecstasy and rapture appeared to free her from what we would call a "normal" pattern of rational thought and allowed her to "see" a reality that was itself influenced by her previous cognitive thought, such as meditation on those biblical images that claimed her attention.

Several genres of visionary literature emerged in the Christian tradition, all of them to some degree influenced by the biblical prototypes just discussed. One of these is the literary tradition of allegorical dream visions, including texts such as *The Shepherd of Hermas*, Boethius's *Consolation of Philosophy*, and Alan of Lille's *Complaint of Nature*. Theodore Bogdanos has outlined the dramatic pattern underlying most of these allegorical visions as follows:

> The dreamer-hero finds himself in a profound spiritual crisis. One or several authoritative figures appear to him in one or several visions and help the dreamer place his crisis in a new perspective of truth, thus inducing its resolution. Such truth is communicated to the visionary hero through symbolic imagery and through rational, conceptually articulate dialogue in which the authoritative figure engages the dreamer. Their encounter takes place in a visionary landscape which has an objective reality of its own (as a supernatural realm, for example), while at the same time functioning as an imagistic concretization of the dreamer's psychic reality—an objective correlative of his inner state at each stage of his spiritual development.[43]

Elisabeth's visions correspond to this model to some degree. The initial spiritual crisis, the appearance of authoritative figures, and the communication of a new perspective through imagery and conceptual dialogue are paralleled in her visionary descriptions. Even some of the most significant images found in the allegorical dream visions are also found in Elisabeth's visions. For example, the building of a structural center such as a tower or city can be seen in her vision of angels building the walls and streets of the heavenly Jerusalem.[44]

Despite these similar elements, Elisabeth's visions do not fit neatly into the literary genre of dream vision. Her authoritative, pedagogical figures—for example, her familiar angel, the Virgin Mary, and Saint Verena—remain exactly these personalities and never become quasi-mythic characters such as Ecclesia, Philosophia, or Natura. More significantly, the visionary diaries are not unified expositions of a new perspective of truth revealed as allegory. They are much more miscellaneous, more reflective of her actual experience, than the focused subjects explored in the dream visions. The *Liber Viarum Dei* can be more profitably compared with the allegories. Here, a more unified composition results from the systematic exposition of the original allegorical visions. However, because the *Liber Viarum Dei* comes relatively late in Elisabeth's career, her language and her conventions of visionary experience are already largely set and tend to be continuous with her earlier imagery, rather than showing much influence from the allegorical dream tradition.

In addition to allegorical narratives, visionary experience was also recorded in hagiographical sources. This type of material, to a greater extent than the dream visions, would have been more accessible to Elisabeth as part of her monastic background. One of the most important early collections of pious deeds that included accounts of visionary experiences was the *Dialogi de miraculis* of Gregory the Great.[45] In this collection, Gregory affirms the continuation of divine revelation through visions granted to certain divinely chosen individuals. "It seems," he writes in the voice of Peter, his interlocutor in the dialogues, "that the spiritual world is moving closer to us manifesting itself through visions and revelations."[46] In addition to the eschatological expectation underlying this belief in the growing frequency of visions, Gregory explains how it is possible for the holy person to learn God's secrets. He maintains that, although corporeal existence obstructs humans from learning all the judgments of God, the spiritual union between genuinely holy people and God enables them "to understand [God's] judgments and pronounce them with their lips."[47]

Most of Gregory's stories of visionary experience focus on deathbed visions of the otherworld. For Gregory, holy people are "sometimes divinely inspired when they are on the point of leaving the body, and thus enabled to gaze upon the secrets of the heavenly kingdom with the incorporeal eye of their mind."[48] Other than the restriction to near-death circumstances, this report accords well with the way in which Elisabeth described her own experience. In fact, the phrase *mentis oculus* appears in the records of Elisabeth's visions, a phrase that has no precedent in the biblical visionaries.[49] Several of Elisabeth's visions are particularly reminiscent of the tales Gregory narrates. For example, her vision of two angels receiving the soul of a dying sister echoes one of Gregory's favorite themes in the fourth Dialogue.[50] Gregory's explanation of Saint Benedict's vision of the entire universe at a glance may have suggested the possibility of such an experience to Elisabeth, who reports that she was "lifted up into the height so that I could see all the ends of the earth."[51] And Gregory's accounts of souls who left their bodies for a tour of the otherworld, and returned to this world to report the sights seen and edifying, if not terrifying, messages, afforded a model for Elisabeth's travels to the otherworldly realm.[52]

The kinds of stories about visionary experience told by Gregory in the *Dialogues* were typical of those found in later hagiographical collections and of accounts of otherworld journeys. Even Guibert of Nogent (died c. 1125), a thoughtful critic of superstitious piety, narrates contemporary examples of otherworld journeys and clairvoyant or prophetic dreams, and he establishes a rational criterion for ascertaining the divine origin of visions.[53] Yet there are significant differences between the records of Elisabeth's visionary experience and the earlier hagiographical and otherworld journey narratives. First, unlike these traditional visionary narratives, which "reveal so much of hell and purgatory and so little of heaven,"[54] Elisabeth frequently reports gazing upon the heavenly inhabitants arrayed in their glorious hierarchy around the throne of God.[55] Carol Zaleski has drawn a distinction between visionary literature that concentrates on the lower realms and contemplative writings in which attention is turned to heaven. While acknowledging that the distinction is not absolute, she suggests that this division of labor reflects the common assumption that, although graphic images are appropriate for portraying hell or purgatory, they are incommensurate with transcendent, heavenly experience.[56] Elisabeth's narratives, departing from this general pattern, thus indicate a new direction in visionary literature, one that brings it much closer to the genre of contemplative writings.

A more far-reaching distinction between the earlier visionary literature and the Schönau corpus of texts is the essentially autobiographical character of the latter. While the didactic element begins to eclipse the confessional atmosphere in the *Liber Viarum Dei*, Elisabeth as seer of the visions usually remains in the foreground of her reports. Otherworld journey narratives are, almost by definition, recounted in the first person, and enough of the seer's life must be detailed to give a context for the inevitable post-journey conversion.[57] But the focus of attention is not the individual who made the otherworldly tour; rather, attention is directed to what was seen and its implications for inducing conversion in the audience hearing the tale. In these accounts, as in most hagiographical texts before the twelfth century, little effort is made to give an intimate portrayal of the personality at the center of the story.[58]

In surveying a wide range of medieval visionary literature, Peter Dinzelbacher concludes that a significant shift took place in the twelfth century. The otherworld journey narratives, so common between the days of
Gregory the Great and the twelfth century, began to give way to a new
type of visionary literature. In this new genre, the seer is not transported
to another realm but rather is visited, in his or her own world, by an
apparition of an otherworldly figure, who then imparts revelation to the
seer.[59] Dinzelbacher correctly sees Elisabeth of Schönau marking this transition, for Elisabeth recounts being both transported out of the mundane
world and into the other realms and being visited by celestial beings who
impart revelation to her.[60]

Another crucial aspect of this new type of vision is that it does not
occur "out of the blue," as, for example, in the otherworld journeys narrated by Gregory the Great. In each of Gregory's cases, there is nothing in
the seer's life that prepares him (all three of Gregory's otherworldly trav-
elers are men, a point to be considered later) to be swept out of his body
and carried away to hell. In contrast, the second type of vision usually
occurs within the framework of an ongoing life of prayer, the visions can
be prepared for and sought in prayer, and they occur repeatedly, thus in
every way distinguishing them from the unexpected, dramatic, singular
occurrence of the otherworld journey.[61] Again, Elisabeth's experience is
clearly a harbinger of this new type of vision. Dinzelbacher notes that it is
this new condition of visions as experienced and prepared for in an ongoing spiritual life that allowed others to turn to the visionaries and seek
information from heaven about affairs concerning themselves. The case of
Elisabeth's involvement in the identification of the Cologne relics is exemplary in this regard.[62]

Finally, Elisabeth's visions depart from the existing tradition in that
they are not understood to inspire a radical conversion in her life. As in
the cases of the visionaries who follow her, her visions tended to confirm
her existing life rather than lead her to embrace a new one.[63] Thus the
visions are part of an integrated spirituality, which underscores the similarity between her visionary records and contemplative literature.

Dinzelbacher also notes that the change in visionary records corresponds to a major shift in the types of people who have visions, most
notably the shift from male to female visionaries.[64] This observation sheds
some light on the differences between the two types and, again, signals
Elisabeth's place with the visionaries who followed rather than preceded
her. As Caroline Walker Bynum has demonstrated, when women of this
period recounted their lives, the stories usually did not follow the plot line

of a climactic conversion. Instead, the images they used enhanced and continued what the woman's ordinary experience already was.[65] Thus it should not be surprising that Elisabeth did not understand her visions to lead to a radical change in her life, but rather saw them as part of her deepening relationship with God. In this aspect, Elisabeth stands with Gertrude the Great, Mechtild of Hackeborn, and other female visionaries of the thirteenth and fourteenth centuries.

One can see that Elisabeth stood within a long tradition of visionary literature that formed her own spiritual background. The visions of the apocalyptic seers in the Bible were her source for certain conventions of visionary experience and even for particular visionary subjects. And from hagiographical literature, Elisabeth knew that certain individuals were still granted the spirit of prophecy and were even lifted out of their bodies to glimpse the secrets of the otherworld. All of this background influenced her perception of her own experience. Her reflection on these visionary motifs led to their reappearance, sometimes modified by her own imagination, in her attempts to articulate what she believed she perceived. Yet numerous elements in Elisabeth's visions have a greater affinity with the visionary texts that emerge in the centuries following her than with the material she herself knew. Thus, in an age in which the written word increasingly shaped new areas of cultural life, Elisabeth, along with her great contemporary Hildegard of Bingen, must be seen as forging new literary genres to express her experience.[66]

The Language of Vision

"From the day on which I began to live under the Rule up until this hour, the hand of the Lord has been fixed upon me" (cf. Psalm 37:3).[67] So Elisabeth describes the course of her visionary life. But what exactly was going on when the hand of the Lord was upon her, or more precisely, what did Elisabeth think was going on when she perceived that God was working through her? Not surprisingly, Elisabeth never volunteers a detailed analysis of her experience. She often refers to her customary or typical experiences (for example, "videbam sicut mos mihi est"; "cum solito more essem in extasi"[68]), but she gives no general framework or ideal scheme of what takes place in these visionary trances. Ekbert attempts such a description, but obviously from only an observer's point of view: "Frequently indeed and as if by habit, on Sundays and other feast days around the hours in which the devotion of the faithful especially burned, a certain suffering of the heart fell upon her, and she was violently disturbed, and finally she was quiet as if dead, such that sometimes no breath or vital movement could be discerned. But after a long trance, when she had gradually resumed her breath, suddenly she would announce certain most divine words in Latin."[69] Here Ekbert mentions several noteworthy features that can be traced in the visionary records, for example, the physical pain preceding the ecstasy, the frequent occurrence on Sundays and other feasts, and her verbal pronouncements after recovering.

In one of the late additions to the visionary collection, a vision in *Liber Visionum Tertius* that bears more the mark of Ekbert's language and interests than of Elisabeth's, a similar reflection on the nature of Elisabeth's visionary experience is given. Elisabeth had been directed to ask her angel-guide to explain Paul's description of being caught up into the third heaven (cf. 2 Cor. 12:2–4).[70] Included in the report of the angel's rather academic response is the following remark to her:

This thing of which I speak, you have frequently experienced within yourself. It sometimes happens to holy people that their spirit, which vivifies the carnal senses for sensing things which are external, is suddenly seized inwardly by such a force for sensing those things which are spiritual, that it leaves the flesh without feeling or motion, and then the person cannot discern whether his or her spirit is in the body or outside of the body. Paul was seized in such a way when he ascended in spirit up to the third heaven.[71]

The description of the senseless, motionless body recalls Ekbert's description of Elisabeth's external appearance. Here, however, he goes beyond just description and attempts an explanation of what is happening internally, an explanatory endeavor characteristic of Ekbert and never matched by Elisabeth, who strains to describe her experience but betrays no interest in the theoretical aspect of the process.

Ekbert's description of the nature of Elisabeth's experience includes certain important aspects, but it is nonetheless only a composite portrait based on Elisabeth's external appearance. He has noted several important recurring features of Elisabeth's descriptions, but his characterization does not reflect the many distinctions made by Elisabeth herself when describing her experience. The only point at which Ekbert acknowledges that *different* things happened to his sister is in his introduction to *Liber Visionum Secundus*. *Liber Visionum Primus* ended with the angel's announcement to Elisabeth that she would no longer receive her customary visions until she was about to die. The visions in *Liber Visionum Secundus* occurred after this warning, so Ekbert needed to account for the continuation of the visions. He did this by deciding that the angel's warning referred to only one particular type of vision—those visions in which Elisabeth described herself as looking through a door into the heavens. Although he satisfied himself that this distinction resolved the issue, he seems not to have noticed that the *per ostium* visions do not correspond in type to any of the categories that Elisabeth herself used in characterizing her visions.

Despite Elisabeth's references to "typical" visions, there is considerable variation in her descriptions of her experience. The most consistent pattern to this variation in the visionary records has already been noted: in the records of events occurring after Ekbert joined her at Schönau, much less emphasis is given to the details of her experience. As the focus of the visionary records shifts from Elisabeth herself to the revelation she receives, less information is given about her perception of her mental and physical states. Thus the material for analysis of the language of vision is found mainly in the earliest records. Since we are examining the words themselves (the most delicate task when working with the visionary records), it is an advantage that most of the relevant material is found in the earliest texts, which were least subject to Ekbert's influence.

In characterizing her physical and mental experience, Elisabeth consistently describes herself as passive. She underlines her passivity by frequent assertions such as "hec fecit mihi dominus" ("The Lord did these things for me") and "que operatus es [domine] mecum" ("The things which you have worked in me").[72] Elisabeth saw her physical suffering as a sign that clearly expressed her passivity, that is, God's use of her which was beyond her control. Ekbert noted her physical pain and, in *De Obitu*, he tells of the hand of the Lord, which always wasted her body with "pressures and distress."[73] Elisabeth herself refers to *angustiae, invalitudo, inbecillitas, labores agoni, languor corporis, concussio corporis, passiones*, and *febris*. Without giving any clinical description of her state, she does repeatedly emphasize two aspects of this suffering: pain and weakness. An unusually detailed description gives some sense of Elisabeth's feeling of physical distress: "I languished in my whole body, and first the tips of my hands and feet, and then all my flesh, began to crawl, and sweat broke out all over me. My heart was made as if it had been cut in two parts by a sword."[74] Elisabeth never repeats her description of crawling flesh, although there are other references to profuse sweat and severe pain. Her weakness is sometimes so extreme that she cannot hold herself up and she simply collapses.[75] She emphasizes the unnaturalness of these bouts. For example, in one case where she has collapsed, the combined strength of the sisters standing around her was not enough to raise her head to place pillows under it.[76] And when she was not incapacitated with weakness, she was sometimes immobilized by paralysis.[77]

Often these seizures strike immediately before a vision or ecstatic experience, and they end with the ecstasy itself. Elisabeth asserts that no human medicine would be effective for relieving these agonies,[78] although she occasionally makes reference to a specific cure of her illness. Once she describes herself languishing for four days during which she could not eat. But then she began to taste a honeycomb sweetness in her mouth which, she claims, refreshed her and led her to emit profuse sweat.[79] Here, as Ernst Benz notes, Elisabeth perceives the cure of her weakness as the reception of a kind of heavenly medicine, which leads in turn to a physical sign (*sudorem copiosum*) of her recovery.[80]

Elisabeth portrays herself as dreading these ordeals of physical suffering. She tells of one episode in which she tried to escape the suffering. She is severely chastised by the angel for this and is reminded that the glories she sees in her visions outweigh the suffering she must endure.[81] Three years after her visions began, Elisabeth recounts an episode in which the apostle Peter tells her she will no longer suffer so greatly in her visions.[82] From this point in the visionary corpus, there are many fewer descriptions of physical pain, and these are less detailed.

Elisabeth applies the characteristic of passivity not only to her suffering the illnesses inflicted upon her and receiving the visions sent to her, both inherently passive processes, but also to her proclamation of revelation, an inherently active process. After seeing the vision, she bursts out in words praising God or repeating what she learned in her vision. These utterances are usually introduced by phrases such as "verba hec ori meo affluxerunt" or "in hec verba prorupi."[83] Sometimes these utterances take the form of proclaiming a well-know prayer or biblical passage, and often these formulaic responses are not even recorded in full in the transcript of the event. Instead only the first line of the prayer or biblical passage, followed by *et cetera*, is included. These outbursts correspond to what Ekbert described as Elisabeth's "testimonies of canonical scripture and other words of divine praise."[84] At other times, her outbursts are the often lengthy narration and explanation of what she learned in her vision. Elisabeth considers these utterances as part of the inspired experience and not part of her own personal reaction to what she saw.[85]

Thus Elisabeth portrays herself as having lost control over her own faculty of speech—words which she did not intend to speak pour out of her mouth.[86] At other times, she describes herself as having been struck dumb, yet another form of powerlessness over her verbal faculty.[87] This physical aspect of her experience—her loss of control of her own body—is dramatically illustrated when she claims that she is not always aware that in her trance she is speaking out loud.[88] In one such case, Elisabeth reports that all her sisters around her heard the words she spoke during a vision of Mary. She did not believe what the sisters told her until they repeated all of her own words in the order she had said them.[89] Her sisters may have even taken advantage of Elisabeth's perceived loss of control during her visions. Elisabeth recounts one incident in which her sisters reminded her of some of her words spoken in her vision which she apparently forgot: "And leaning myself on the breast of the mistress, I came again into ecstasy, and I saw those same things which I had seen before. And again, returning to myself, I seized these words: 'Help me, Lord, my God' [cf. Psalm 108:26], et cetera. And I added: 'By the grace of God I am what I am,' et cetera [cf. 1 Cor. 15:10]. They told me that I also said: 'Let not the greatness of the revelations exalt me' [cf. 2 Cor. 12:7], and no more."[90] This may be an instance in which the sisters used Elisabeth's vulnerability—her inability to control her speech and her inability to know that she has lost control—to ensure that she would not lose her humility despite the marvels that God was working through her. Their reminder is especially striking in that it immediately follows Elisabeth's assertion, "I am what I am." Perhaps here can be perceived the twinge of jealousy or fear of disorder that the nuns at Schönau could easily have felt at the extraordinary claims made by the young sister in their midst.

Despite Elisabeth's extensive emphasis on her passivity, it is clear that both she and Ekbert believed it was possible for her to provoke or elicit visions. For example, Elisabeth prays to receive a vision about the dedication of Ekbert's church at Bonn, and she then receives such a vision.[91] At points, the entire Schönau community is involved in prayer and penance so that Elisabeth will receive a hoped-for vision.[92] Prayer and penance, like the more dramatic practice of fasting, need not be techniques for actually coercing divine revelations,[93] but the claim to pure passivity becomes more attenuated in these cases. And this belief in the possibility of eliciting visions becomes crucial in the later phase of Elisabeth's visionary activity when she is viewed by Ekbert and others as a medium for acquiring specific knowledge otherwise out of their reach.

As noted above, Ekbert's general description of Elisabeth's appearance during her visions does not suggest that there was any variation in her experience. In contrast, the language Elisabeth uses to describe these events varies. Although her usage is not thoroughly systematic, it is clear that she struggled to distinguish among what she perceived to be her divergent experiences.

By far the most frequent event Elisabeth describes is what may be called a simple vision or apparition. She uses two basic formulae in describing these visions. Either something appears to her (e.g., "a great light in the heavens appeared to me" [*michi apparuit*]) or she just describes herself as seeing something (thus the ubiquitous use of the word *vidi*). Elisabeth does not appear to distinguish between something appearing to her and her seeing something. For example, there is no distinction between vision and apparition according to content: both demons and saints appear to her and likewise she *sees* both celestial and this-worldly visions.[94]

Elisabeth is careful to note that the process by which she sees these images is not the same as normal physical sight. She expresses this distinction in several ways, saying that she sees with the eyes of her heart or of her mind, by seeing in her mind's gaze (*mentis intuitu*), by seeing in or through the spirit.[95] In this spiritual vision she usually claims to see apparitions of saints or demons, or symbols such as a cross or dove. But several times Elisabeth's spiritual vision allows her to see earthly events that normally would not be available to her because of physical limitations of time and space. So, for example, she sees the celebration of Mass or the divine office when she is not actually present at the rites.[96] In these cases, she sees nothing that a little imagination would not have provided, but nonetheless these episodes are interpreted by Elisabeth as visions she received through divine favor.

The next category of events is somewhat more complex. These too are visions, but in these cases Elisabeth describes herself as being in ecstasy, "in the spirit," or *in mentis excessu*, when she has the vision.[97] She seems to use these three phrases interchangeably to indicate a state of trance in which her mind has been withdrawn from its normal functions. Although ecstasy is a state in which she has visions—rare is the mention of ecstasy without explicit elaboration of a vision[98]—it is not a necessary condition for having a vision, as witnessed by explicit references to non-ecstatic visions.[99] It appears that Elisabeth understood ecstasy to be a state that could be part of a process. She could approach ecstasy and she could hold back from it (or be held back from it).

In many cases, the beginning of the process is physical suffering. Thus ecstasy is not just a state of consciousness; it has distinctive physical correlates.[100] The notion of ecstasy as a release from physical sufferings is expressed several times,[101] but although bodily pain and exhaustion is a common prelude to entering the ecstatic state, it is by no means a necessary precondition. Not every description of ecstasy refers to bodily effects (although many do), and there is one explicit description of ecstasy without initial suffering.[102]

Elisabeth also describes ecstasy as a state that could last for an extended period of time.[103] Not only could the ecstasy be prolonged, but the recovery itself is not always achieved instantaneously.[104] Also, according to Elisabeth, the physical and mental effects of the ecstatic experience could still be felt after she had revived. For example, she describes an ecstasy in which she saw Judas's betrayal of Jesus. She then describes the aftereffects of the ecstasy: "After this throughout that whole night, whether I was sleeping or awake, I saw how those impious ones blasphemed the Lord by scourging and spitting upon him and beating him with strikes and blows. And indeed I did not come into ecstasy, but all my sense was there and I could not turn to anything else, with the result that I seemed almost insensible."[105] Elisabeth's characterization of herself as *insensata* recalls Ekbert's statement that sometimes no breath or vital movement could be discerned in her. This passage also indicates that Elisabeth was able to distinguish between being in ecstasy and her later contemplation of what she had seen while in ecstasy.[106]

Something of Elisabeth's perception of her ecstatic condition can also be seen in the ways she describes the end of the state. She tells of coming back (*reversa sum*), recovering (*respiravi*), rising (*surgens*), or awakening (*expergiscens*) from ecstasy. She also refers to returning to or being restored to herself ("ad me rediens"; "reddita sum mihi"), or having regained her spirit ("resumpto spiritu").[107] In some of these expressions, Elisabeth indicates that her ecstasy is something other than her natural self, and thus the end of ecstasy is the return to her self. Her use of words such as recovering, awakening, and arising suggests comparisons with natural conditions such as sleep and sickness, conditions that have recognizable physical as well as mental components. Although all of these expressions connote a sense of return to a normal physical and mental state, none of them gives any hint about the place from whence Elisabeth is returning.

In addition to these reports of ecstatic states, Elisabeth tells of one other type of visionary experience, which could best be described as rapture. "On the vigil of All Saints Day, at Vespers, I struggled in agony for a long time, and while I was doubled over with violent pain, I tightly bound the sign of the crucified Lord to my breast, and at last coming into ecstasy I became quiet. Then, in an unusual way, it seemed to me as if my spirit had been snatched up into the height, and I saw an open door in the heavens and such a multitude of saints, more than I had ever seen before."[108] The distinctiveness of this experience seems to refer to Elisabeth's perception that her soul was forcibly taken up into heaven, and there, in heaven, she saw visions.[109] She continues this narration with the report that the next day, also at Vespers, she was again raised up.[110] In both of these cases, Elisabeth says that she was already in ecstasy when she was lifted up into heaven. But the rapture is not the same as the ecstasy; it is always something beyond the initial experience of ecstasy. It is most clearly distinguished from ecstasy or *mentis excessus* in that Elisabeth always perceived herself to be taken away from her room or her place in the chapel and brought somewhere else. Unlike the other types of experience described, here Elisabeth clearly emphasizes the separation between her body and her spirit.[111] In each of these cases of rapture, Elisabeth perceives her soul to be lifted up into heaven or, at least, lifted up into "the height," which is ostensibly closer to heaven and thus affords a better view of what is going on among the celestial citizens.

In her first reports, Elisabeth strives to communicate what this experience is like, and the difficulty of expressing her perceptions is evident in her descriptions. Her first four attempts to describe it are qualified: "It seemed to me as if . . . "; "I felt as if. . . . "[112] Elisabeth never qualified her descriptions of her other experiences in this way. If she reported a vision, she did not say that *it seemed to her* that she had a vision, nor does she ever say that she *sensed* she was in ecstasy. In contrast to these more comprehensible experiences, her initial perceptions of rapture appear to have been more ambiguous or more difficult to interpret than her other visionary episodes.

Another significant aspect of the raptures is that, in the context of the new experience of rapture, Elisabeth begins to perceive herself having a special relationship with a particular angel who comes to play such an important role in the rest of the visionary corpus. Sandwiched directly between accounts of her first two experiences of rapture is Elisabeth's first reference to seeing the angel, "a very lovely boy, clothed and girded in a white robe."[113] She identifies him as the angel who was with Jacob (cf. Gen. 48:16) and prays that he be with her in her earthly pilgrimage. Later,

Elisabeth perceives that this angel is the agent of her rapture and at this point she ceases to qualify her descriptions of rapture. Her variations on the formula, "It seemed to me that my spirit was seized," give way to a new model: "The angel of the Lord seized my spirit."[114]

As the one who grabs her soul out of her body and lifts it into another world, the angel now becomes Elisabeth's steady companion, comforting, exhorting, or chastizing her, preaching divine messages to her, and interpreting her sometimes puzzling visions.[115] Elisabeth compares him to a father kindly instructing his daughter, a surprising image for "a very lovely boy," but throughout the later visions, the angel takes on a persona that is more paternal and powerful than her initial vision of him as a comely boy. He is frequently "ductor meus," and even becomes "procurator meus" in a vision in which he saves Elisabeth from eternal damnation.[116] But according to Elisabeth, the angel's sphere of influence is not limited to bearing her soul in celestial transports or communicating divine secrets to her. He also wields power over her body: he cures her from illness by placing his hand on her head; he enfeebles her by flagellation.[117]

All the experiences described so far are similar in that they share a visual component. A striking exception to this general pattern is found in one episode in which Elisabeth describes hearing "a great and dreadful voice from heaven." Elisabeth says that she was already in rapture, but instead of seeing anything while in this state, she only heard the voice.[118] Theologically, it is entirely appropriate that Elisabeth should see nothing at this point, for here she reports a direct experience of God. Usually her visions are not of God but of other heavenly (or demonic) beings.[119] The verbal aspect of this experience is not unusual—the visual experiences themselves have very extensive verbal components. What is unusual is the total lack of any visual element.[120]

Ekbert's characterization of the timing of her visions—"around the hours in which the devotion of the faithful especially burned"—is corroborated by Elisabeth's own accounts, which often cite the Mass or a service of the divine office as the context for her visions. Symbolically, this liturgical setting is appropriate. It is in the context of the liturgy, particularly in the celebration of the Eucharist, that a recognized channel of communication and grace between heaven and the community of believers is established. Elisabeth's experience is understood to be yet another form, albeit a highly individualized example, of this connection between the divine and the human spheres. In fact, some of the visions that Elisabeth describes depict a visualization of this connection as, for example, when she sees a ray of light extending from heaven to the altar in the church, and the Virgin Mary, accompanied by a troop of angels, descending via the ray and standing by the priest during the Mass.[121]

In addition to the symbolic weight of the liturgy as the context for her visions, the physical aspect of the liturgy is also influential. The daily round of the monastic office with its particular dedication to chanting, an activity which focuses the attention on a rhythmic pattern, may have enhanced Elisabeth's tendency to go into a trance. This tendency could have been further enhanced by other physical factors. Her visions and trances occur in the context of ongoing undernourishment and other forms of physical mortification. Elisabeth makes several references to her inability to eat, which she often describes not as a voluntary form of penance but as part of her spiritual torment.[122] In the long version of *De Obitu*, Ekbert lists her abstemious consumption as one among many corporeal penitential practices, including extensive weeping, genuflections, and the tearing of her flesh by coarse garments and a harsh belt which cut into her sides.[123] Whether or not one understands Ekbert to be describing anything beyond the normal monastic practices here, such as wearing a penitential haircloth, it is clear that Elisabeth's daily existence was one of continued physical hardship. To these forms of mortification must be added her life of celibacy, another disruption of natural physical existence.

None of these factors serves to explain the occurrence of trance or Elisabeth's perception that she was seeing things not present to physical eyesight. But noting these physical aspects of Elisabeth's life contributes to an understanding of her experience, especially as modern scientific inquiry continues to demonstrate the connection between different modes of consciousness and various physical states.[124] Elisabeth's physical austerities and her attention to her liturgical environment may have been part of a cultivation of a mode of consciousness that was distinct from a normal process of perception and thought. In this alternative mode of consciousness, she was receptive to seeing in her world a configuration of reality that differed from the perception of others. But this perceptual mode was always enriched by her absorption of traditional symbols and beliefs which naturally affected what she saw and highly influenced her interpretation of her experience.

Elisabeth as Prophet and Visionary

In the earliest records of Elisabeth's experience, a transformation in her self-consciousness can be traced. She begins her self-portrait with descriptions of being overwhelmed by spiritual tedium ("obscuritas animi" or "tristiciae").[125] She reports being tormented by visions of the devil, who appeared to her in frightening human and bestial shapes.[126] The transformation begins as she moves from this state of turmoil and fear to a state of greater confidence enabled by the appearances of Mary and other saints who show her their favor and strengthen her in her sufferings.[127] Not only is Elisabeth granted the grace of these visions, but soon she finds herself proclaiming the word of God through her own mouth, proclaiming it in such a way that she does not even have control over what she says or understand how the words she speaks got into her mouth.[128]

This is not the end of the process. On the vigil of the Feast of All Saints, slightly less than six months after the beginning of her visionary life, Elisabeth has her first experience of rapture. Soon she begins to see the angel as the one who lifts her soul up into the heavens and mediates divine revelation from God to herself.

Although one might expect that Elisabeth's sense of direct contact with heaven was decreased by the new presence of this intermediary who served to communicate and interpret what she learned in her ecstatic trance, this is not the case. In fact, once she began having regular visions of this angel, it is almost as if she now understood her own role more clearly. As the angel served as an intermediary between God and herself, so now she was to serve as an intermediary between heaven and earth. And as the angel exhorted her to a greater perseverance in her faith, so now was she to exhort her fellow Christians to return to a faithful dedication to their vocation as Christians.

This shift in Elisabeth's perspective, the widening of her vision from her own personal experience to a sense of her role in the moral improvement of the universal church, can be seen in the final chapters of *Liber Visionum Primus*. She describes herself praying alone in the church on the day before Palm Sunday, 1154. While she was praying, a ray of copious light poured over her which, she said, warmed her like the sun. Like the Apostle Paul, who was overwhelmed by a light from heaven on the road to Damascus, she fell to the earth with a violent force (cf. Acts 22:6–7). She continues:

> After a little while, the angel of the Lord came and quickly raised me up and stood me on my feet, saying: "Rise up, o human, and stand on your feet, and I will speak to you, and do not fear, because I am with you all the days of your life. Act manfully and let your heart be strengthened, and uphold the

Lord. And you will say to the transgressors of the earth, 'Just as once the people crucified me, so I am crucified daily among those who sin against me in their hearts.'" [129]

The angel continues this sermon excoriating the faithlessness of the people who have turned away from God.

Here and several more times in the course of the book, the angel is represented as commissioning Elisabeth to take on the prophetic role of communicating God's displeasure to sinful humankind. The entire scene evokes the memory of the biblical apocalyptic seers and the events on the Damascus road. Elisabeth's initial response to this commission echoes the biblical motif of the prophet's hesitance to become the mouthpiece of God. "Lord," she cries to the angel, "I do not know how to speak, and I am slow in talking," [130] recalling Jeremiah's protest of ignorance when God called him to be a prophet (Jer. 1:7) and Moses' excuse of a speech impediment when God called him to deal with Pharaoh (Ex. 4:10). But the angel assures her: "Open your mouth and I will speak, and whoever hears you, also hears me," [131] recalling Jesus' words as he sent his disciples off to preach his message (Luke 10:16). At another point, Elisabeth confides to the angel that she does not know what to say or do because she was unlearned in divine Scripture. Again the angel assures her: "My grace is sufficient for you," this time recalling Paul's description of God's response to his own request for aid (2 Cor. 12:9). [132]

Other reminiscences of biblical prophets can also be seen in these last chapters of *Liber Visionum Primus*. Elisabeth reports the angel addressing her in these words: "And you son of man [*fili hominis*] will say to those people who inhabit the earth: Listen people! The God of gods has spoken." [133] Here Elisabeth retains the exact formula, *fili hominis*, found so frequently in the book of the prophet Ezekiel, when God addresses Ezekiel and tells him to prophesy to the people of Israel. Elisabeth's use of this explicitly masculine form of address, "son" (*fili*), and her report of the angel's earlier command to act manfully (*viriliter age*) are the two moments at which she transposes the gender of an image or phrase referring to herself. The angel's order to "act manfully" reveals her sense that courage, a virtue not frequently associated with women, is required to fulfill her duty of announcing God's word. Elisabeth understood this virile courage, a phrase reminiscent of Old Testament images of preparation for heroic endeavor, to be something required not just of a would-be prophet, but of all spiritual leaders, including other women. Thus she exhorts the abbess of Dietkirchen, "Act manfully and let your heart be strengthened, and endure the temptations of this world." [134]

Likewise, her sense of herself as *filius homini* reveals a self-consciousness about doing something (preaching the word of God), that is traditionally the exclusive vocation of men. But her recognition of "doing something male" does not mean that Elisabeth sees herself as male, as having moved onto a new and different plane. Rather, her use of the phrase seems to indicate her extreme fidelity to biblical prophetic tradition as a way of understanding, communicating, and protecting her own preaching activity, to the extent that she forces the traditionally gender-specific phrase to function in a new, androgynous way, just as she explodes the traditional conception of courage as a predominantly male virtue.

The angel's orders for her to preach repentence come to fruition on the day after Palm Sunday, when Elisabeth suddenly proclaims, in the middle of Matins, the words which she says the Lord put into her mouth. Although the brief sermon she delivers is very similar in tone to the messages the angel gave to her, a slightly different nuance can be detected. The same sins of hypocrisy and faithlessness are chastised, but the audience is slightly different. Whereas the earlier sermons spoken by the angel were general enough to be directed to all Christians, Elisabeth's sermon is clearly directed toward the clergy, the ecclesiastical leaders of the church whose celebration of ritual sacrifices are polluted by their evil deeds.[135]

Elisabeth's new sense of herself as a prophet and preacher to the church, especially to its failing leaders, was foreshadowed by her earlier visions in which she expressed concern for the morality of the "professional religious" of her day. She had seen, for example, a vision of the Day of Judgment and had been dismayed to recognize so many priests as well as men and women from her own order among the unhappy crowd at Christ's left hand who were condemned to eternal punishment.[136] And at another point she had asked the angel about the will of God regarding "clergy and nuns not walking in the good path."[137] These are the first hints that Elisabeth was beginning to see herself in the role of a preacher of penance, although this new image is not fully realized until the later scenes in which Elisabeth describes herself flooded over by the light, knocked down in a trance, raised up by the angel, and then ordered by him to carry God's word of condemnation and exhortation to the sinful people.[138]

At the end of *Liber Visionum Primus*, Elisabeth reports an experience that was a crucial turning point in her visionary career. The angel of the Lord demands to know why she has not made public her revelations: "Why do you hide gold in the mud? This is the word of God which has been sent to earth through your mouth, not so that it could be hidden, but so that it could be made manifest for the praise and glory of our Lord and for the salvation of his people."[139] Here we see Elisabeth's explicit identification of her revelations with the word of God that is to be publicly proclaimed to the people of God for their own salvation. Thus the broadening of her perspective is confirmed in a most concrete way: no longer does she understand her experience of divine grace to be solely for the purpose of her own spiritual comfort and edification. Instead, she sees herself as chosen by God to bear the message of divine wrath and the call to conversion.

This new image of divinely ordained preacher and prophet could not but collide with Elisabeth's sense of herself as a woman whose sole technique of affecting the world was prayer within her cloistered community. Some of this inner conflict can be glimpsed in this scene where she describes the angel's angry accusation of her silence. After asking why she has dared to hide her revelations, the angel resorts to physical violence. Elisabeth, in her trance, perceives that she has been whipped by the angel, and she is so visibly shaken by this experience that her sisters around her can see her physical response.[140] Elisabeth then finds that she cannot speak until she has handed over to her abbot the book of revelations recorded thus far by her brother Ekbert and the other nuns. She and Ekbert had previously agreed that, although her revelations should be recorded, they should not be published until her death. But Elisabeth made this agreement before she came to see her private, interior experiences in terms of a divine mission to preach the word of God.

Abbot Hildelin's preaching of Elisabeth's prophecy exposed her to derision, and Elisabeth's fear that her words would be regarded as *muliebria figmenta* haunted her commitment to revealing God's word. But this fear that her words would be mistaken for "womanish fictions" did not lead Elisabeth to relinquish her role as a prophetic revealer of God's words, as can be seen in *Liber Visionum Secundus*, which records events dating after Hildelin's fateful preaching. Yet new tensions appear in this book, especially in the involvement of men in her life. This can be seen, for example, in the increased presence of Abbot Hildelin in the records of Elisabeth's visions.

The abbot's priestly and liturgical role is repeatedly emphasized: Elisabeth suffers in physical agony until she receives an indulgence from the abbot; three women in purgatory ask Elisabeth to enlist the abbot to celebrate the office of the dead for them; Elisabeth goes into ecstasy when the abbot blesses her; she sees the Eucharist under the species of flesh and blood while the abbot is blessing the host; when the Virgin Mary is displeased with Elisabeth's tepid service, Saint Peter advises Elisabeth to ask the abbot to celebrate the office of the Virgin; later, when Mary has been appeased, she tells Elisabeth that the abbot as well as Elisabeth herself will receive a reward for their service; Saint Peter likewise promises special patronage to the abbot because of his devotion.[141]

Throughout these visions, Elisabeth's role as channel of communication between her community and the otherworld is repeatedly paralleled to the abbot's role in sustaining the community's relation with heaven through his liturgical activities. Hildelin's increased presence in *Liber Visionum Secundus* must reflect his greater involvement in Elisabeth's activities, which itself can be traced back to the episode recorded at the end of *Liber Visionum Primus* where Elisabeth submits her hidden book of visions to him.

The increased presence of Hildelin and the interest in his liturgical role is not a direct emphasis on his authority as abbot, as one to whom Elisabeth owed obedience, although this dimension of their relationship cannot be ignored. Nor does the heightened notice of the abbot dominate the narrative to the exclusion of emphasis on Elisabeth's prophetic, preaching role. Early in the book, Elisabeth reports a message she received from John the Baptist. He urged her to persuade her brothers and sisters at Schönau to learn from what God has worked in her.[142] She continues to image herself in terms of prophetic prototypes in the Bible.[143] And one of the most dramatic affirmations of her role as someone chosen by God to reveal God's secrets to the world is found in this book. She tells of being swept up into the heavens and hearing a great and awful voice speaking to her, a mighty voice that unequivocally asserts the divine origin of Elisabeth's revelations and her duty to proclaim them "on account of the unbelief of many and for the confirmation of the faith."[144] In this speech, Elisabeth is placed within a telescoped view of salvation history: God created humans, who in their pride followed the counsel of the serpent. The obedience of one regained what the earlier disobedience had lost. But now, despite the many who are called Christians, "there are few who wish to follow the one whose name they have received."[145] The visions therefore have been given to Elisabeth in these wicked times to strengthen the nominal Christians in their faith.[146] Thus despite any circumstances that may seem to limit the efficacy of Elisabeth's extraordinary power, such as a liturgical context controlled by the priestly office from which she was excluded or the mockery of those who think themselves better than she, here Elisabeth clearly articulates the significance of her experience for the entire church.

Each of Elisabeth's subsequent visionary compositions builds on this image of herself as God's vessel of continuing revelation. For example, in the *Liber Viarum Dei*, Elisabeth reports a conversation in which the angel tells her that she has begun the Book of God's Ways. The revelation of this book had already been foretold to her in a vision:

> When I was in the spirit, [the angel] led me to a place like a meadow, in which a tent was pitched, and we entered it. And he showed me a great pile of books stored there and he said, "Do you see these books? They all are yet to be drafted before the Day of Judgment." Lifting one of them, he said, "This is the Book of God's Ways, which is to be revealed through you, when you will have visited sister Hildegard, and heard her." And indeed it began to be fulfilled in this way, immediately after I had returned from her.[147]

Not only is this passage what Barbara Newman has called Elisabeth's graceful acknowledgment of her debt to Hildegard of Bingen,[148] but it also indicates something of Elisabeth's understanding of her own book. In meeting with Hildegard, Elisabeth appears to have come to understand her revelations as something not unique to herself, but as part of a larger genre of books that were still to be announced through other people, as part of a larger scheme of divine revelation of which she herself was just one, albeit a significant, participant.

Thus it is possible to discern in the *Liber Viarum Dei* a different persona of Elisabeth emerging. With several years' experience behind her, with the sympathy and encouragement of Hildegard, whose visionary gift Elisabeth deeply respected, and with the presence of Ekbert and her confidence in his discretion about publishing her visions, Elisabeth had come some distance from the time of her earliest frightful experience of demonic apparitions. Given Ekbert's interest in specific theological questions and his obvious guidance of Elisabeth toward these issues, it is not surprising that she turned her attention to larger questions of spiritual interest. Ekbert's willingness to allow her voice to be heard in a text that was not overloaded with his apologies or her expressions of self-doubt shows that he too had come to a new sense of confidence in what Elisabeth was doing. There are still affirmations of the authenticity of her revelations, but these declarations are no longer coupled with her protestations of inability or hesitancy to proclaim the revelations she is receiving. In fact, one of these affirmations of the divine origin of the visions indicates Elisabeth's new self-consciousness as the creator of a literary product, a book, which will be copied and read by many. Elisabeth declares that the angel told her: "Blessed is the one who shall read and hear the words of this book because they are true."[149] This assertion plays on the words of the apocalyptic seer John, who introduces his own visions with a declaration of their divine origin and the need for the faithful to heed their message (cf. Apoc. 1:3). Elisabeth's sense of her sermons and visions as a literary creation is echoed at the end of the text as well. The conclusion of the *Liber Viarum Dei* is followed by a brief *adjuratio* to all future copyists of the book. She solemnly charges "through God and his angel" that anyone who copies this book should carefully proofread the copy and include this adjuration.[150]

Elisabeth's sense of herself as one divinely commissioned to reveal God's word, whatever its power for transforming her self-understanding, did not radically transform the structures of her life. She recognized this and accepted it by accepting a somewhat attenuated sense of what it meant to preach God's word. Unlike Hildegard, who summoned the necessary interior as well as exterior resources to leave her cloistered walls and travel the countryside preaching God's word in cathedrals and monasteries, Elisabeth relied on others to serve as her mouthpiece. In a thundering letter to the bishops of Trier, Cologne, and Mainz, she commanded them to preach the sermons of the *Liber Viarum Dei* to all the people of the Roman church and to repent for their own sins in the process.[151] Even though Elisabeth accepted restrictions on her personal condition by not attempting the life of itinerant preacher, we can see from this letter that she allowed no limitations to be imposed on her revelations. In fact she urgently sought the broadest audiences and the most authoritative messengers for the latest installment of God's continuing revelation.

The continuation of divine revelation took a surprising turn when Elisabeth was confronted with the bones from the newly discovered Cologne graveyard. The revelations Elisabeth pronounced in response to the requests sent by Abbot Gerlach of Deutz could only stand in contradiction to the received tradition about the martyrdom of Saint Ursula and her eleven thousand companions. Elisabeth knew well the tradition and equally well understood the pressure she was under to mediate between the authoritative tradition and the desire to see in the bones the remains of the martyred virgins. In her reflection on the traditional legend, she came to "see" how both the tradition and the new discovery could be genuine.

The fact that the material she reveals is surprising ceases to be a liability. For Elisabeth, the novelty of her message begins to enhance her sense of her special role in the divine order of history. She portrays herself questioning the credibility of the new discovery and then reports the response she received when one of the martyred virgins appeared to her: "A long time ago God predestined you for this, so that those things about us which had been unknown up until now, would be made manifest through you."[152] Here Elisabeth offers a new and ostensibly incontrovertible defense to her self-portrait—ancient predestination. Like the words of God warning the prophet Jeremiah that his divinely ordained prophetic mission preceded his birth (Jer. 1:4–5), these words lift Elisabeth out of the constraints of contemporary expectations.[153] Not even the threat of revealing novelties, a possibility that sometimes worries Elisabeth, stands in the way of her visionary re-creation of the legend of Saint Ursula.[154]

It is possible that Elisabeth's confidence in her role as revealer of divine mysteries, as well as the confidence of others such as her brother Ekbert and Gerlach of Deutz, may have been strengthened by the example of another woman's visionary revelation. The end of *Regnante domino*, the best-known version of the legend before Elisabeth's adaptation of it, relates the case of the nun Elyndruda, to whom the virgin Saint Cordula was said to have appeared and ordered the veneration of her memory as one of the Cologne martyrs. The author of the *passio*, by mentioning numerous biblical examples of people who learned great celestial mysteries through dreams, emphasizes that this was not just a deceptive dream.[155] But Elyndruda did not have to announce a revelation that contradicted the received tradition. Elisabeth, however, refers to her detractors and her own hesitation, and well she might, given the unexpected content of her new revelations. It is this very awareness of presenting something in tension with tradition, however, that she now interprets as confirmation of her role as a divinely predestined vessel of communication.

In her letters, Elisabeth couches her identity in a striking image of both grandeur and abject humility: "A certain small spark sent forth from the seat of great majesty, and a voice sounding in the heart of a certain wormlike person speaks. To H[illin], Archbishop of Trier. The one who was, is, and is to come warns you."[156] Elisabeth's description of herself as the *vermiculus homo* through whom the voice of God speaks is her image expressing in graphic terms the Gospel verse she later quotes: "You have hidden these things from the wise and prudent and revealed them to the little ones" (Matt.11:25, Luke 10:21). She is one of the little ones to whom God has revealed hidden things, and now it is the voice of God speaking through her that Elisabeth usually sends in her letters. This perspective thus eliminates any need for conventional forms of address, or for apology for her outspoken criticism or commands, even to archbishops. This sentence about the spark from the great majesty and the voice sounding in the heart of the worm-person appears in six of Elisabeth's letters.[157] Where it does not appear, other phrases usually warn the reader that the message which follows is from God: "A certain divine inspiration warns you"; [158] "Receive with thanksgiving my words, which have been brought forth from me by God's gift without human effort"; [159] "The divine voice speaks to you." [160]

The most explicit association of Elisabeth's experience with that of Old Testament models comes from the hand of Ekbert. In his introduction to *Liber Visionum Secundus*, Ekbert offers an apologia for the fact that divine revelation is being announced by a woman:

> Indeed, [Our God] is not restrained by the murmuring of those who, judging themselves great and despising those which things appear weaker, are not afraid to insult the riches of his goodness in [his handmaid]. . . . This thing scandalizes them, that in these days, the Lord deigns to magnify exceedingly his mercy in the weak sex. But why does it not come to mind that it happened likewise in the days of our fathers, when, while men were given over to negligence, holy women were filled with the spirit of God so that they prophesied, vigorously governed the people of God, and even triumphed gloriously over the enemies of Israel, women such as Huldah, Deborah, Judith, Jael and others of this kind? [161]

Here Elisabeth is placed in the Old Testament series of women who boldly spoke God's word and courageously acted in the face of danger when men were too foolish or indolent to do so.[162] Ekbert's choice of Huldah for comparison is particularly striking in that Huldah's prophecy failed: her prediction of peace for King Josiah was betrayed by his death in battle (4 Kings 22:14–20, 23:29). Ekbert may have had in mind Elisabeth's own failed prophecy when he recalled the model of this Old Testament prophetess.

Elisabeth never makes such an explicit comparison of herself with biblical prophets. For all her language that evokes biblical models of prophecy or divine inspiration, she never calls herself a *propheta* or claims to have a *spiritus prophetiae*. This remains the business of her apologist, who tries to give a rational explanation for an untraditional event by drawing a parallel with tradition. Elisabeth rarely descends to the level of mere rational comparisons. Instead, she has absorbed the theological force of the models that inspired her, and she speaks their words rather than speaks about them. This is not to imply that she offers no apologies of her own. She is highly aware of the questionable nature of what she is doing, but she defends it without stepping out of the language of her experience.

If they diverge in their explanations of her role, Elisabeth and her brother share an understanding of its purpose. Their agreement may be due in part to Ekbert's ability to convince Elisabeth, but her consent appears genuine, for it surfaces in many of the most confessional passages of the visionary corpus. In her opening address to Ekbert in the expanded version of *Liber Visionum Primus*, Elisabeth explains that she has been taught by certain wise individuals that her visions have been given to her not only for her sake.[163] This confession indicates the influence of others on Elisabeth's interpretation of her own experience, which is a well-documented aspect of the visionary canon. It also is realistic for what it hints of Elisabeth's initial interpretation of her visions. Elisabeth's descriptions of her earliest experiences treat them largely as a private phenomenon with relevance only to her own spirituality. For example, an apparition of a particular saint is recounted in such a way that its significance is largely its demonstration of that saint's favor toward Elisabeth,[164] but this interpretation soon widened so that Elisabeth began to perceive her role as one divinely ordained to proclaim the revelations she received. In the words of her opening remarks to *Liber Visionum Primus*, these revelations were not intended merely for herself, but for the confirmation of the faith and consolation of the church at large. Ekbert echoes this sentiment in his own introduction to the same book, asserting: "All these things which took place around her appeared to pertain to the glory of God and the edification of the faithful."[165]

But with her widened understanding of her experience, why were even the early, ostensibly only personal, events recorded? Why were not only the obviously didactic texts such as the *Liber Viarum Dei* or the obviously "revelatory" texts such as the visions about the bodily assumption of Mary or about the Cologne martyrdom retained in the visionary canon? What could Elisabeth have understood as the universal edifying and consoling purpose of those visions that were focused more narrowly on her own spiritual state?

To some degree, the marvelous quality of the experience was in itself a reason for publishing the accounts and a reason for believing the accounts to be edifying for others. Throughout the texts there are repeated references to the fact that God has acted wonderfully, has done marvelous things with Elisabeth. Therefore, the revelations should not only inspire their hearers to praise God, which is certainly one of their purposes, but they should also give hope to the faithful, because, as Elisabeth repeatedly stresses, she has been the beneficiary of these marvels not due to her own merit but due to God's compassion.[166] In Elisabeth's view, her experience stands as a witness to God's merciful grace to the faithful. The recording of her experience fulfils its role as confirmation of the faith and consolation to believers in that it is an account of God's marvelous actions.

But her didactic role is not exhausted thereby. She also has visions about central tenets of the Christian faith, such as the ineffable mystery of the Trinity. In reporting her experience of the three persons in one divine substance, however, she offers no explanation of this mystery, nor does she even describe the visual images by which she came to understand it.[167] Yet she offers her report of having actually perceived this mystery as effective confirmation that the church's faith is true.

Her many reports of the otherworld, the activities of the saints and angels, and Gospel events also serve as a type of eyewitness proof to what the church already believes. Even when she is not revealing something new or delivering the message of God's call to repentence, in other words, even in what twentieth-century audiences may judge to be her most mundane accounts, Elisabeth still understands herself to be confirming the faith of the church and edifying and consoling its members in their pilgrimage on earth. In an age in which there was a recognized gap between belief and knowledge, when Peter Lombard, certainly one of the most influential theologians of the day, could assert that many people believe what they do not know, Elisabeth's visions offer a kind of evidence for the professed faith that did not require formal training in logic or even in theological study in general.[168]

In offering her visions as proof of the faith and as a call to renewal, Elisabeth sees herself as nothing less than a vehicle of salvation for her fellow Christians. No hint of megalomania accompanies this—her ambivalence is too strong. When she reports that the angel told her she had received revelations "for the salvation of the people of God," it is in the context of her bitter punishment and humiliation.[169] But even humiliation has its prophetic prototypes, and Elisabeth's emphasis on the didactic role of her experience would be easily appreciated by her readers. After all, Elisabeth's words reassuringly recall that crucial criterion of genuine prophecy established by the Apostle Paul: the one who prophesies speaks to others for their edification, exhortation, and consolation.

6. The Religious Vision of Elisabeth

Elisabeth of Schönau is of historical and religious interest for what made her unusual in her own day: her claim to receive divine revelation through the medium of visions; her compulsion to proclaim to the world what she learned in her visions; the credence she was given by the members of her community, by those who wrote to her and visited her, and by those who copied and read her revelations. But she is also of interest for what may or may not have been unusual in her own day: her religious attitudes and the images she used to express them; her moral indignation at sin and corruption; her fear about death and what follows it. Elisabeth was not a theologian. This fact makes the visionary corpus, its shaping by Ekbert notwithstanding, a precious series of documents for eliciting some picture of what it meant to a mid-twelfth-century woman to call herself a Christian.

God, the Saints, and the Worlds Beyond

Underlying many of Elisabeth's visions is a concern, sometimes urgent, sometimes curious, with the otherworld. To some degree this preoccupation may be due to Elisabeth's exposure to the tradition of visionary literature that documented journeys to hell and purgatory, but Elisabeth's visions of the otherworld are not limited to the traditional didactic concern to inspire moral conversion with tales of fire and brimstone. Rather, they illustrate her tendency to focus her attention on a larger, more important, inherently more interesting reality than the immediate world of her convent life.

TRANSCENDENCE AND IMITATION

This interest in the otherworld functioned on many levels. Let us begin with Elisabeth's visions of heaven, already noted as a relatively untraditional subject. In *Liber Visionum Primus*, there are eight examples of fairly detailed visions of heaven (chapters 20, 21, 27, 31, 41–42, 53, 54, 73) and numerous less extensive accounts. The more detailed visions describe the population of heaven—the angels and saints neatly arranged in order around a throne, usually singing praises to God, sometimes falling prostrate before the majesty on the throne. These visions reveal Elisabeth's familiarity with the comparable scenes in the Apocalypse (4:1ff; 7:9ff), which also influenced the artistic representation of the orderly choirs of heavenly inhabitants.[1] But citing the biblical and iconographic models does not exhaust the meaning of these visions, for Elisabeth's repeated return to this image, often with new detail added, suggests that this subject had a powerful attraction for her.

Elisabeth's descriptions of the heavenly citizens usually emphasize hierarchy. Evangelists, elders, apostles, martyrs, virgins, angels, archangels, cherubim, and seraphim are reported in their proper places. The saints and angels always appear in vast multitudes, and their numbers imply glory and order, never jumble. The sense of marvel is enhanced by her description of the four animals and the flaming wheels of Ezekiel, which also find their place in the celestial crowd.

These are some of Elisabeth's most voyeuristic visions, that is, where she is purely spectator, almost eavesdropper. Unlike most of her other visions which focus on some communication between herself and the heavenly personalities she sees, in these visions there is no interaction. Attention, hers and that of the personalities she sees, is directed away from herself and toward the center of the heavenly stage. At the center Elisabeth sometimes sees the mystery of the Trinity somehow communicated to her ("modo quodam, quem explicare non audeo").[2] More frequently she refers to the throne of great majesty in the center, and once even to "one sitting on the throne, whose appearance was frightful."[3]

In her one report of a direct audition of God's voice, God is portrayed as referring in particular to these visions of heaven as the ultimate secrets.[4] Thus for Elisabeth, her glimpses of the celestial world were an essential part of her experience as recipient of divine mysteries. But more importantly, heaven, with its hierarchical order and awesome hub, exerted a continuing fascination for her. Her sense of divine power as she perceived it working in her own life—its glorious as well as frightful aspects—was concretely mirrored in this celestial scene.

Elisabeth's inactivity as she gazed on the scene of divine majesty stands in sharp contrast to her extreme identification with the physical passion of Jesus. Especially during the season of Lent, she experiences in her own body the agony of Jesus that she sees *in oculis mentis*:

Then after a little while the brothers began to celebrate the office of the day, and when they had continued as far as the reading of the passion, I began to agonize and be pressed beyond every limit in such a way that I could tell no one. Indeed, my brother, if all my flesh were torn to pieces, it seems to me that I would endure it more easily. Finally, however, I came into ecstasy and again I saw the Lord on the cross, and then at that time he gave up the spirit.[5]

From here Elisabeth goes on to detail the physicality of Jesus' death—the bent neck, the lowered head, the folded knees, the inactive limbs. Meditation on the sufferings of Jesus on the cross in prayer and in artistic representation had flourished since about the middle of the eleventh century.[6] In Elisabeth's case, compassion for the sufferings of Jesus becomes a literal reality of *compassio*, "suffering with."

Her identification with the humanity of Christ was grounded in a continuing life of Eucharistic devotion. Elisabeth frequently reflected on the Eucharist in her visions. Her visions of the Eucharist as flesh and blood,[7] her visionary participation in the Mass when she was not physically present in the church,[8] her vision of blood from the side and feet of the crucified Jesus pouring into the chalice on the altar,[9] her vision of a dove depositing tongues of fire above the heads of her sisters as they approached the altar to receive communion,[10] her miraculous recovery from illness which enabled her to receive communion,[11] her vision of the Eucharistic bread tipping the scales of her eternal judgment in her favor,[12] the angel's command that she receive communion even though she did not consider herself sufficiently prepared,[13] all reveal the significant place of the sacrament in her life. And in addition to these specific visions involving the Eucharist, frequently Elisabeth's ecstasies occurred during the Eucharistic celebration.[14]

For Elisabeth, the Eucharist is an intimate experience—it nourishes her and reveals its true nature to her spiritual eyes. Representing the moment when the chasm between heaven and earth is bridged, it becomes a moment when this chasm is likewise bridged through her visionary experience. Given through the supreme physical suffering of Jesus, it precipitates her own physical torment.[15]

Elisabeth's devotion to the humanity of Christ, which can be seen in her visionary re-creation of the events of Jesus' life,[16] her sympathetic identification with his physical suffering, and her attachment to the Eucharist, reaches a remarkable expression in a vision in which Christ's humanity is represented by a female virgin. A beautiful virgin with her hair spread out over her shoulders sits in the middle of the sun, holding a golden cup. A dark cloud repeatedly comes and obscures the sun, causing the earth to be covered in darkness and the virgin to cry. Elisabeth learns from the angel that the virgin represents "the sacred humanity of the Lord Jesus" ("domini Jesu sacra humanitas"), the sun represents the divinity of Christ, and the cloud is sin reigning in the world.[17] The virgin's actions are those characteristically associated with women: she cries in lamentation and she offers refreshment to the world from her cup. When questioned by her hearers about this unexpected female image for Christ's humanity, Elisabeth expands the interpretation: the virgin also represents the blessed mother of Christ. Elisabeth's further reflection on this image, coaxed by Ekbert, produced the more conventional interpretation. But this second signification is not meant to replace the first. As Elisabeth reports, the Lord provided the image in such a way that "it could more suitably be adapted to signify also his blessed mother."[18]

The multivalence of the symbol functions so easily because of the intimate connection between Christ's humanity and his birth from Mary. The vision occurred during Mass on Christmas Eve, which provided the liturgical context for reflection on the nativity of Jesus, the point at which his humanity is most explicitly linked to his birth from a human woman. In the case of Jesus, where no human fleshly father had any part in the conception of the infant, the connection between Mary and Christ's humanity was direct, strengthened at least implicitly by medieval associations between femaleness and flesh.[19] Thus Elisabeth's attribution of the second interpretation of the image of the virgin should not be dismissed as merely a capitulation to a rationalized, conventional theology under pressure from her brother.[20] Rather, it further illuminates her association of Christ's humanity with femaleness.[21]

All of these aspects of Elisabeth's spirituality, her Eucharistic piety, her devotion to the humanity of Christ, her identification with his physical suffering, and her sense of Christ's humanity sharing her own female nature, correspond to the religious experience of many women in the thirteenth century, as it has been analyzed by Caroline Walker Bynum.[22] Like these women, Elisabeth found in her meditation on the humanity of Christ and her devout reception of the Eucharist a possibility of ecstatic religious experience that affirmed her life as a physical, female being receiving the divine and being redeemed by it.

There remains, however, a fundamental difference between Elisabeth and the women Bynum describes. According to Bynum, many women of the thirteenth century sought to become the crucified Christ whom they imitated, to fuse with the body on the cross. They were unitive mystics, a characterization difficult to ascribe to Elisabeth of Schönau. Whatever may be Elisabeth's rapture at her perception of God's intervention in her life, whatever may be her sense of transcending the normal human level of communication with God, whatever may be her craving for a continuation of this experience, Elisabeth never expresses any sense of herself as becoming anything other than what she is, nor any hint of union with the one whom she perceives to be invading her life.

That Elisabeth does not seem inclined to envision her spiritual life in this way is not surprising in light of several other important aspects of her religious perspective. Consider her visions of heaven—thousands of saints and angels arranged in order according to their status around the throne of indescribable majesty.[23] Elisabeth's spiritual goal is to join that company in her appropriate rank, to fall on her face in front of the one "whose appearance was frightful," and to sing ceaselessly God's praises.[24] These recurring visions underscore the abyss that remains, even in the eschatological state of celestial beatitude, between God and creature. This awareness continually tempers any inclination on Elisabeth's part to envision union with the divine.

But what is to be made of Elisabeth's visions that reveal her identification with the humanity of Christ? Does this identification not stand in tension with her pervasive sense of differentiation from God? For Elisabeth, there is no tension because the identification itself springs from her image of Christ:

> Moreover, in my trance I saw the opened heavens and the Lord Jesus with infinite thousands of saints. . . . And there was no splendor or beauty in him; rather he was as if but recently crucified, so pitiable did he appear. And when to the whole world he brandished the cross on which he had hung, and the wounds of his passion dripping as if with fresh blood, he shouted with a loud and exceedingly dreadful voice: Such things have I endured for you, but what have you suffered for me?[25]

The bloodied image of savior hardly beckons the visionary toward union. Rather, this vision, which resonates with Elisabeth's other visions of the awesome, forbidding divinity, reveals a quite different type of identification with Christ. Her imitation of his physical suffering originates in her powerful sense of what is owed to him. Similarly in the *Liber Viarum Dei* sermon on martyrdom in which Elisabeth encourages her hearers to embrace suffering in this life, she again emphasizes the debt owed to Christ: "Servant of God, what will you repay to your savior?"[26] In this same context is also found her most explicit expression of a physical identification between believer and Christ. She refers to Zechariah 2:8 ("The one who touches you touches the pupil of my eye") to remind her hearers that they are so closely joined to Christ ("ita sibi te coniunxit") that anything they suffer he too will suffer with them. Of course, this conjunction does not imply similarity. It is not until the final transformation (*reformatio*) of the believer's body that it will become like the brightness of Christ's body.[27]

Elisabeth's sense of the female aspect of Christ's humanity heightens the degree to which she is able to imitate his agony and allows her to understand her own suffering, both self- and divinely inflicted, in terms of the ongoing process of redemption. But redemption is clearly not becoming, not melting into, the wounded body of Christ nor into his glorified, bright body at the end of time. Instead, even when the "thorn of Adam" is removed from her resurrected body, redemption means taking her place in the celestial hierarchy.

Such a view of her relationship with God, both present and eschatological, is rooted in Elisabeth's experience of "the hand of the Lord upon her." Her perception of her life being invaded, invaded to such an extent that she no longer even has control over her own body, is the experiential basis for a powerful sense of God as other. True to the biblical prophetic models which so influenced her, Elisabeth exhibits the "psychology of captivity": the experience of being overwhelmed by an external power fundamentally different from herself.[28] And for all of Elisabeth's devotion to the humanity of Christ, the incarnation of the Word of God in Christ does not bridge the gulf between creator and creature. For Elisabeth, the God that became incarnate remains essentially God, one who now appears to be owed an even greater debt than before the sacrifice of the crucifixion. In the same vision in which she saw the virgin identified as the humanity of Christ, she explains that human beings have been oblivious to all that God has done for them. Instead of honoring and thanking God for the gift of the Incarnation, they have "vilely trampled the benefits of his redemption."[29]

For Elisabeth the world is only saved from total destruction at Christ's wrath by the constant prayer of his merciful mother.[30] The emphasis is again on distance, otherness, and imitation directed toward repayment rather than fusion. This is why Elisabeth's visions so frequently focus on the otherworld, rather than the inner world of her own soul. Although she experiences "the hand of the Lord" in her innermost being, both physically and psychologically, the effect is not primarily interior. She understands its purpose as drawing her and her hearers back to the path of righteousness that leads to the membership among the celestial crowd thronging around the throne of great majesty, a scene which at present she can only gaze upon passively.

POWERFUL INTERCESSORS: DEVOTION TO MARY AND THE SAINTS

For Elisabeth, mediation between earth and this glorious heaven takes place when some of those saints and angels so perfectly arranged *coram maiestate magna* occasionally leave their contemplative stance to come somewhat closer to earth. Many of Elisabeth's visions recount celestial visitations—saints deigning to show her their favor by granting her their presence. It is these visits, especially the earliest visits by the Virgin Mary, that comfort and strengthen Elisabeth in her times of spiritual malaise.

Elisabeth's devotion to Mary, which must in some ways be distinguished from her veneration of other saints, holds a prominent place in her spiritual life. As already noted, Mary played a crucial, salvific role in her constant prayer to her son, restraining him from condemning the sinful world to perdition. In addition to this role of universal patronness, Elisabeth saw Mary as her own personal protector. Elisabeth's earliest celestial visitations, occurring during a period of grave spiritual unrest, were of Mary. Interspersed among the episodes of demonic manifestations are apparitions of a regal, even priestly Mary.[31] Elisabeth sees Mary sign her with the sign of the cross (a sacerdotal act) and assure her that these threats will not harm her.[32] After several such appearances, Elisabeth no longer remains passive in the face of her terrifying visions, but she boldly, in the name of God, orders her tormenter to cease vexing her.[33] These appearances of Mary provide the basis for Elisabeth's newly found confidence which, in turn, is the beginning of Elisabeth's developing sense of herself as a chosen vessel with a prophetic mission. Thus it is Mary, not as a tender, maternal figure, but a figure almost male in her symbols of authority, whom Elisabeth envisions as her inspiration and protector.

Elisabeth's devotion to Mary and her growing sense of herself as the recipient of heavenly mysteries were channeled by Ekbert into the production of a visionary text about the Virgin. He draws Elisabeth squarely into the center of the theological debate about the corporeal resurrection of Mary. As Elisabeth states at the beginning of *De Resurrectione*, she wanted to learn whether Mary was resurrected in body as well as in soul, because of the uncertainty about this found in the writings of the Fathers.[34]

The patristic sources of doubt are not cited by name, but the controversy and its major positions can be reconstructed. The issue was whether Mary was distinguished from the rest of the human race by being bodily raised into heaven before the general bodily resurrection at the Last Judgment. The question was succinctly put by Atto of Vercelli: "We do not dare to affirm that the resurrection of [Mary's] body has already taken place, since we know that this has not been declared by the holy fathers."[35]

The silence of Scripture about Mary's death had led to enthusiastic elaboration of the events surrounding her last days, most significantly in the form of apocryphal *Transitus* legends which flowered in the fifth century. Occasional warnings against an uncritical acceptance of unauthorized belief were heard from the ninth to twelfth century, including an influential letter by Paschasius Radbertus (d. 860), written in the name of Saint Jerome.[36] No theological articulation of the belief was advanced, and the word *assumptio* was commonly understood to refer to the ascent of Mary's soul into heaven after her death.[37] Despite this lack of theological definition, the tendency of the ever-growing medieval Marian piety was to highlight the glorious aspect of Mary's death and the events that took place thereafter.

The beginning of the twelfth century brought a new theological perspective to the issue. An anonymous treatise that came to be ascribed to Augustine used reason as a basis for argument on matters where Scripture was silent. The author advanced several rational arguments for the belief that Mary's body had already been lifted up and that Mary's full person—body and soul—was residing in heaven. As Hilda Graef has pointed out, the reasoning in this text echoes the argumentation of Eadmer of Canterbury in his treatise on the Immaculate Conception of Mary.[38]

Several decades later another theologian moved beyond both Scripture and reason to find the solution to this question. Ekbert of Schönau turned to a new source of authority, to the Virgin Mary herself, from whom he could learn the truth through the medium of Elisabeth and her extraordinary relationship to Mary. Ekbert's concern to verify this apocryphal legend sets him apart from certain other monastic writers of his day. Unlike, for example, Aelred of Rievaulx, who recognized the contemplative value of apocryphal stories while cautioning against rashly asserting their authenticity, Ekbert was disturbed by the conflict of authoritative opinions.[39] Thus he formulated his questions and engaged Elisabeth to present them to Mary during her customary appearances to Elisabeth. Elisabeth describes herself obediently posing the questions to Mary, but she reports that Mary is not yet ready to reveal such mysteries to her. She says that for one year she refrained from asking either Mary or the angel for this information. Finally, however, she was coerced to pray for the revelations. On the Feast of the Assumption, Elisabeth describes a vision in which she sees a woman rise out of a tomb, be lifted into heaven, and there be greeted by the Lord. Later Elisabeth asks the angel what the vision means, and he explains that it signifies that Mary was assumed into heaven in body and soul.[40]

Elisabeth then reports that seven days later the angel returned, and she asked yet a further question concerning the length of time between Mary's death and her resurrection. The angel's response is forty days, and he goes on to clarify any potential ambiguity. Although the holy fathers did not *know* for certain of Mary's bodily assumption, they *believed* it, thus they called the day of her death (*dormitio*) her Assumption.[41]

This new revelation was at odds with the traditional church calendar. Elisabeth concludes from her visions that the church should celebrate September 23 as the Feast of the Assumption, and August 15, the presently established date for the Assumption, should commemorate only Mary's death. Elisabeth's uneasiness with her own proclamation of this new data was manifested in another vision one year later when she confides to Mary that she hesitated to publish the revelation lest she appear "as an inventor of novelties."[42] To allay her own uneasiness, Elisabeth reports that Mary warned her not to publish these revelations among the people, because they would not understand due to the evil of the time. But Elisabeth also affirms that Mary does not want the records of these visions totally destroyed—the revelations have not been made so that they can pass into oblivion, but they should be shared with those who are genuinely devoted to her.

The affirmation that these revelations were only intended for a certain group of special devotees is not characteristic of Elisabeth's records. Elisabeth declared that after learning the true date of Mary's corporeal Assumption, they did celebrate that solemnity. The twelfth-century Schönau necrology notes September 23 as *Resuscitatio sancte Marie XL° dies post dormicionem eius*, thus indicating the recognition of the new feast within the Schönau cloister.[43] In fact, the new observance spread beyond Schönau. *De secunda assumptionis* gives liturgical directions for celebrating the feast,[44] and fifteenth-century missals from Brandenburg, Freising, Mainz, Passau, and Regensburg, noting September 23 as "the bodily assumption of Mary" or the "commemoration of the assumption of Mary," suggest an enduring tradition of Marian devotional practice that originated in Elisabeth's visionary proclamations.[45]

In both *De Resurrectione* as well as the other visionary texts, Elisabeth awaits the visits of her celestial callers and understands these visits to depend on her devotion to the saints in question. Thus a mutual relationship is established between saint and devotee. Elisabeth honors Mary by commemorating her feast and, in return, Mary honors Elisabeth by a visitation. When the expected visitations do not occur, Elisabeth understands this to be due to her own failure of devotion.[46] These instances are always followed by Elisabeth's renewed veneration in the form of more prayers to the saint, and the consequent reestablishment of celestial favor. In this way, the status of both the saint and the visionary is enhanced by the text that documents this mutual relationship.

Furthermore, the visionary relationship that Elisabeth establishes with the saints in general serves to soften the awesome scene in heaven by virtue of the fact that heaven is now populated with Elisabeth's friends. When the saints come to visit her, she commends the eternal welfare of herself and her community to these powerful intercessors, who then return to heaven and become her advocates in the celestial court. Thus the importance of the mutual relationship goes beyond the honor it confers on Elisabeth in this life. She cultivates these visionary relationships for what she thinks is the advantage in having the patronage of these saints. Through her visions a concrete bond of obligation is established between this world and the other.

The most dramatic example of this aspect of her spirituality can be seen in her revelations about the Cologne martyrs. Although the context for producing a book is a situation set up by others who had a vested interest in Elisabeth's confirmation of the relics' identity, her visionary creations went far beyond a perfunctory concession to "certain men of good repute who . . . compelled" ("quidam bone opinionis viri qui . . . compulerunt") her to investigate these mysteries. This is because the subject of the visions, the martyrdom of Ursula and the eleven thousand virgins, offered Elisabeth a distinctive source of motivation. Her revelations would have tangible effects in the increased devotion to the Cologne martyrs both within the walls of Schönau and beyond. This, she hopes, will have an almost tangible effect on herself. The book both begins and ends with references to the reward one may receive for contributing to the increased honor of these martyrs.[47]

Whatever its origins in the desires of "certain men of good repute" to guarantee the value of their possessions, Elisabeth's book about Ursula and her companions expresses her own deep commitment to the veneration of these martyrs. These saints were mostly women, women who were martyred for their dedication to virginity, a focus of Elisabeth's own religious life, and they dwelled in heaven where they could graciously intercede for someone who had done so much to promote their honor. Like the conclusion of the most influential earlier version of the Ursuline legend, *Regnante domino*, which exhorts a community of nuns to seek the patronage of the Cologne martyrs in striving to preserve their own virginity,[48] Elisabeth's *Revelatio* ties together two crucial aspects of the spiritual life of her community—the dedication to virginity and the veneration of exemplary, powerful saints. Despite the fact that, of the entire visionary corpus, this book is probably the most foreign to modern sensibilities and is the text in which we see Elisabeth most clearly being manipulated by others, nonetheless, here we also see Elisabeth undertaking her keenest imaginative work on a subject that profoundly expresses her religious life and commitments.

Elisabeth's fear of divine judgment provokes the urgency underlying her desire to establish and maintain these relationships with saintly intercessors. In addition to the glorious scenes of the celestial hierarchy, Elisabeth also has visions of the darker side of what takes place in the otherworld. She sees Christ with his fresh wounds still oozing blood, and he shouts to the earth demanding an account of repayment for his suffering. The scene that follows is no less unsettling. Elisabeth sees this grim judge consign a large crowd to eternal flames, a crowd full of confused and mournful clergy and Benedictine nuns and monks.[49] With this image of her redeemer, it is not surprising that Elisabeth felt the need for celestial patrons to intercede for her, especially because of her frequent illness and her perception of imminent death.[50]

THE PIETY OF PURGATORY

Integral to Elisabeth's view of the otherworld is her belief in the power of intercessory prayer. As noted above, her devotion to the saints was founded on her belief that their prayers for her were especially effective because of their proximity to God, a belief that underlies many of her earliest visions. In the visions recorded in *Liber Visionum Secundus*, another aspect of her spiritual worldview blossoms. This is her belief in the power of intercessory prayer performed by the faithful still living in this world. Not only do the dead pray for the living, but the living pray for the dead.

The constituency of the dead is, of course, not the same in these two cases. The dead who pray are those who crowd around the throne of great majesty, singing God's praises. The dead who are prayed for are those souls who are presently tortured for their sins but will eventually join the celestial hosts in eternal joy. Concomitant with Elisabeth's growing concern about prayer for the dead is a growing tendency to have visions of the dead in their purgatorial environment.

Elisabeth did not have a systematic interpretation of purgatory. According to Jacques LeGoff, no one of her day could have had a systematic view, for the fully elaborated notion of purgatory did not exist until 1170. Tracing a history of the concept of a purgatorial place between heaven and hell, LeGoff argues that the last quarter of the twelfth century saw the first use of the word *purgatorium*. Although there was much in the tradition reaching back to Augustine about the purgation of sins after death, LeGoff credits the cathedral school of Notre-Dame in the decade 1170–80 with the first articulation of a named, spatial purgatory.[51]

Elisabeth's visions, a source that LeGoff did not refer to in his study, present an interesting slant on the question of the birth of purgatory.[52] The word *purgatorium* does occur in the visionary records, and she did envision the existence of a place in which souls were punished after death for their sins.[53] This place was distinguished from hell, from which there was no departure. Her conceptualization of this place, based as it was on a visual rather than verbal reflection, was not entirely consistent and seems to have developed over the course of several years. Her earliest apparent reference is in fact very ambiguous. In the later version of *Liber Visionum Primus*, on the feast commemorating the souls of the dead, Elisabeth describes a high mountain with a glorious building on its peak, and a deep smokey valley beside it, in which souls were horribly tortured. She continues:

> The place which appeared in the middle between this building and the aforementioned valley, appeared to be completely filled with very rough and seemingly scorched thorns. And while I looked on, behold, a numerous crowd of shining people rising up from the valley appeared to head through the middle of those impassable thorn-bushes with great speed and much effort toward that aforementioned building and, finally reaching it, they entered. Some of them, however, chose a path outside the briars and arrived without any effort. This crossing occurred many more times at intervals.[54]

Elisabeth clearly envisions a third place situated between the valley of torture and the celestial mansion, but this cannot be a simple heaven/purgatory/hell scheme. It appears that the crowd of people who begin their ascent to the glorious building have already been purged of their sins—they emerge from the valley and are already bright white. Yet most of them still have suffering to endure until they reach the peaceful scene at the top of the mountain.

Although aspects of this image of a tripartite otherworld will be retained, this particular vision will later serve as the basis for Elisabeth's reflection on a very different subject. The *Liber Viarum Dei* opens with several visions of a high mountain with various paths leading to the brightly illuminated summit. Some of these paths look inviting and easily negotiable while others are only traversed with great hardship.[55] The sojourn up the mountain has been transformed from an image of otherworldly purgation into an image for life in this world, with each of the paths representing a different way of Christian life.

While the mountain ascent ceases to be associated with an otherworldly purgation, the place of heavenly beatitude continues to be portrayed as a glorious supernal building.[56] Hell receives remarkably little attention. It is a dark, fiery abyss where souls are tormented, offering no hope of liberation.[57]

Purgatory is not a single venue but several places of punishment. One of these is a smokey underground cave in which the soul is punished with fire; another is a dry field in which the soul lies tormented with hunger and thirst. There is even some incipient sense of the law of *contrapasso*, which will reach its classic expression in Dante's *Commedia*: Elisabeth sees the soul of her great-uncle Helid "who was harshly tormented in his mouth, and [the angel] said that he was tortured in this way because of his habit of undisciplined words."[58]

Elisabeth's interest in these visions is not primarily focused on the gruesome details of the punishments that the souls endure. She always notes the extremity of the situation—vast numbers of souls or excruciating pain. But despite the didactic possibilities of these horrible scenes, conversion, either in her own life or that of her hearers, is not the intended effect of these visions. Rather, she pays much more attention to the question of the souls' liberation. She is very much concerned to see the souls receive some kind of respite from their ongoing agony. This desire is projected onto the otherworldly geography: a pleasant island surrounded by burning water is a place where souls can rest for an entire night through the intercession of Saint Michael.[59]

Usually Elisabeth asks her angelic guide or the tormented souls themselves how they can be freed from their sufferings. The answer, though varying in detail, is always basically the same: the celebration of Masses in their memory. Sometimes the giving of alms is also mentioned and sometimes the number of requisite Masses is specified, but the emphasis on the celebration of the Mass is usually explicit.[60] This emphasis on the Mass for the liberation of souls is striking for what it reveals about Elisabeth's spiritual life. Her new attention in *Liber Visionum Secundus* to the importance of the Mass does not necessarily suggest a radically new focus in her devotional life. It is clear from the earliest records that Elisabeth had a deep devotion to the Eucharist, yet there is a subtle difference between her Eucharistic devotion, so prominent in *Liber Visionum Primus*, and her growing sense of the centrality of the celebration of the Mass, a consistent feature of her visions of souls in purgatory in *Liber Visionum Secundus*.

Elisabeth's devotion to the Eucharist is, as I noted above, intimately linked with her ecstatic experience. The Eucharist is often the occasion of her ecstasy and, like her ecstasy, it is a moment of connection between the otherworld and this world. Although the Eucharist is an embodiment of Christ's corporeal suffering which she herself is reliving in her own body, the celebration of the Mass, while encompassing the Eucharistic experience, is another order of devotion.[61] It is a formalized ritual which, no matter what the intensity of Elisabeth's devotion and intimate relationship with God, highlights the sacerdotal power to which she did not have access. Thus in *Liber Visionum Secundus*, an emphasis on the necessity of Masses for freeing souls from purgatory meant that Elisabeth's private prayer life, even when endowed with the extraordinary grace of divine visions, was not particularly effective in freeing souls from purgatory.

The implications of this shift toward an emphasis on the celebration of the Mass can be seen in a series of visions recorded in *Liber Visionum Secundus*. Elisabeth reports a conversation with three deceased women who were detained outside the gates of Paradise because no one had prayed for their liberation. They ask Elisabeth to request that her abbot "offer the divine sacrifice for [their] liberation and that of all the faithful departed."[62] Before telling Hildelin of the request, Elisabeth tells her sisters of the women's plight. These nuns immediately "agreed with a pious intent to undertake together bodily affliction for them and, with the psalter divided among them, they prayed with all diligence to the Lord for their liberation."[63] But when the departed women are released from their punishment, they refer only to Hildelin's intercession. Elisabeth then reminds them of the nuns' role in their liberation.[64] Thus neither Elisabeth's visionary gift on its own, nor her visions in conjunction with the piety of the women of her community, can produce the desired effects of liberating the women and insuring their patronage on behalf of the Schönau community once they have entered the realm of powerful saints.[65] A tension seems to underlie this series of visions, a tension that results in this attempt to balance the charismatic, visionary power of Elisabeth with the liturgical power controlled by the abbot.

A similar tension is found in another vision in *Liber Visionum Secundus*. This time Elisabeth asks the soul of her departed uncle what is required to free him from his punishment. He replies that he could be comforted by the offering of Masses for forty days. Elisabeth inquires if any other prayers would aid him. His response: "Anything other than that bread of life and cup of salvation which is offered for me, has as much value to me as when a starving person is refreshed by other foods without bread and wine."[66] The ambiguity of this scene, which begins with an emphasis on the necessity of Mass (an emphasis Elisabeth explicitly questions) and ends with a suggestion that other prayers could be equally effective, again indicates Elisabeth's ambivalence about the centrality of the Mass.

This ambivalence is particularly striking when these episodes from *Liber Visionum Secundus* are compared with an earlier example of Elisabeth's participation in intercessory prayer. In chapter 56 of *Liber Visionum Primus*, Elisabeth relates that they received the announcement of the death of a sister at Dirstein, at which point, "according to custom," the nuns undertook "the divine service" under the "ministry" (*ministerio*) of the *magistra*. Elisabeth declares that she saw an angel of the Lord standing near the *magistra* and the Virgin Mary looking down from heaven upon this praying, female community.[67] In the record of this incident, which antedates both Ekbert's permanent arrival at Schönau and Elisabeth's increased attention to Hildelin's liturgical power, there is no trace of ambivalence about the efficacy of women's prayer. Thus the tension found in records of similar incidents in *Liber Visionum Secundus* seems to suggest a change in Elisabeth's understanding of her own spiritual life.

As noted earlier, *Liber Visionum Secundus* also shows the increased influence of Ekbert, and one of the most noticeable aspects of his presence is the new attention to the otherworldly status of departed souls. Because it is mostly in the records of visions occurring after Ekbert's arrival at Schönau that Elisabeth's visualization of purgatory is found, it appears likely that Ekbert, with his theological training in the intellectual milieu in which, according to LeGoff, the concept of purgatory was articulated, provided this impulse toward Elisabeth's new visionary subject.[68] An essential part of this complex of ideas that were being consolidated into the concept of purgatory was that the most effective way of liberating suffering souls is by offering them Masses.[69] The possible introduction of a more theologically developed concept of purgatory together with Hildelin's heightened involvement in Elisabeth's life created an environment that helped shift her spirituality from a more autonomous, intimate experience of direct contact with the divine to a heightened awareness of herself as a member of a hierarchical community dependent on sacerdotal supremacy.[70] What has been noted as women's perception of the power of their piety for the plight of the dead is somewhat more complex in the case of Elisabeth, who seems to have struggled with the role of her own spirituality within this community that supported but also demonstrated the limits of her power.[71]

If Elisabeth's relationship with the otherworld was constrained in some way by the presence of Ekbert and Hildelin, her newly developing perspective also appeared to have certain implications for her sense of her own eternal destiny. It is striking that the only visions Elisabeth had of her own final judgment preceded the events recorded in *Liber Visionum Secundus*. Each of these two visions depicts a contest between Elisabeth's good and evil deeds, with salvation or damnation as the possible outcomes.[72] Neither scenario leaves room for a period of otherworldly purgation. Thus it might seem that the idea of purgatory would have provided some comfort for Elisabeth, who all too clearly feared the judgment of eternal damnation.

Yet the idea of otherworldly purgation seems to have provoked its own anxieties. Elisabeth's prolonged attention to the three women in purgatory seems to indicate her concern over their particular case. She learns that they are three religious women, one of whom took the veil as a child, another as an adolescent, and the third at an advanced age. The reason for their thirty-year detention outside the gates of heaven is significant: because they appeared to have led holy lives on earth, nobody had thought of them as needing prayers after their death.[73] Elisabeth identifies with these women, religious women who were basically pious during their lives, but whose piety led others to neglect the offices still needed for their total liberation. No longer does she seem concerned about being eternally condemned to hell. This new fear is much more realistic, and therefore much more nagging. This anxiety haunts her even on her deathbed as she

pleads to Abbot Hildelin and her fellow sisters: "Faithfully and with ear-
nest intent take care of my soul, and do not neglect any of those matters
which pertain to my debt, in that you may judge that I do not need the
suffrages of your prayers. I say this because often people who appear religious tend to be neglected because those who were familiar with their
good lives think that they do not particularly need their help."[74] Hildelin
reminds Elisabeth that she has already received divine assurance that she
would find eternal rest. Elisabeth replies that she does not distrust the
promises of the Lord; nonetheless, she wants the assurance of the community's commitment to offer the necessary suffrages for her soul.

In her earlier visions of judgment, she was saved each time from eternal punishment by a last-minute intervention. In one case her guardian
angel places a piece of Eucharistic bread on the scale, representing Elisabeth's devotion to the sacrament, and in the other case, Mary and other
saints respond to Elisabeth's plea for intercession. Although in each of
these cases the saving power is something otherworldly, it is not something out of Elisabeth's reach. For Elisabeth, it is her devotional life of
seeking refuge in the Eucharist and cultivating the patronage of the Virgin
and other saints that finally saves her. But in the new scheme, where one's
final liberation is entrusted to the sometimes negligent care of an all-too-
human community, Elisabeth found serious cause to be nervous. Just as
the new articulation of purgatory limited her power in effecting the salvation of others, so it also tended to de-emphasize the role of her own
piety in determining her salvation.

The Path of Righteousness

Elisabeth's attention to the otherworld, whether expressed in her awe of
the glorious scene of the celestial choirs, her terror at scenes of judgment,
or her interest in the status of departed souls, is complemented by the
other major concern of her visionary spirituality—her fervent meditation
on the proper Christian life in this world. Her condemnations of present
corruption and her exhortations to righteous living are scattered throughout most of the visionary texts and comprise the entire subject of *Liber
Viarum Dei*.

Elisabeth, like so many other writers of the twelfth century, seized
upon the image of journeying to express the spiritual life.[75] For her, the
Christian life was equivalent to following the path to God. Each indivi-

dual's life was the difficult ascent up the mountain to celestial beatitude.[76] With the *Liber Viarum Dei*, Elisabeth elaborates a universal picture of this upward Christian journey. The high mountain is marked with ten different paths leading to the summit, each described in terms of its relative degree of difficulty. These ten paths represent the diverse ways in which the elect climb the mountain to reach the realm of eternal life: contemplation, the active life, martyrdom, marriage, continence, the paths of religious and secular leaders (*rectores*), widowhood, the solitary life, the life of children, and the life of adolescents.

I have already noted that Elisabeth reflected the contemporary concern to articulate a picture of Christian society by classifying various religious and social roles. In the *Liber Viarum Dei*, she incorporates but goes far beyond the traditional scheme of three orders inherited from Gregory the Great: leaders of the church, the chaste, and the married.[77] Obviously Elisabeth's ten *viae* are not mutually exclusive, nor is this a thoroughly systematic scheme. Elisabeth was aware of the ambiguities within the overall picture and expresses her misgivings at its potential confusion by noting that as a member of a monastic community she must locate herself on the path of virginity as well as on the path of contemplation.[78] Some of the difficulty in this scheme results from the amalgamation of several traditional distinctions within the same picture: the distinction between the marrieds, celibates, and ordained; the distinction between the active and the contemplative lives; the distinction between the cenobitic and the eremitic vocations. These traditional classifications focused largely on permutations within what can be called the professional religious life, thus accounting for overlap in areas such as contemplation and celibacy. But in the *Liber Viarum Dei*, the paths representing the active life, the married life, children, adolescents, and secular rulers are Elisabeth's affirmation of the diversity of ways in which a Christian can follow in the footsteps of Christ.

As a complete picture of the Christian life, these visions represent the earthly counterpart to the visions of the celestial ranks seen in heaven. After the visions that include the ten paths, Elisabeth again sees, as in so many of her earlier visions, the orderly population of heaven; but this time the vision is graphically linked to the geography of this world. The heavenly tableau is located at the top of the mountain with the ten paths, and the angel explains that the blessed ones have arrived at their present state by walking along these various paths.

There is no clear hierarchy among the various paths. Elisabeth emphasizes that all these ways lead to celestial beatitude, although there is a certain preeminence associated with the path of divine contemplation. This special dignity is symbolized by its position as the center path, the path in which the Christ-image is standing. The way of contemplation is the only way that will last forever, whereas the other paths will not endure beyond this life. Furthermore, all paths leading to eternal life are in some way subsumed under contemplation, for "in all ways of truth, God is to be contemplated."[79] Although much of the exhortation is general enough to apply to several, if not all, of the paths described in the original visions, there is usually some reflection within each sermon on the specific nature of the path being described.

THE FAILURE OF THE CHURCH

The exhortation in the *Liber Viarum Dei* often shades into criticism of those who fail to walk righteously in their paths. It is striking that when the discourse is focused on the life of ecclesiastical leaders, exhortation practically disappears and condemnation prevails. This note first appears in the sermon on the contemplatives and is later given full play in the sermon on prelates. Clergy are castigated for neglecting to care for their flocks, for their external show of piety while they are polluting the church, their greed and their tolerance of "selling and buying sanctification," their disregard for venerable traditions, and their intrusion into the affairs of the world. While all of these practices are roundly condemned, none is elaborated in any specific detail. The result, however, is clear: "On account of this, behold, religion suffers contempt, faith suffers schism."[80]

The sermon on prelates builds to a climax in an uncharacteristically pointed accusation: "The head of the church has grown weak and its members have died since the Apostolic See has been obsessed with pride and avarice is cultivated, and it is filled with iniquity and impiety and they scandalize my sheep and make them wander when they should protect and guide them."[81] Although even here the accusations are still general—pride, avarice, iniquity, and impiety—this passage reappears several years later in a context where the source of her frustration with the papacy is explicit. In a letter to Hildegard of Bingen, Elisabeth again bemoans the languishing head of the church and its moribund limbs. Several other images amplify the message: God sought workers for his vineyard but now the vineyard perishes; the rock of foundation of the church has been thrown away and the church of God is drying up.[82] All of this criticism is directed at ecclesiastical leaders who will not take decisive action against the Cathars.

Even though Elisabeth's criticism in the *Liber Viarum Dei* is not always as specific as it is in this context, it is usually similar in its motivation. Rarely does she appear to be interested in the degeneracy of the clergy for its own sake—there is no particular interest in the purity of the church per se. Always the criticism of avarice, worldliness, or corruption is related to the impact that this corruption has on the members of the church. In contrast to this failure, the example of the great priest Jesus, who led and protected his flock in humility, is offered.[83] To some extent, all the ways of Christian life involve imitation of Christ, but here the specific example of the *pontifex magnus*, who exercises his role through humility and service, is offered to the current *pontifex magnus* and those surrounding him.

That Elisabeth should locate the source of clerical negligence and corruption in the Roman papacy is striking. This connection is heightened in her letter to the bishops of Trier, Cologne, and Mainz, in which she orders them "to announce to the Roman church and all the people and every church of God these words which you will find in the present book [i.e., the *Liber Viarum Dei*]."[84] Thus Elisabeth envisions the three German bishops proclaiming the failure of the papacy to the papacy.

Her condemnation of the sluggishness of the Roman leadership of the church became yet more explicit. Two years after her initial letter to the three German bishops, Elisabeth returns to the same subject, this time in a letter addressed only to Hillin, the archbishop of Trier. She begins with her usual admonitions to conscientious pastoral care, but then takes up the issue at hand.

> Again the Lord warns you saying, "Give the reason why you have cheated me of my chosen pearls, and have thrown behind your back the precious gems which were sent to you from the realm of great majesty, and have been unwilling to obey me. Don't you know that I said, 'You have hidden these things from the wise and prudent and revealed them to the little ones?' [Luke 10:21]. Take up again and open the book and you will find what I said and what has been done: 'The apostolic seat is obsessed with pride and avarice is cultivated,' et cetera. But if you will not tell them what has been revealed to you and they should die in their sins, you will bear the judgment of God."[85]

In her visionary style Elisabeth accuses Hillin of neglecting his earlier divine commission to bring her message of condemnation to Rome. She orders him to go back to the *Liber Viarum Dei*, especially the passage which explicitly indicts the sins of the papacy and, with his own salvation at stake, she exhorts him to relay the sentence of judgment.

But since the time of her first letter to Hillin, a new development had occurred, a genuine schism in the church, which had been prefigured in her description of the results of ecclesiastical corruption. Upon the death of Hadrian IV, a contested election led to the existence of two popes. Elisabeth allowed herself a visionary pronouncement on this situation, one that was intended to influence the policy of Hillin by telling him that God's preferred candidate is Victor IV, the German pope: "And it should be known to you that the one who was chosen by the emperor is more acceptable before me."[86]

This letter is significant for its evidence of her interest in ecclesiastical events outside of Schönau as well as her interpretation of local clerical abuses in terms of a withering head of the church. Elisabeth's move to rally the moral voice of the German church against the perceived inadequacy of the head of the Roman church must be seen in the context of old resentments and dissatisfactions. By the late eleventh century, the elaboration of the papal office as part of the Gregorian reform program had led to a strong reaction among German bishops who saw the dignity of their spiritual leadership vitiated by papal claims to ultimate ecclesiastical jurisdiction.[87] In her own day, this reaction in its most extreme form had taken shape in the thought of Rainald of Dassel, friend of Ekbert, archbishop of Cologne, and, most significantly, chancellor of Emperor Frederick.[88]

Ekbert's association with Rainald and Elisabeth's assertion of Victor IV's legitimacy have led some to the conclusion that Elisabeth herself nurtured the ideal of a German church independent of papal authority,[89] but there is no further evidence in the visionary texts for Elisabeth's concern with the schism. Ekbert himself takes up the question of schism in his letter to Rainald upon the latter's appointment as archbishop of Cologne. He describes the greed that encourages the abomination of simony and warns that it is in this setting of clerical failure that schism occurs: "Behold, strife has been poured out over the princes of the chief church, which is mother of all, and they have sundered the unity of the high priesthood, broken the bond of ecclesiastical peace, in such a way that they devour each other, destroy each other, anathematize each other. Still, it is uncertain which of the two sides strikes with the sword of Peter, because it cannot be divided into parts, nor, undivided, can it be turned against itself."[90] Ekbert is less willing than Elisabeth to voice publicly his preferred papal claimant. His remarks, disapproving yet not explicitly accusatory, may indicate his perception of Rainald's role in the schism.[91] It is striking that in this letter of congratulations, Ekbert has taken the opportunity to voice his concern about the broken unity of the church. His letter is hardly a ringing affirmation of the recent turn of events, and he appears to indict both sides for their responsibility in creating the schism.[92] Thus any interpretation of Elisabeth's ecclesiastical politics should not be based on an assumed link from Rainald through Ekbert to Elisabeth.

The few but pointed accusations that Elisabeth makes about the languishing head of the church certainly suggest her frustration with what she perceives to be the cause of widespread pastoral degeneration within Christendom. But these accusations also illuminate her distance from the actual events in Rome. Her description of Victor as "electus est a Cesare" betrays a certain ignorance of the actual events that led to the enmantling of Victor IV in 1159.[93] Her later criticism of the papal neglect of the Cathar threat suggests that she was not aware of the fourth canon of Pope Alexander III's Council at Tours (May 1163), in which Cathar sects were condemned.[94] This canon, which preceded the execution of Cathars at Cologne by only months, also suggests the gulf between the Roman papacy and the imperial territory at this time: the canon refers only to the heretical sects spreading in southern France and makes no mention of the similar circumstances in the Rhineland.

My point here is not to emphasize Elisabeth's ignorance of these events but rather to suggest that ecclesiastical "politics" is not her primary interest. Her criticism of the "head of the church" and her advocacy of Victor IV are not linked to any theoretical musings about the proper relationship between imperial and papal power in leading Christendom. In her sermon on *rectores*, she affirms that both secular and religious authority come from God, but she never delineates the proper spheres of those powers or their mutual relationship.[95] Her reference to God's favor of Victor IV is followed by her adaptation of a quotation from Ezekiel: "If he fears me and executes my judgment, I will give him a new heart and I will place my spirit within his heart" (cf. 36:26). This suggests the *ad hoc* aspect of Victor's prerogative. It has nothing to do with the nature of the office, with his claims to the papal mantle, or even with his "choice" by Frederick.[96] Unlike the original passage in Ezekiel, in which Israel is assured by God, "I will put my spirit in your midst; and I will make it so that you will walk in my precepts" (36:27), Elisabeth offers no divine guarantees of Victor's ability to walk in God's ways. His prerogative is provisional; the conditional clause ("if he fears me") affirms that his right to the office is based on his piety, on his faithful response to God's laws.

Elisabeth's willingness to attribute responsibility for current ecclesiastical abuses to the Roman papacy was probably influenced by contemporary German rejection of papal claims to ultimate spiritual jurisdiction.

Her desire for three German bishops to voice her opinions to Rome indicates her sense of the tension between the German and Roman churches. Yet her proclamations on the schism and the failure of ecclesiastical leadership are not just anti-papal propaganda as part of an imperial strategy for an independent German church. Rather, they are a small but integral part of her larger vision of the renewal of Christendom which requires the spiritual regeneration of its pastors.

THE WAYS TO SALVATION

In the face of so much depravity Elisabeth feels herself called to counsel perseverance in each of the paths up the rocky mountain. To those climbing the path of the active life, she offers a series of exhortations. Their lives are to include regular participation in the church's sacraments, deferential obedience to the ministers of God, honesty in interaction with others, compassion and charity for the widow and orphan, loans given without interest, and the instruction of the unlearned by the more prudent.[97] In the sermon for infants, parents are admonished not to neglect the moral formation of even the youngest children, not to laugh at their faults, nor lead them to pride by an indulgent upbringing ("per delicatam educationem").[98] This last warning originates in Elisabeth's sense of her own parents' failings. In the *Vita* of Ekbert written by his successor Emecho, Elisabeth is reported as having visions that revealed that she should encourage her brother to renounce the world, that is, to enter the monastic life. Elisabeth, however, hesitated to communicate this revelation to him "because she knew that he had been delicately brought up since his infancy," and therefore feared "that he would not be able to endure the rigor of our rule in fasts, vigils and abstinences."[99] Thus Elisabeth's own experience of family life provides her with insight that inspires her prophetic exhortation in God's name.

Although Elisabeth affirmed that each of the ten paths leads to heaven if properly followed, her monastic instincts make her very suspicious of the two ways most dissimilar to her own life—the order of married people and the way of hermits. The path trod by hermits is envisioned as an extraordinarily difficult one. It is free from the thorns that represent worldly cares and obstruct the path of married people, but it is dry and, like a plowed field, filled with large clods of earth. Elisabeth's own cenobitic context is in the foreground as she announces this sermon: she anticipates receiving this sermon on the feast of the translation of Saint Benedict; the angel appears to her when she is standing in prayer after the hour of chapter; the angel concludes the sermon "while we were sitting in chapter listening to a reading of the rule."[100] Thus it is not surprising that Elisabeth begins this sermon with a meditation on discretion as the mother of all virtues.[101] Hermits are warned not to follow every impulse of their own will, not to exceed the measure of their strength, and not to subvert human understanding and thereby turn themselves into dumb animals. Such abuses "suffocate the devotion of contemplation," and she urges them to attend to what she already proclaimed about contemplation.[102] In emphasizing contemplation as the genuine life of hermits, Elisabeth has likened their goal to that of cenobites but sees them as having, for somewhat dubious reasons, chosen a more difficult path to that goal. This sermon reveals that Elisabeth, like many of her fellow Benedictines, did not notice that contemporary hermits were not like the hermits of old who sought to live in total solitude. Rather, the hermits of her own day generally embraced various forms of communal life and sought to structure their lives according to a rule.[103] Elisabeth's criticism of the hermit's dangerous self-sufficiency seems to be based more on a traditional interpretation of the Rule of Saint Benedict than on accurate knowledge about the contemporary variations on the eremetical life.[104]

When she turns to the life of married people, Elisabeth has harsh words for women who are immodest in their demeanor and spend money needed by the poor for their extravagant clothes "which are useful for nothing except suffocating births."[105] This immoral softness of women is now affecting men who also seek the pomp of extravagant clothes and delicate hairstyles and, in so doing, have relinquished the manly seriousness of traditional morality. Elisabeth's characterization of this moral crisis in terms of gender associations recalls Hildegard of Bingen's condemnation of the present "effeminate age" (*muliebre tempus*), although Elisabeth does not quite hypostasize the current moral scene into an historical epoch.[106]

Elisabeth devotes much attention to sex in this sermon. She reminds her hearers that fear of God is the ornament of the conjugal bed. This means that feast days should be honored with sexual continence and that propagation of offspring is to be the principal cause of intercourse (any other coupling is due to weakness but can be forgiven by the offering of alms). Partners are to exhort each other to continence and to pray for the strength of self-control, resorting only to the "remedy" of the marriage debt when weakness prevails. Her concern for sexual control also permeates the sermons on the ways of adolescents and of children. In the former she seems to be thinking of adolescents who have already come to live at the monastery and may eventually adopt the celibate life of the cenobite. In the latter case, she warns parents to train even young children to refrain from polluting themselves. Behind each of these exhortations lies her simple, universal assessment of human nature: "All flesh inclines to evil."[107]

Yet this picture is not as simple as it may seem. Although Elisabeth can wave the standard of continence in front of everyone from infants to legitimately married couples, she recognizes that an extreme ascetic life can have its own dangers. It is her familiarity with Cathar piety that led her to curb her zeal for universal virginity. The pious rectitude of the Cathars, which seems so praiseworthy, is rejected in favor of a more tolerant (and more orthodox) acceptance of marriage between people who have not preserved their virginity. This passage is particularly significant, for it comes after a section in which Elisabeth strongly condemns sexual intercourse before marriage.

Unlike the sermons about the ways of *rectores*, hermits, and married people, the discourses on the paths of contemplatives, virgins, and even martyrs are much more directly related to the life with which Elisabeth identifies. She urges contemplatives to be like angels who never cease to gaze at God.[108] In the sermon on the life of celibates, Elisabeth anxiously asks whether the integrity of virginity can be lost by the lust that one experiences in temptation if one refrains in deed from the lustful act. Here the question is not only of theoretical significance (as was an earlier question about the distinction between adultery and fornication), but pertains directly to the life Elisabeth lives. Her impassioned cry for an answer also indicates the personal urgency of this subject. Elisabeth articulates the answer to her own question in what is one of the more surrealistic episodes of visionary imagination. She describes a scene in which she was commanded by the angel to thrust her hand into a pile of filth.[109] The angel then compares the external impurity of her hand to the superficial pollution caused by lust that is not brought to fulfillment in carnal action.

This attempt to articulate the relationship between thought and action and to determine the culpability of thought that is not executed in deed is a striking dynamic of the *Liber Viarum Dei*. It can also be seen in the sermon on children, where Elisabeth ponders the guilt of children who naively pollute themselves.[110] Unlike other parts of the *Liber Viarum Dei* where she confidently encourages or condemns particular acts, in these two cases Elisabeth portrays herself as uncertain about the moral implications of these situations. In each case, her conclusion reflects her awareness of the ambiguity of intention: pollution occurs and thus guilt and the need to atone for it ensue. But still these situations are contrasted to deliberate acts of carnality.

Elisabeth, of course, was not alone in her attention to questions about the ethics of intention and deed. As John Benton has shown, the sophisticated ruminations of Peter Abelard and Gratian on intention should be seen in the context of a culture shaped by penitential literature that often raised the issue of thought and intention.[111] Like her more learned predecessors, Elisabeth too absorbed the impetus toward introspection encouraged by the great expansion of penitential literature in the twelfth century. Elisabeth's introspection—her urgent examination of her own interior spiritual ebb and flow, which was so evident in the early visionary diaries—leads her to this reflection on the moral value of intention. As she tries to articulate a universal moral vision in the *Liber Viarum Dei*, it is this most delicate problem that particularly troubles her.

It is also striking that Elisabeth usually ponders the question of intention in the context of sex. Both the urgency of her query about the culpability of impure thoughts and the scatological tableau by which she constructs an answer are unusual within the visionary texts. I already noted that sexual activity claims much of her attention in the sermon on married life, as well as the fact that she uses gender as a metaphor for describing the morality of men and women of the world. But when she considers the possibility of sexual sin within her own life, a life founded on the explicit and public rejection of sexual activity, she pushes herself to a more subtle level of moral analysis. That her analysis reveals her close association between sexual sin and excrement should not be surprising; it illustrates the degree to which she understood sexual sin as pollution, as the defilement or violation of her most basic identity as virgin.

Elisabeth's concern for virginity should not be viewed in an anachronistic fashion that would flatten the ideal of virginity into mere physical intactness or the denial of pleasure. Like most contemporary authors writing for the guidance of religious women, Elisabeth emphasizes that rejection of sexual activity is genuine virginity only when it is inspired by and "ornamented" with other virtues.[112] Although John Bugge's assumption that virginity embraces all aspects of monastic spirituality does not exhaust the complexity of medieval women's religious lives,[113] nonetheless, for Elisabeth (as well as for many of her contemporaries) virginity is a very profound symbol that integrated many features of her spirituality.

One of the most important aspects of this spirituality of virginity is its association with contemplation. In the sermon on virginity, Elisabeth describes the virgin whose "innocence of flesh" is inseparable from her love of her heavenly spouse. The means to this exercise of love-inspired virginal existence is, in addition to chastening one's body, meditation on Christ, the virgin's spouse. Thus meditation, a mental activity, as well as discipline of the body constitute the techniques of virginity. Elisabeth, reflecting on 1 Corinthians 7:34, emphasizes the priority of mental discipline in viriginity: "It is the mark of virgins to withdraw their mind from the cares and anxieties of the present life and to ponder only those things that are of the Lord, so that they may be holy in body and spirit."[114] Direction of the mind ensures sanctity of body as well as spirit.

Most of Elisabeth's reflection on virginity in her letters is elaborated in terms of the virgin's relation with her celestial spouse. It is not surprising that, although virginity was obviously a central part of the life of all monastics, Elisabeth's references to virginity are limited to her letters to women; and the *Liber Viarum Dei* sermon on virginity is the only part of that text that includes direct address to an explicitly female audience. It is when Elisabeth discusses the spiritual life of women that she can most fully reflect upon her own her identity as bride of Christ.

The successful monastic life, however, not only is predicated on the lofty ideals of contemplation and virginity but also requires the coordination of the lives and personalities of the specific individuals involved. Elisabeth's recognition of this fact is shown in her recurrent interest in the pastoral leadership of abbesses and abbots. Many of her letters urge these monastic leaders to wield their pastoral staves gently but firmly. The goal that she seeks is always the continuation of the simple, communal life of devotion and penance. For example, when a monk from the abbey of Odenheim asks Elisabeth to seek God's will about his proposed pilgrimage to Jerusalem, Elisabeth's reply is unequivocal. In the voice of God she contrasts evildoers, who must go to Jerusalem to seek the patriarch and his penance, with monks who are sons of light, who need only to seek God in their hearts. She warns against this dangerous seduction and then proceeds to remind the abbot of his duties within the community.[115] In this way Elisabeth makes it clear that the daily life of the monastery, not the exotic distraction of the pilgrimage, should be the focus of his concern.[116]

But for all of Elisabeth's interest in the monastic life, the *Liber Viarum Dei* stands as a testimony to her vision of the diversity of ways to approach

God. It is unlike certain other medieval prophetic texts that have been characterized as merely offering consolation in time of despair.[117] In contrast, the *Liber Viarum Dei* represents a genuine call for reform and steadfastness articulated in terms of bitter invective against abuse and urgent instruction and command. What makes this program so compelling is that it is fueled by Elisabeth's sense of the glory that awaits at the summit of the mountain, the same glory she has glimpsed in her moments of ecstatic transport.

Conclusion. The Prophetic Voice of a Twelfth-Century Woman

AMONG THE MARTYRS whose lives Elisabeth portrayed in *Revelatio* was Saint Gerasma, the queen of Sicily and aunt of Saint Ursula herself. Elisabeth's characterization of Gerasma follows the pattern of other portraits in this text: a rather complex family history relates her to several other holy people martyred outside of Cologne; she is given a British birth; her decision to bring several children on the pilgrimage accounts for the presence of children's bodies among those exhumed from the cemetery outside of Cologne. In addition to these rather typical aspects of Gerasma's portrait, Elisabeth also adds a few brush strokes of a more personal character. When Ursula discussed her plans for her pilgrimage and martyrdom with her father, he wrote a letter to Gerasma, asking to hear her advice, "because he knew that she was a woman of great wisdom."[1] His judgment was correct: "She, inspired with divine strength, and understanding that the word had come from the Lord," gathered her children and set sail for Britain.[2] Upon arrival, she took charge of organizing the massive pilgrimage which was to end in death: "Moreover, in accordance with her counsels, that whole sacred company of virgins was gathered and put in order, and by the governance of her counsels she was the leader of them all in all the ways of their pilgrimage, and she suffered the final martyrdom with them."[3] Gerasma emerges as a woman who was recognized for her wisdom. Elisabeth does not portray this wisdom as a product of native intelligence. Rather, Gerasma was divinely inspired; she "was from the faithful root of Aaron, and she abundantly possessed the spirit of the Lord."[4] Nor was this wisdom theoretical knowledge, but it was counsel—advice about managing a particular situation.

It goes without saying at this point that Elisabeth never talked of herself as a woman of great wisdom. Such a declaration would have been at odds with her posture of humility and unworthiness to be the vessel of divine revelation. Yet the picture she paints of Gerasma, the inspired woman abundantly possessing the spirit of God, called upon to use her wisdom to guide others in need, is not far from Elisabeth's perception of her own divinely ordained vocation. Elisabeth's sketch of Gerasma thus provides us with a clue for understanding the voice we hear when we read the records of her visionary experience, a voice sometimes prompted or muffled by Ekbert.

The scholarly assessment of Elisabeth has been haunted by the peculiarities of her relationship with Ekbert. One of the primary efforts of this study has been the disentangling of the various strands of Ekbert's influence on his sister and his involvement in the production of the literary records of her visions. But this influence was not one-way. The development in Elisabeth's self-consciousness about her prophetic role led her to feel compelled to have her visions proclaimed to the public, and it was only after this transformation in her own identity that Ekbert was moved to abandon his earlier plans for a career among the clergy at Bonn and to devote himself to a life of monastic retreat and service to his sister. Elisabeth's development in her understanding of her interior experience—influenced by others around her, including Ekbert—was paralleled by Ekbert's own developing spiritual identity, influenced by Elisabeth.

Ekbert's decision to join his sister did not render him a passive secretary. Rather, he took on the active role of managing her career. In this role, his influence took two different forms: he directed Elisabeth's attention to particular subjects of interest to himself, and he transformed Elisabeth's oral accounts of her visions into visionary texts. Elisabeth's response to his direction was varied—resistance and hesitation at points, dutiful obedience at others, and adoption of his concerns at still other times. My examination of the visionary texts has distinguished among these responses and, most importantly, has demonstrated that in many cases where Elisabeth accepted Ekbert's program (or shared an interest with him, not necessarily originating in his suggestion) her pronouncements reveal her own visionary reflection on the question, often resulting in an expression distinctly different from Ekbert's own. Thus we can see how Elisabeth absorbed certain spiritual concerns from people around her; but only in relatively rare circumstances, such as in some of the technical theological discussions recorded in *Liber Visionum Tertius*, did she become merely a mouthpiece for Ekbert's thoughts.

Ekbert's role in creating written records of Elisabeth's spoken pronouncements was extensive. Elisabeth appears not to have taken an active part in overseeing the production of the literary texts that record her experience, although she also appears never to have capitulated fully to the order that she tell Ekbert everything. With Ekbert's almost free rein over the selection, arrangement, editing, translating, and polishing of the visionary records, even the apparent freedom to add to Elisabeth's words, we recognize that the picture of Elisabeth that emerges is largely the picture Ekbert allowed to emerge. Although the picture remains partial—both Elisabeth and Ekbert withheld parts of it—the foregoing analysis demonstrates that the written record still reflects much evidence about Elisabeth herself. For example, after Elisabeth's death (obviously the point at which Elisabeth ceased to have any possible control over Ekbert's editorial role), Ekbert revised the original version of *Liber Visionum Primus*, the records of Elisabeth's earliest experience. While the revision shows Ekbert's willingness to make some changes in Elisabeth's words, the descriptions of her experience nonetheless remain largely intact. As for the descriptions of Elisabeth's later visions, much less revision would have been required. Ekbert's active involvement in her life during this later period insured his influence on the level of her experience itself, thus reducing the need for major changes on the editorial level. The evidence for this remains overt in the visionary records.

It was Ekbert's fundamental belief in the authenticity of Elisabeth's experience that led him to attempt to use Elisabeth as a channel for his divine information-seeking, and his belief in its authenticity allowed him to let the evidence for this process remain within the published texts. Ekbert did suppress what he thought would be suspicious or "unedifying" about his sister's claims. If he had thought that his own questions and directions, rather than the divine will, were the source of Elisabeth's pronouncements, he could easily have not included his questions in the texts lest they compromise the authority of the visions in the eyes of the world. The historian is grateful for Ekbert's belief. It allows for a more precise understanding of his influence and of Elisabeth's response to his intervention. And if Ekbert can be considered a forger for those parts of the visionary texts in which his own theological concerns are expressed as part of Elisabeth's visionary experience, it is again his belief in the authenticity of Elisabeth's experience that lies behind this action. Unlike more typical theological forgeries in which works are reattributed to give them antiquity and authority,[5] Ekbert has chosen to support his thoughts not with the names of unimpeachable *auctoritates*, but with the revelations of his "unlettered" sister.

As we have seen, it was often in situations of intervention, either by

Ekbert, by Abbot Hildelin of Schönau, or by Abbot Gerlach of Deutz, that Elisabeth most clearly articulated her view of her visionary gift. With this evidence we are able to piece together a picture of her understanding of herself as prophet and visionary. Hildelin's interest in Elisabeth's charismatic claims led to one of the most significant events of her life: the uncritical publication of one of her most inflammatory prophetic visions. This event seems to have had numerous ramifications: exposing Elisabeth to ecclesiastical scrutiny as well as to both public approbation and mockery, giving Ekbert greater cause to join his sister and offer his more experienced hand at managing her public career, and making Elisabeth wary of appearing in the public eye as a creator of novelties and announcer of womanish fictions. The records of events following Hildelin's intervention show his increased presence in Elisabeth's visionary life: he appears in many of the experiences recorded in *Liber Visionum Secundus*. Although his performance of his liturgical office is often highlighted in these visions, Elisabeth's developing sense of herself as divinely appointed preacher of repentance is hardly diminished by her awareness of the tension between his liturgical power and her own charismatic authority. Not surprisingly, it is this situation of potential conflict that gave rise to one of her most explicit assertions of her role within the divine scheme of human salvation. Similarly, the delicacy of the situation created by Abbot Gerlach of Deutz and his desire to have his relics authenticated led to Elisabeth's claim of yet another aspect to her role. Like the prophet Jeremiah, who was told that before his birth he was predestined for his prophetic role (Jer. 1:4–5), Elisabeth learns in her vision that long before her lifetime God predestined her to be the one to reveal the truth about the Cologne martyrdom.

This is not the only aspect of Elisabeth's self-understanding that shows her use of biblical prototypes of prophecy and visionary experience. Her reports of looking through an open door in the heavens, of falling on her face and being raised up by an angel who delivers a message to her, her protestations of inadequacy for the divine commission she has received, and her visions which parallel those of the prophet Ezekiel or the apocalyptic seer John all attest to her consciousness of being within a tradition of divinely appointed revealers of truth. Her surprising retention of the form of address found in the Book of Ezekiel, "filius hominis," illustrates the extent to which she identified with the biblical models, even when, ostensibly, they ceased to be applicable. Yet this identification also appears to reveal something of Elisabeth's self-image—her awareness that her preaching of the word of God is an activity traditionally reserved for men. Unlike Ekbert, Elisabeth did not make the logical move of identifying herself with the prophetic women of the Old Testament. Ekbert, the careful apologist, tried to explain Elisabeth's unconventional activity by a comparison with something from the tradition, that is, the divine empowerment of holy women. If Elisabeth knew the stories of Deborah, Jael, Hulda, and Judith, they apparently did not move her or seem applicable to her own life. In fact, she seems not to have felt the need to rationalize her activity by pointing to models from her own sex, but instead, she legitimated her activity by describing her interior experience. The invasion of her body and mind by an exterior power, an experience so incontrovertible to her, was the proof of the authenticity of her message.

Ekbert's explanation of Elisabeth's proclamation of divine revelation also hints at his sensitivity to Elisabeth's critique, sometimes implicit, sometimes explicit, of the church's failure. According to Ekbert, the great women of Israel were filled with the spirit of God when the men were too negligent to rule the people. Unlike Hildegard of Bingen, Elisabeth herself did not declare a causal relationship between her divine commission to preach repentance and her recognition that the present leaders of the church were neglecting their duties.[6] But Ekbert, as one who was potentially indicted in that critique and who introduced Elisabeth's visions to the world she was condemning, felt the need to cite a precedent for this unusual turn of events.

We have also seen how Elisabeth stands in relation to the visionary and devotional traditions of her day. Several aspects of her descriptions of her experience distinguish her accounts from those of the hagiographical and allegorical genres that formed the tradition of Christian visionary literature. Her visionary records, especially the earliest, retain a frankly autobiographical character. Even when Elisabeth begins to understand her experience as having meaning for the church at large, she does not cease to describe her personal life as the context for the visions. As she becomes increasingly aware of a larger audience for her revelations, she more extensively reflects on her role as messenger of divine revelation.

This autobiographical aspect of her reports is to some degree due to the type of experience she describes. Her experience is not a sudden, unexpected, single event that radically changes her life. On the contrary, her visions are part of her ongoing spiritual life shaped by her intensive private prayer and participation in the regular worship of her community. Nor, except to some extent in the *Liber Viarum Dei* and *Liber Visionum Tertius*, are her visionary texts unified, allegorical expositions. For these reasons,

Elisabeth's revelations have much more in common with the later visionary literature of women in the thirteenth and fourteenth centuries than the
tradition of hagiographical and allegorical visionary literature, largely produced by men, that preceded her. Thus Elisabeth marks the transition
from these earlier accounts to the more confessional, contemplative literature of the later Middle Ages. In Hildegard of Bingen, Elisabeth had a
model of a woman divinely inspired to announce celestial secrets in the
form of visionary revelations, but Hildegard's allegorical exposition of her
visions into a systematic treatment of the Christian faith was not followed
by Elisabeth. Instead, Elisabeth presented her revelations by describing
what happened to her body and her soul, and how this experience affected
her life. Thus the boldness and originality of Elisabeth's visionary accounts
must be recognized.

But the fact that Elisabeth is more a harbinger of the new develop-
ments in visionary literature than a representative of the traditional genres
does not mean that her piety is more easily assimilable to what followed
her than what preceded her. In fact, her piety was very complex and does
not neatly fit into a periodized scheme. Her veneration of saints as powerful intercessors is quite traditional, and her special devotion to the Virgin Mary likewise reflects the ever-growing veneration of Mary in her day.
Missing from her devotion to the Virgin, however, is much of the tender-
ness, even sentimentality, that comes to mark Marian piety in the twelfth
century and beyond. Apart from an occasional, cursorily described vision
of Mary with her baby, Mary remains a figure of regal, even priestly, power
who deigns to visit and bless Elisabeth.

A constellation of Christocentric themes underlies much of Elisabeth's piety, themes that also come to the fore in the piety of some women
in the thirteenth century. Elisabeth's physical identification with the corporeal suffering of Jesus, her devotion to the Eucharist and the Eucharistic
context of many of her ecstatic experiences, her visualizing the humanity
of Christ in a female form, attest to the centrality of the Incarnation
for her.

Yet the face of this incarnated God is almost fierce, and certainly
threatening. Neither the impassive majesty of images of Christ in the early
Middle Ages nor the beckoning humanity of Christ in the piety of her
own day and later exactly corresponds to Elisabeth's picture of her bloodied savior who demands a sacrifice from those for whom he suffered. Elisabeth's imitation of Christ's suffering, facilitated by her association of
Christ's humanity with femaleness and by her sense of being afflicted by

the hand of God, is motivated by this picture of Christ. The otherness and even intimidation of this Christ, not likely to nurture a desire for union, is perfectly consistent with her understanding of perfect bliss: to stand among the heavenly crowds and gaze at the fearful majesty on the throne.

The route to that state of celestial beatitude was also of great concern to Elisabeth. Her anxiety about her own afterlife, manifested in her visions about her judgment, was hardly eased by the thought of a place of purgation. On the contrary, the idea of purgatory seems to have reduced Elisabeth's sense of her efficacy in liberating the souls of the deceased or in assuring her own eternal blessedness. Elisabeth's concern with the route to heavenly reward also took concrete expression in her description of the ten ways to that destination. Her attempt to articulate the diversity of Christian lives is based on her conviction that the heavenly crowd gathered round the throne of great majesty is comprised of people from each of these ten paths. Her elaboration of this vision of the diverse constituency of the church gave her the opportunity both for exhortation to the faithful and for condemnation of those who abused the power or neglected the responsibilities of their *ordo*.

The vivid records detailing Elisabeth's ecstatic experience as well as her manipulation by those who sought access to divine information through her are the product of her attempt to articulate her vision of her faith and her dismay at the evil of the world. And this attempt to articulate her vision based on her interior experience generated a new type of spiritual literature. The fact that a twelfth-century woman's voice has so rarely survived, a voice expressing her religious impulses, hopes and anxieties, only enhances the value of her words.

Appendix. The Transmission of Elisabeth's Works

Two major problems arise from an examination of manuscripts transmitting Elisabeth's works. The first is the development of the visionary corpus and its arrangement in various collections. The second is the relationship between the dispersion of Elisabeth's works and the dispersion of relics from the excavation of the reputed site of the Ursuline martyrdom.

The Redactions of the Visionary Collections

Köster divided the forty-nine manuscripts known to him that transmit more than one visionary text into six redactions which he ordered chronologically, the major contents of which can be seen in the following list. (The records from the visionary diaries and many of the letters were only titled or numbered as such in the final redaction, but they are listed below in the earlier redactions by their later titles in parentheses for convenience of reference.)

REDACTION A   (BETWEEN 1159 AND 1164/65)[1]

Liber Viarum Dei and *Adjuratio conscriptoris*
De Resurrectione Marie and (Ep. 20)
Revelatio de sacro exercitu virginum Coloniensium, and (Ep. 5, 11, 6), and
    Ekbert's vision[2]

REDACTION B[3]   (BETWEEN 1159 AND 1164/65)

(*Liber Visionum Primus*, Ch. 1-mid 25, with short preface by Ekbert, and
    concluding with Elisabeth's prophecy)

Liber Viarum Dei and *Adjuratio conscriptoris*
De Resurrectione Marie and (Ep. 20)
Revelatio de sacro exercitu virginum Coloniensium, and (Ep. 5, 11, 6), and
    Ekbert's vision

REDACTION C   (BETWEEN 1164/65 AND 1184)[4]

(*Liber Visionum Primus*, Ch. 1–79, with an expanded preface by Ekbert)
De Obitu

REDACTION AD   (BETWEEN 1164/65 AND 1184)

Liber Viarum Dei and *Adjuratio conscriptoris*
De Resurrectione Marie and (Ep. 20)
Revelatio de sacro exercitu virginum Coloniensium, and (Ep. 5, 11, 6)
[Vision of Hildegard of Bingen about the Cathars][5]
(*Liber Visionum Tertius*, Ch. 20–28: Letter of Elisabeth to Hildegard
    about the Cathars)
(*Liber Visionum Tertius*, Ch. 1–4, in various orders, and Ep. 22)

REDACTION D   (BETWEEN 1164/65 AND 1184)

Liber Visionum Primus, Ch. 1–79, with expanded preface
(*Liber Visionum Secundus*, Ch. 1–18, in various orders)
Liber Viarum Dei and *Adjuratio conscriptoris* and (Ep. 20)
De Resurrectione Marie
Revelatio de sacro exercitu virginum Coloniensium, and (Ep. 5, 11, 6), and
    sometimes (Ep. 1, 4, 3, 2, 9,10)
[Vision of Hildegard of Bingen about the Cathars]
(*Liber Visionum Tertius*, Ch. 20–28)
(*Liber Visionum Tertius*, Ch. 4, 1, 2, 3, and Ep. 22)
De Obitu (sometimes)

REDACTION E   (BETWEEN 1166 AND 1184)[6]

Ekbert's prologue to the collection
Liber Visionum Primus, Ch. 1–79, with expanded preface

Liber Visionum Secundus, Ch. 1–32, including *De Resurrectione Marie*
Liber Visionum Tertius, Ch. 1–31
Liber Viarum Dei
Revelatio de sacro exercitu virginum Coloniensium and Ekbert's letter to Ul-
    rich of Steinfeld.
Epistolae
De Obitu

Köster indicated the relationship between these versions in the following
stemma:[7]

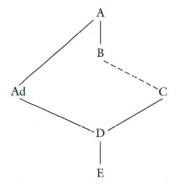

Köster's interpretation of how the collection developed involves at
least one assumption that is open to question—his theory of the relationship between A and B. There is no conclusive reason for assuming that
Redaction B must follow A just because it includes the contents of A plus
additional material. The texts included in both redactions are virtually
identical. The material unique to B is the original version of *Liber Visionum Primus*. This is a collection of earlier records, and thus they do not
push the *terminus ad quem* for the collection any later than the date for
Redaction A. Furthermore, Redaction B opens with a brief biographical
introduction of Elisabeth, and the entire book is autobiographical. *Liber
Viarum Dei*, the first text in Redaction A, presumes a familiarity with Elisabeth and the type of experience she describes in the text. It seems likely
that when putting together the first collection of visionary books, Ekbert
would have included the first visionary diary which would have been at
hand as a completed text and which sets the stage for all the later
revelations.

Whether or not Redaction A is the earliest compilation, there is yet another qualification to be made about it. Among the manuscripts Köster lists in Redaction A, three do not transmit *Liber Viarum Dei*.[8] There is evidence that these manuscripts represent a separate redaction which never included *Liber Viarum Dei*, not merely, as Köster implies, examples of Redaction A in which *Liber Viarum Dei* was not copied. An examination of one of these manuscripts, St. Omer, Bibliothèque Municipale, MS 710, leads to this new conclusion. Within the body of the text *De Resurrectione*, three references are usually made to the composition of *Liber Viarum Dei*. However, the St. Omer manuscript omits two of these references. Also, neither the St. Omer manuscript nor the other two manuscripts in question transmits Elisabeth's letter (Ep. 20) in which she exhorts the bishops of Trier, Mainz, and Cologne to preach the message revealed to her and recorded in *Liber Viarum Dei*, a letter included in the other manuscripts of Redaction A. The relatively constricted geographic area of the origins of these three manuscripts (Benedictine monasteries in St. Bertin, Liège, Arras) also supports the possibility of these manuscripts representing a separate transmission. Let us call this separate version of the collection F and note that it shares the same *terminus ad quem* as both A and B.[9]

There is one other place in the redactionary scheme where perhaps room must be made for another version of the collection. As was noted in Chapter 3, there are two versions of Ekbert's text, *De Obitu*. In addition to the text printed by Roth in *Visionen*, there is an alternative, short form of *De Obitu* in the thirteenth-century Vienna, Österr. Nationalbibliothek Vindob. Pal. MS 488. One of the major differences between the two forms is that the short version in Vienna MS 488 lacks a substantial section. This section, found only in the long version, includes reference to the selection of Elisabeth's successor as *magistra* of the nuns at Schönau and to a grave concern for the eclipse of Elisabeth's reputation. Both of these things seem to indicate a lapse of time between Elisabeth's death and the composition of the text. In addition to the substantial block of material found only in the long version, throughout much of the text every third or fourth sentence is found only in the long version. Among these sentences found only in the long form is Elisabeth's elaboration of the divine favor bestowed upon Schönau.[10] Also, one of these single sentences depicts Elisabeth exhorting Ekbert to observe his commitment to stability and not leave Schönau even if called to a more prestigious place.[11] This sentence, too, indicates a lapse of time after Elisabeth's death. Sometime after Ekbert became abbot at Schönau in 1167, he was offered a position in the diocese of Utrecht.

The discovery of this short form of *De Obitu* suggests another version of Redaction E, one which transmits this ostensibly earlier edition of the text. Yet it is difficult to account for this variant transmission. The Vienna manuscript is the only short version of *De Obitu* known, and its provenance has never been established.[12] Some clues for tracing its origins do, however, exist. In a library catalogue of the Cistercian abbey at Eberbach, there is the description of the manuscript H11. No extant manuscript has ever been identified with Eberbach MS H11. Although the description of Eberbach H11 is not very detailed, it appears to conform closely to the contents of Vienna, Österr. Nationalbibliothek Vindob. Pal. MS 488.[13] There is no conclusive proof that the Vienna manuscript is the one described in the sixteenth-century Eberbach catalogue, but such an identification is not precluded by any known facts about the Vienna manuscript and is supported by circumstantial evidence.[14]

Vienna, Österr. Nationalbibliothek Vindob. Pal. MS 488 is the only one of the three manuscripts of Redaction E that circulated outside the walls of Schönau. This fact may account for the absence of certain material that reflected Schönau's private concerns (e.g., the election of Elisabeth's successor as *magistra* and the honor of the Schönau monastery). Thus it appears that Ekbert created the final redaction of the visionary collection with two versions of *De Obitu*, one for the members of the Schönau community and one for those outside who did not share the same concerns or sympathies. Two observations must qualify this picture. First, the long version of *De Obitu* had already circulated outside of Schönau in Redactions C and D, thus lessening any effect of preparing a special public version of the text. Second, while it is plausible that Ekbert may have suppressed the one long section in the text that includes the election account, it is more difficult to see him systematically suppressing every third or fourth sentence throughout the text. With these two observations in mind, it seems likely that in preparing a public version of the complete visionary corpus, Ekbert used an edition of *De Obitu* he had written earlier but never included in a collection. This explanation allows the earlier date to be maintained for the shorter version, while recognizing that the longer version was initially published but later reserved only for the Schönau community.

The foregoing discussion operates within the basic framework proposed by Köster while suggesting modifications for its beginning (Redactions A, B, and F) and its end (Redaction E). A revised scheme to accommodate these modifications is the following:

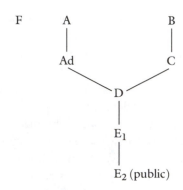

Here the transmission A to Ad is separated from that of B to C. B and C evince an interest in the biographical materials that give the most attention to Elisabeth herself, while A and Ad transmit the texts of greater theological interest, that is, *Liber Viarum Dei*, the revelations about Ursula, the visions about the Assumption, and the writings of Hildegard and Elisabeth about the Cathars. This scheme, however, as well as the one designed by Köster, both recognize that the many variations, especially in the contents of Redactions Ad and D, defy simple categorization into cleanly distinguished branches.[15]

The Dispersion of Elisabeth's Works

The dispersion of Elisabeth's works has been seen as part of the general dispersion of texts recording the legend of Saint Ursula, which in turn has been seen as the result of the dispersion of relics from the Cologne excavation. Below is a list of the manuscripts that come from places that had Ursuline relics. The MS number refers to the enumeration given in Köster's catalogue (1951, pp. 251–311; 1952, pp. 114–16), and the provenance and date of the MSS are taken from the same source. MSS not listed in that catalogue are preceded by a dash. The dates of relic acquisition are from

Tervarent, I, pp. 39–43. An asterisk marks the MSS that include Elisabeth's revelations about Ursula (*Revelatio*) and which chronologically follow the acquisition of relics; an asterisk preceded by a question mark indicates inconclusive but no counterindicating evidence.

MANUSCRIPT	RELIC ACQUISITION
Benedictine Abbey of St. Martin, Tournai	1170, 1267
*3. Brussels, Bibliothèque Royale MS 18421–29; c. 1200	
40. + Metz, Bibliothèque de la ville MS 1183; 2nd half of 12th c.; no *Revelatio*	
?*123. + Middlehill, Phillipps 2014; date unknown	
Benedictine Abbey, Anchin	c. 1260
5. Douai, Bibliothèque Municipale MS 865; end of 12th c.	
Benedictine Abbey, St. Bertin	1178–86
*6b. St. Omer, Bibliothèque Municipale MS 710; after 1316	
Cistercian Abbey, Vauclair	1270–72
12. Laon, Bibliothèque Municipale MS 178; end of 12th c.	
Carmelite Convent, Paris	1262
14. Paris, Bibliothèque Nationale lat. MS 2873; end of 12th c.	
Cistercian Abbey, Himmerod	?1134–1381
24. Paris, Bibliothèque Nationale Nouv. acq. lat. MS 760; 12/13th c.; no *Revelatio*	
*112. Berlin, Öffentl. Wissensch. Bibl. Lat. fol. MS 744; 13th c.; *Revelatio* fragment	
Premonstratensians at Windberg	1142
*26. Munich, Bayer. Staatsbibl. MS CLM 22253; end of 12th c.	
Benedictine Abbey, Laach	1156
31. Trier, Bistumsarchiv MS 10; 12th c.; no *Revelatio*	

Benedictine Abbey of St. Eucharius-Matthias, Trier   1148, 1278, 1279

45. Trier, Stadtbibliothek MS 718; 15th c.; no
   Revelatio

—. +Trier, St. Eucharius MS 148; date and contents
   unknown

?*—. +Trier, St. Eucharius MS 524; date unknown;
   does contain *Revelatio*

Cistercian Abbey, Lilienfeld   1262

74. Lilienfeld, Stiftsbibliothek MS 60; 13th c.; no
   Revelatio

Benedictine Abbey, Mariazell

79. Lilienfeld, Stiftsbibliothek MS 91; 14th c.; no   1325
   Revelatio

Benedictine Abbey, St. Trond

*86. Liège, Bibliothèque de l'Université MS 210 II;   1270–72
   1366

Cistercian Abbey, Clairvaux   1272

93. Montepellier, Ecole de Médicine MS I, 1; c. 1200

—. Troyes, Bibliothèque Municipale MS 946;
   1173–78; no *Revelatio*

Cistercian Convent, Brussels   c. 1260

*95. Brussels, Bibliothèque Royale 8609–8620; early
   14th c.

Köster declares that Tervarent's list could be considerably lengthened, and
he adds nine other sites where Ursuline relics were acquired.[16] Of these
nine sites, two correspond to places where there were MSS of Elisabeth's
visions, although Köster does not date the relic acquisition in comparison
with the date of the MS. The MSS which could possibly be added to the
list then are:

Cistercian Abbey, Eberbach

?*100. +Eberbach, Liberaria minora H7; date and contents not known

?*124. +Eberbach, Liberaria minora H11; date and contents not known;
   if it can be identified with Vienna, Österr. Nationalbibliothek Vindob. Pal. MS 488, then it does contain *Revelatio*

Cistercian Cloister, Aldersbach

?*116. Munich, Bayer. Staatsbibl. MS CLM 2610; 13th c.

These lists reveal that six of the 145 medieval manuscripts known to transmit the works of Elisabeth may have been produced or obtained by a religious house as a means of validating their previously acquired relics from the Cologne site of the Ursuline martyrdom. A further five manuscripts may also fit this scenario, although not enough information is known either about the relic acquisition of the monastery or the date and contents of the book to confirm it. Allowing for incorrectly dated manuscripts, manuscripts of unknown provenance, and additional sites of relic acquisition, the number of manuscripts copied as a result of the spread of the Ursuline relics is perhaps greater than the six certain and five possible cases indicated by my count. Yet this number would have to be considerably multiplied to come to a significant proportion of the total of 145 manuscripts. Thus the dispersion of the Ursuline relics does not appear to be an adequate explanation for the dispersion of Elisabeth's visionary works.

Abbreviations

De Obitu	Ekbert of Schönau, *De Obitu Elisabeth*
LVD	*Liber Viarum Dei*
LV1, 2, 3	*Libri Visionum Primus, Secundus, Tertius*
De Resurrectione	*Visio de resurrectione beate virginis Marie*
Revelatio	*Revelatio de sacro exercitu virginum Coloniensium*
AASS	Acta Sanctorum, 3d ed. Paris, 1863–.
BHL	*Bibliotheca Hagiographica Latina Antiquae et Mediae Aetatis.* 2 vols. Brussels, 1898–1911.
CCCM	Corpus Christianorum, Continuatio Mediaevalis
Ep.	Epistola
JL	Phillippus Jaffé. *Regesta Pontificum Romanorum.* 2d ed. Vol. 2. Ed. S. Loewenfeld. Graz: Akademische Druck- und Verlag, 1956.
Köster (1951)	Kurt Köster, "Elisabeth von Schönau: Werk und Wirkung im Spiegel der mittelalterlichen handschriftlichen Überlieferung." *Archiv für mittelrheinische Kirchengeschichte* 3 (1951): 243–315.
Köster (1952)	Kurt Köster, "Das Visionäre Werk Elisabeths von Schönau: Studien zu Entstehung, Überlieferung and Wirkung in der mittelalterlichen Welt." *Archiv für mittelrheinische Kirchengeschichte* 4 (1952): 79–119.

Köster (1965)   Kurt Köster, "Elisabeth von Schönau: Leben,
Persönlichkeit und visionäres Werk," in *Schönauer
Elisabeth Jubiläum 1965: Festschrift anläßlich des
achthundertjährigen Todestages der heiligen Elisabeth
von Schönau*. Limburg: Pallottiner Druckerei, 1965,
17–46.

MGH   Monumenta Germaniae Historica.

MGH, SS   Monumenta Germaniae Historica, Scriptores.

Pitra   *Analecta Sanctae Hildegardis*. Ed. J.-B. Pitra.
Analecta Sacra, vol. 8. Monte Cassino, 1882.
Reprint. Farnborough: Gregg Press Limited, 1966.

PL   Patrologia cursus completus: Series Latina. Ed.
J.-P. Migne. Paris, 1844–64.

Roth (1911)   F. W. E. Roth, "Aus einer Handshrift der
Schriften der heil. Elisabeth von Schönau,"
*Neues Archiv der Gesellschaft für ältere deutsche
Geschictskunde* 36 (1911): 219–25.

SC   Sources Chrétiennes.

Visionen   *Die Visionen der hl. Elisabeth und die Aebte Ekbert
und Emecho von Schönau*. Ed. F. W. E. Roth.
Brünn: Verlag der Studien aus dem Benedictiner-
und Cistercienser-Orden, 1884.

Biblical citations are from the Vulgate.

Notes

Chapter 1

1. For the prevalence of visions as a part of women's spiritual life, see Simone Roisin, "L'efflorescence cistercienne et le courant féminin de piété au XIIIe siècle," *Revue d'Histoire Ecclésiastique* 39 (1943): 373–76; Michael Goodich, "The Contours of Female Piety in Later Medieval Hagiography," *Church History* 50 (1981): 30–31; Caroline Walker Bynum, *Holy Feast and Holy Fast: The Religious Significance of Food to Medieval Women* (Berkeley: University of California Press, 1987), 26 et passim; André Vauchez, *La sainteté en Occident aux derniers siècles du Moyen Age*, Bibliothèque des Ecoles Française d'Athènes et de Rome, vol. 241 (Rome: Ecole Française de Rome, 1981), 445–56; Elizabeth Alvilda Petroff, "Introduction," in *Medieval Women's Visionary Literature* (New York: Oxford University Press, 1986), 3–59.

2. *Die Visionen der hl. Elisabeth und die Schriften der Aebte Ekbert und Emecho von Schönau*, ed. F. W. E. Roth (Brünn: Verlag der Studien aus dem Benedictiner- und Cistercienser-Orden, 1884), 1 (hereafter cited as *Visionen*). The visions attributed to Elisabeth in P. Livarius Oliger, "Revelationes B. Elisabeth: Disquisitio critica una cum textibus latino et catalaunensi," *Antonianum* 1 (1926): 24–83, are not in fact part of Elisabeth's works. See Kurt Köster, "Das visionäre Werk Elisabeths von Schönau: Studien zu Entstehung, Überlieferung und Wirkung in der mittelalterlichen Welt," *Archiv für mittelrheinische Kirchengeschichte* 4 (1952): 98–101 (hereafter cited as Köster 1952).

3. This count includes references to MSS no longer extant. The MSS are catalogued in Köster, "Elisabeth von Schönau: Werk und Wirkung im Spiegel der mittelalterlichen handschriftlichen Überlieferung," *Archiv für mittelrheinische Kirchengeschichte* 3 (1951): 243–315; and Köster (1952), 114–19. To this list should be added Troyes, Bibliothèque Municipale MS 946; Cologne, Stadtarchiv MS GB 8° 60; Cologne, Stadtarchiv MS W133; +Trier, St. Eucharius-Matthias Abbey MS 148 (D56); and +Trier, St. Eucharius-Matthias Abbey MS 524 (I66). From this list should be deleted Trier, Stadtbibliothek MS 646/869 8°, in which letters of Hildegard of Bingen are attributed to Elisabeth.

4. See, e.g., Penelope D. Johnson, *Equal in Monastic Profession: Religious Women in Medieval France* (Chicago: University of Chicago Press, 1991); Jeffrey M. Hamburger, "The Visual and the Visionary: The Image in Late Medieval Monastic Devotions," *Viator* 20 (1989): 161–82; Sharon K. Elkins, *Holy Women of Twelfth-Century England* (Chapel Hill: The University of North Carolina Press, 1988); Ursula Peters, *Religiöse Erfahrung als literarisches Faktum: Zur Vorgeschichte und*

Genese frauenmystischer Texte des 13. und 14. Jahrhunderts, Hermaea, N.F., Bd. 56 (Tübingen: Max Niemeyer Verlag, 1988); Peter Dinzelbacher and Dieter R. Bauer, eds., *Religiöse Frauenbewegung und mystische Frömmigkeit im Mittelalter* (Cologne and Vienna: Böhlau Verlag, 1988); Dinzelbacher and Bauer, eds., *Frauenmystik im Mittelalter* (Ostfildern: Schwabenverlag, 1985); John A. Nichols and Lillian Thomas Shank, eds., *Medieval Religious Women*, 2 vols. (Kalamazoo, MI: Cistercian Publications, 1984–87).

5. See, e.g., Jo Ann McNamara and Suzanne F. Wemple, "Sanctity and Power: The Dual Pursuit of Medieval Women," in *Becoming Visible: Women in European History*, ed. R. Bridenthal and C. Koonz (Boston: Houghton Mifflin Company, 1977), 90–118; Eleanor Commo McLaughlin, "Equality of Souls, Inequality of Sexes: Women in Medieval Theology," in *Religion and Sexism: Images of Women in the Jewish and Christian Traditions*, ed. Rosemary Radford Ruether (New York: Simon and Schuster, 1974), 213–66; Jane Tibbetts Schulenburg, "Sexism and the Celestial Gynaeceum—from 500–1200," *Journal of Medieval History* 4 (1978): 117–33.

6. See especially Bynum, *Holy Feast and Holy Fast*, 277–96.

7. For a wide-ranging and comprehensive introduction to this debate, see Robert L. Benson and Giles Constable, eds., *Renaissance and Renewal in the Twelfth Century* (Cambridge, MA: Harvard University Press, 1982).

8. Elkins' valuable study, *Holy Women of Twelfth-Century England*, analyzes the unparalleled increase of English women in the monastic and anchoretic life during this period, and links this increase to other historical factors. However, because of the paucity of surviving spiritual texts written by women in England in this period, her work does not focus primarily on the spirituality of these women.

9. For an attempt to delineate such a category see Petroff, 6–20.

10. For example, the conflict between the individualistic "religion of the spirit" seen in women's mystical writings and the "religion of authority." See C. H. Lawrence, *Medieval Monasticism: Forms of Religious Life in Western Europe in the Middle Ages*, 2d ed. (London: Longman, 1989), 233–34.

11. While this may seem an obvious point, the lives and thought of some medieval women have been appropriated as representing some twentieth-century perspectives that are rather different than their own. See the astute rejection of Matthew Fox's interpretation of Hildegard of Bingen in Barbara Newman, *Sister of Wisdom: St. Hildegard's Theology of the Feminine* (Berkeley: University of California Press, 1987), 250.

12. See, e.g., the books listed in the bibliography in *Visionen*, LX–LXXXVI.

13. "His etiam diebus in sexu fragili signa potentiae sue Deus ostendit in duabus ancillis suis, Hildegarde videlicet in monte Roperti iuxta Pinguiam, et Elisabeth in Schonaugia, quas spiritu prophetie replevit, et multa eis genera visionum . . . revelavit" (*Annales Palidenses*, MGH, SS, vol. 16, 90). For Ruotger's dates, see Norbert Backmund, *Monasticon Praemonstratense* (Straubing: Cl. Attenkofersche Buchdruckerei, 1949), vol. I, 238.

14. See, e.g., Edith Ennen, *Frauen im Mittelalter* (Munich: Verlag C. H. Beck, 1984), 116–17. A more extended comparsion is Josef Loos, "Hildegard von Bingen und Elisabeth von Schönau," in *Hildegard von Bingen, 1179–1979: Festschrift*

zum 800. Todestag der Heiligen, ed. Anton Ph. Brück (Mainz: Selbstverlag der Gesellschaft für Mittelrheinische Kirchengeschichte, 1979), 263–72, which depends heavily on Köster (1965).

15. For the manuscripts of Hildegard's works, see Hildegard, *Scivias*, ed. Adelgundis Führkötter and Angela Carlevaris, CCCM 43 (Turnholt: Brepols, 1978): XXXII–LVI, and Marianna Schrader and Adelgundis Führkötter, *Die Echtheit des Schrifttums der heiligen Hildegard von Bingen: Quellenkritische Untersuchungen*, Beihefte zum Archiv für Kulturgeschichte, 6 (Köln-Graz: Böhlau Verlag, 1956), 42–85, 193–96. Cf. Schrader, "Hildegarde de Bingen," *Dictionnaire de spiritualité*, (Paris: Beauchesne, 1932–), vol. 7, 519–20, for an interpretation of the cause of Hildegard's relative lack of influence on her contemporaries.

16. Wilhelm Levison, "Das Werden der Ursula-Legende," *Bonner Jahrbücher* 132 (1927): 1–164.

17. Guy de Tervarent, *La Légende de Sainte Ursule dans la littérature et l'art du moyen âge*, 2 vols. (Paris: Les Editions G. Van Oest, 1931).

18. Gertrud Jaron Lewis, "Christus als Frau: Eine Vision Elisabeths von Schönau," *Jahrbuch für Internationale Germanistik* 15 (1983): 70–80; Rudolf Berliner, "God is Love," *Gazette des Beaux-Arts* 42 (1953): 9–26; Elisabeth Gössmann, "Das Menschenbild der Hildegard von Bingen und Elisabeth von Schönau von dem Hintergrund der frühscholastischen Anthropologie," in *Frauenmystik im Mittelalter*, ed. Dinzelbacher and Bauer, 41–42; Barbara Newman, *Sister of Wisdom*, 40.

19. *Visionen*, 60–62.

20. See note 2 above.

21. Köster (1951), 243–315, and Köster (1952), 79–119. Köster's work incorporates and corrects the collection of MSS in Ruth J. Dean, "Manuscripts of St. Elizabeth of Schönau in England," *Modern Language Review* 32 (1937): 62–71.

22. Citations in this study are from *Visionen*, corrected by manuscript readings as listed in the notes. Roth's edition is the only source consulted for other texts, such as Ekbert's letters and other Schönau documents. For MSS examined, see Bibliography.

23. See Hans Wolter, "The Post-Gregorian Epoch (1124–53)," in *From the High Middle Ages to the Eve of the Reformation*, trans. Anselm Biggs. Vol. 4 of *History of the Church*, ed. Hubert Jedin and John Dolan (New York: Crossroad, 1986), 23–24.

24. Haydon V. White, "The Gregorian Ideal and Saint Bernard of Clairvaux," *Journal of the History of Ideas* 21 (1960): 321–48.

25. For a survey of various interpretations of this text, see Elizabeth Kennan, "The 'De Consideratione' of St. Bernard of Clairvaux and the Papacy in the Mid-Twelfth Century: A Review of Scholarship," *Traditio* 23 (1967): 73–115, and most recently, Walter H. Principe, "Monastic, Episcopal and Apologetic Theology of the Papacy, 1150–1250," in *The Religious Roles of the Papacy: Ideals and Realities, 1150–1300*, ed. Christopher Ryan, Papers in Mediaeval Studies, 8 (Toronto: Pontifical Institute of Mediaeval Studies, 1989), 118–29, and the literature cited therein.

26. "Serpit hodie putida tabes per omne corpus Ecclesiae, et quo latius, eo desperatius, eoque periculosius quo interius. . . . Ministri Christi sunt, et serviunt

Antichristo. Honorati incedunt de bonis Domini, cui Domini honorem non deferunt. Inde is, quem quotidie vides, meretricius nitor, histrionicus habitus, regius apparatus. . . . Pro huiusmodi volunt esse et sunt ecclesiarum praepositi, decani, archidiaconi, episcopi, archiepiscopi." *Sermones super Cantica Canticorum*, 33. 15, in *Sancti Bernardi Opera*, ed. J. Leclercq, C. H. Talbot, and H. M. Rochais (Rome: Editiones Cistercienses, 1957), vol. 1, 244.

27. Stanley Chodorow, *Christian Political Theory and Church Politics in the Mid-Twelfth Century* (Berkeley: University of California Press, 1972), 27–39, proposes a theory of politics within the Curia that led to the disenfranchisement of the older Gregorian party with its focus on consolidating the church's institutional sovereignty. Cf. Mary Stroll, *The Jewish Pope: Ideology and Politics in the Papal Schism of 1130* (Leiden: E. J. Brill, 1987), for an alternative interpretation.

28. For a range of reform ideals and programs, see Lester K. Little, "Intellectual Training and Attitudes toward Reform," in *Pierre Abélard, Pierre le Vénérable: Les Courants philosophiques, littéraires, et artistique en Occident au milieu du XIIe siècle*, Colloques Internationaux du Centre National de la Recherche Scientifique, No. 546 (Paris: Editions du Centre Nationale de la Recherche Scientifique, 1975), 235–49. For the general vocabulary of reform, see Giles Constable, "Renewal and Reform in Religious Life: Concepts and Realities," in *Renaissance and Renewal in the Twelfth Century*, ed. Benson and Constable, 37–67.

29. Chodorow, 76–86.

30. For these controversies, see Giles Constable, "Introduction," in *Libellus de diversis ordinibus et professionibus qui sunt in aecclesia*, ed. and trans. Constable and B. Smith (Oxford: Carendon Press, 1972), xi–xxix; Ernest W. McDonnell, "The *Vita Apostolica*: Diversity or Dissent," *Church History* 24 (1955): 15–31.

31. See John Van Engen, "The 'Crisis of Cenobitism' Reconsidered: Benedictine Monasticism in the Years 1050–1150," *Speculum* 61 (1986): 269–304, on the question of Benedictine decline in the mid-twelfth century.

32. Few manuscripts earlier than 1150 survive from Schönau. See Sigrid Krämer, *Handschriftenerbe des deutschen Mittelalters*, Mittelalterliche Bibliothekskataloge Deutschlands und der Schweiz, Ergänzungsband 1 (Munich: C. H. Beck'sche Verlagsbuchhandlung, 1989), 714–15. For the library holdings of other monasteries connected to Hirsau, see Raymund Kottje, "Klosterbibliotheken und monastische Kultur in der zweiten Hälfte des 11. Jahrhunderts," *Zeitschrift für Kirchengeschichte* 80 (1969): 149–52.

33. Urban Küsters, *Der verschlossene Garten: Volkssprachliche Hohelied-Auslegung und monastische Lebensform im 12. Jahrhundert*, Studia humaniora: Düsseldorfer Studien zu Mittelalter und Renaissance, 2 (Düsseldorf: Droste Verlag, 1985), 82.

34. Küsters, 142–55. Küsters also traces other structures of monastic affiliation for women within the Hirsau movement. On the inadequacy of the phrase "double monastery" to describe communities that include both women and men, see Elkins, xvii–xviii.

35. Küsters, 73–75.

36. For another example of the connections between the Hirsau monasteries

and local episcopal offices, see Petrus Becker, "Die Hirsauische Erneuerung des St. Euchariusklosters in Trier," *Studia Anselmiana* 85 (1982): 185–206.

Chapter 2

1. The *Vita* and canonization proceedings listed in Dean, "Manuscripts of St. Elizabeth of Schönau in England," 68–69, are of Elizabeth of Thuringia, not Elisabeth of Schönau. See Köster (1951), 255, 291, 311; and Köster (1952), 98, 118. Köster (1965), 41, suggests that a canonization process was produced but is now lost. He cites no evidence for the composition.

2. For Elisabeth's visions of her great-uncle, see *Visionen*, 48, 66. For the dates of Ekbert's episcopacy at Münster, see *Annalista Saxo*, MGH, SS, vol. 6, 765, 767. Some details of Ekbert's career are examined in Gerlinde Niemeyer's introduction to her edition *Hermannus quondam Judaeus: Opusculum de conversione sua*, MGH, Geistesgeschichte, vol. 4, 3–7, 36–44, and in Hans-Josef Weiers, *Studien zur Geschichte des Bistums Münster im Mittelalter*, Kölner Schriften zu Geschichte und Kultur, Band 8 (Köln: DME-Verlag, 1984), 101–3, 105–7.

3. John H. Van Engen, *Rupert of Deutz* (Berkeley: University of California Press, 1983), 223, 243; Niemeyer, in *Hermannus quondam Judaeus*, 37–39.

4. Ekbert's orders from Lothar were changed before he reached Rome to meet with Anacletus. See Weiers, 105–6; Wilhelm Bernhardi, *Lothar von Supplinburg* (Berlin: Duncker und Humblot, 1975; rpt. of 1879 edition), 341–43.

5. Niemeyer, in *Hermannus quondam Judaeus*, 15–16.

6. "[S]epius, ut solebat, commissis sibi ovibus pabulum verbi Dei bonus ille pastor administraret." (*Hermannus quondam Judaeus: Opusculum de conversione sua*, 73).

7. *Visionen*, 48–49.

8. The fragmentary *Vita* is found in Visionen, 343–55 and was also edited by S. Widmann in *Neues Archiv der Gesellschaft für ältere deutsche Geschichtskunde* 11 (1886): 447–54.

9. For the sister, see *Visionen*, 273. For the other family members, Roth, *Visionen*, XCII.

10. *Visionen*, 270.

11. *Visionen*, 263.

12. The early fourteenth-century necrology of St. Marien at Andernach refers to *Guda magistra secunda*, but the death date of Tengswind, the first *magistra*, is uncertain. See Alfred Haverkamp, "Tenxwind von Andernach und Hildegard von Bingen: Zwei 'Weltanschauungen' in der Mitte des 12. Jahrhunderts" in *Institutionen, Kultur und Gesellschaft im Mittelalter: Festschrift für Josef Fleckenstein zu seinem 65 Geburtstag*, ed. Lutz Fenske, Werner Rösner, and Thomas Zotz (Sigmaringen: Jan Thornbecke Verlag, 1984), 517–19, especially n. 17. Elisabeth addressed one letter (Ep. 9), to the sisters at Andernach and another to *cognatae sue et venerabili magistre* G. (Ep. 15), again suggesting Guda as the *magistra* of the Andernach convent.

13. *Visionen*, 154–55.

14. Roth, *Visionen*, XCII; Köster (1965), 18.

15. Count Dudo of Laurenburg founded the cloister in 1114 as a priory. In 1125 or 1126, Count Rupert, Dudo's son, converted it into an independent monastery, and shortly thereafter the nun's cloister was added. For a sketch of the history of the Schönau community, see Hans Becker, "Das Kloster Schönau (Übersicht)" in *Schönauer Elisabeth Jubiläum 1965*, 80–81. More details about the foundation are given in Wilhelm Günther, *Codex Diplomaticus Rheno-Mosellanus* (Coblenz: B. Heriot, 1822), vol. I, 231, n. 2.

16. *Visionen*, 49–50. Elisabeth's vision of Rupert's torment is probably linked to his offense against the church. On May 13, 1154, Pope Anastasius IV instructed Archbishop Hillin of Trier to threaten Rupert and Count Arnold of Nassau with excommunication for seizing the property of the Worms church (JL 9899). See Stephen Hilpisch, "Erzbischof Hillin von Trier, 1152–69," *Archiv für mittelrheinische Kirchengeschichte* 7 (1955): 14. The monastery at Schönau was directly affected by these events. While describing her vision of Pentecost (May 23), 1154, Elisabeth reports that Mass had been suspended there because of the excommunication (*Visionen*, 35, cf. also 66–67).

17. *Visionen*, 277.

18. On the offering of children to monasteries, see Penelope Johnson, *Equal in Monastic Profession*, 13–27.

19. The remaining part of the introduction printed in *Visionen*, 1–2, is not found in this early version of the introduction.

20. *Visionen*, 264. For a sketch of life in a twelfth-century Benedictine women's community, see Sabina Flanagan, *Hildegard of Bingen, 1098–1179: A Visionary Life* (London: Routledge, 1989), 32–40.

21. "Pene omnis sensus meus subversus erat in me" (*Visionen*, 4).

22. Küsters, 239, 257–59.

23. *Visionen*, 3.

24. For a previously unedited letter of Hildegard to the Schönau *magistra*, see L. Van Acker, "Der Briefwechsel zwischen Elisabeth von Schönau und Hildegard von Bingen," *Instrumenta Patristica* 23 (1991): 415–17.

25. *Visionen*, 38.

26. Cf. Köster (1965), 31, who dates it to 1154, but all that can be determined with certainty is that it occurred in July of 1152, 1153 or 1154. The vision is printed in Roth, "Aus einer Handschrift der Schriften der heil. Elisabeth von Schönau," *Neues Archiv der Gesellschaft für ältere deutsche Geschichtskunde* 36 (1911): 220.

27. For earlier examples, see Bernard McGinn, *Visions of the End: Apocalyptic Traditions in the Middle Ages*, Records of Civilization, vol. 96 (New York: Columbia University Press, 1979), 88–90, and 306, nn. 9–11.

28. The idea of Satan transforming himself into an angel of light appears to become part of a standard interrogation about visionary claims. Similar questions were later posed to Joan of Arc. See Pierre Tisset, *Procès de condamnation de Jeanne d'Arc* (Paris: Libraire C. Klincksieck, 1960), vol. 1, 162, 320–21. It is possible that Augustine's use of this Pauline passage in his explanation of demonic visions is the

source of this connection. See *De Genesi ad litteram*, XII, 13. 28 (PL 34, col. 464–65).

29. Ep. ad Hildegardem, in *Visionen*, 73. It seems quite possible that this unidentified, overzealous believer came from within the walls of the Schönau community. In her introductory remarks in *LVi* (composed no earlier than 1155), Elisabeth reminds Ekbert of the danger if her revelations are improperly publicized such as "per quosdam incautos fratres," as already happened once against her will (*Visionen*, 2).

30. "[S]i non et hi, qui in habitu religionis ambulant, spiritum meum acerbius contristarent" (*Visionen*, 71).

31. *Visionen*, 73–74.

32. According to Köster (1965), 19, Ekbert studied under Adam of Balsham, one of the first medieval commentators on Aristotle. This, however, is unlikely now that Adam of Balsham is thought to have died in 1181 (Wanda Cizewski, "Adam of the Little Bridge," *Dictionary of the Middle Ages*, ed. Joseph R. Strayer [New York: Charles Scribner's Sons, 1982], vol. 1, 51–52). The late date of his death precludes his identification with *magister Adam*, who died c. 1155, according to Elisabeth's report of a vision of Ekbert's former teacher (*Visionen*, 50).

33. Julia Barrow, "Education and the Recruitment of Cathedral Canons in England and Germany 1100–1225," *Viator* 20 (1989): 126–27.

34. Cf. Barrow, 127.

35. Peter Munz, *Frederick Barbarossa: A Study in Medieval Politics* (Ithaca, NY: Cornell University Press, 1969), 93.

36. PL 195, col. 12–93.

37. *Visionen*, 310–17. Another fragmentary letter of Ekbert (*Visionen*, 319–20) may also have been addressed to Rainald, or perhaps to Philipp of Heinsberg, Rainald's successor. See Richard Knipping *Die Regesten des Erzbischöfe von Köln im Mittelalter* (Bonn: P. Hanstein Verlag, 1901), vol. 2, 234. The corpus of Ekbert's works has yet to be defined and several works remain unpublished. See Köster, "Ekbert von Schönau," in *Die deutscher Literatur des Mittelalters: Verfasserlexikon* (Berlin: Walter de Gruyter, 1980), vol. 2, col. 437–39.

38. Köster (1965), 19.

39. "Satis mihi gloria mundi arridebat, satis plena manu rerum temporalium copias supernus provisor michi fundebat, dum adhuc essem canonicus in ecclesia Bunnensi" (Letter to Abbot Reinhard of Reinhausen, in *Visionen*, 318).

40. Köster (1965), 19.

41. Emecho, *Vita Eckeberti*, 450, 452. In the longer version of *De Obitu*, Ekbert adds a passage in which the dying Elisabeth persuades him never to leave Schönau even if he was called to a "more honorable and wealthier place" (*Visionen*, 272).

42. *Vita Eckeberti*, 449–50.

43. *Visionen*, 3.

44. See Köster (1952), 83

45. *Visionen*, 32–33; 38.

46. These numbers exclude chapters comprised of material written by Ekbert

and other material, such as letters, that were not originally dictated and transmitted as part of the visionary diary.

47. See, e.g., Köster (1965), 25; Wilhelm Wattenbach and Franz-Josef Schmale, *Deutschlands Geschichtsquellen im Mittelalter: Vom Tode Kaiser Heinrichs V. bis zum Ende des Interregnum* (Darmstadt: Wissenschaftliche Buchgesellschaft, 1976), vol. 1, 357; Jakob Marx, *Geschichte des Erzstifts Trier als Kurfürstenten und Erzdiözese von den ältesten Zeiten bis zum Jahre 1816* (1860, Rpt. Aalen: Scientia verlag, 1970), vol. 2, 454; Gabriel Bucelinus, *Nenologium Benedictinum sanctorum beatorum ataque illustrium eiusdem ordinis virorum* (Augustae Vindelicorum, 1656), quoted in *Visionen*, 187.

48. *Visionen*, 310–17.

49. "Per te celum mundo erat apertum et effluebant abscondita a seculis archana dei per organum vocis tue ad nos, et erat preciosius auro, dulcius melle eloquium tuum . . . . Gloriam civium celi notam nobis faciebas, et quasi ante oculos mentis nostre ponebas, et inflammabant non mediocriter beate narrationes tue corda nostra in desideriis patrie, quam expectamus" (*De Obitu*, in *Visionen*, 264). The first sentence is not found in the version transmitted in Vienna, Österr. Nationalbibliothek Vindob. Pal. MS 488, fol. 166v. For similar sentiments expressed by the monks of Villers about Hildegard of Bingen, see Ep. 21 in *Analecta Sanctae Hildegardis*, ed. J.-B. Pitra, Analecta Sacra, vol. 8 (Monte Cassino, 1882; rpt. Farnborough: Gregg Press Limited, 1966), 395. For the attribution of this letter, see Newman, *Sister of Wisdom*, 2, n. 6.

50. Roth (1911), 222–23.

51. "Et dixi: Non ego nunc presumo ad similitudinem prophete: orate, ut fiat spiritus tuus duplex in me, sed si simpliciter mihi dare spiritum tuum dominus vellet, sufficeret mihi. Et ait: Karissime! voluntas domini fiat in te" (*Visionen*, 271). This passage is only found in the long version of *De Obitu*.

52. See Bynum, *Holy Feast and Holy Fast*, 229–30.

53. On the relationship between women's visions and illness, see Petroff, 37–44.

54. On the expansion of Cologne's fortifications which led to the discovery, see Paul Strait, *Cologne in the Twelfth Century* (Gainesville: University Presses of Florida, 1974), 30–31, and the maps on 48–49.

55. *Visionen*, 123–24.

56. Tervarent, 39–43.

57. *Visionen*, 124.

58. *Visionen*, 124–25. Levison doubts that Gerlach sent Elisabeth actual stones and suggests it is more likely that he sent pieces of painted wood (114).

59. MGH, SS, vol. 14, 569–70. Levison concludes that the inscriptions represent a single great deception (111). For Thioderic's possible involvement in creating other records for the abbey of Deutz, see Joseph Milz, *Studien zur mittelalterlichen Wirtschafts- und Verfassungsgeschichte der Abtei Deutz*, Veröffentlichungen des Kölnischen Geschictsvereins e.V., 30 (Köln: Verlag der Buchhandlung H. Wamper GMBH, 1970), 99–110, and the literature cited therein.

60. *Visionen*, 123.

61. This letter is printed in *Visionen*, 178–79, and PL 197, col. 216–18. This

exchange of letters is translated and discussed in Kathyrn Kerby-Fulton and Dyan Elliott, "Self-Image and the Visionary Role in Two Letters from the Correspondence of Elizabeth of Schönau and Hildegard of Bingen," *Vox Benedictina* 2 (1985): 204–23. Another letter of Hildegard has been thought to be addressed to Elisabeth, but see Hiltrud Rissel, "Hildegard von Bingen an Elisabeth von St. Thomas an der Kyll: Die heilige Hildegard und die frühesten deutschen Zisterzienserinnen," *Cîteaux* 4 (1990), 5–44.

62. *Visionen*, 179.

63. "Qui opera dei perficere desiderant, semper adtendant, quod fictilia vasa sunt, quoniam homines existunt, et semper aspiciant, quid sint, et quid futuri sint, et celestia illi relinquant illi, qui celestis est, quoniam ipsi exules sunt, celestia nescientes, sed tantum mistica dei canentes sicut tuba, que solum sonum dat nec operatur, sed in quam alius spirat, ut sonum reddat" (*Visionen*, 179). On Hildegard's prophetic role, see Barbara Newman, "Hildegard of Bingen: Visions and Validation," *Church History* 54 (1985): 163–75.

64. Kerby-Fulton and Elliott, "Self-Image and the Visionary Role," 207.

65. Hildegard explains her perception of "the living light" in a letter to Guibert of Gembloux, Ep. 2 in Pitra, 331–34. See also Newman, *Sister of Wisdom*, 6, n. 15.

66. Elisabeth refers to this visit at the beginning of *Liber Viarum Dei* (*Visionen*, 91).

67. For the triangular column, see *Visionen*, 41, and *Scivias*, 462–63. For the heavenly Jerusalem, see *Visionen*, 60, and *Scivias*, 571.

68. *In matutinis laudibus*, in *Symphonia: A Critical Edition of the "Symphonia armonie celestium revelationum*," ed. and trans. Barbara Newman (Ithaca, NY: Cornell University Press, 1988), 236, cf. 8, 307–10. I thank Barbara Newman for suggesting this possible influence to me.

69. Jeffrey Burton Russell, *Dissent and Reform in the Early Middle Ages* (Berkeley: University of California Press, 1965), 84–86; R. I. Moore, *The Origins of European Dissent* (New York: St. Martin's Press, 1977), 168–82.

70. According to the *Chronica Regia Coloniensis*, four men and a young woman were burned on August 5. Ed. George Waitz, Scriptores Rerum Germanicarum in Usum Scholarum, 18 (Hanover: Bibliopolium Hahianionum, 1880), 114.

71. *Vita Eckeberti*, 452–53, and the dedicatory letter of his *Sermones contra catharos*, PL 195, col. 13–14.

72. The setting for Hildegard's preaching is a public sermon delivered at the cathedral of Cologne around 1163. This sermon is transcribed in Ep. 48, PL 197, col. 244–53. See Newman, *Sister of Wisdom*, 11–12, 234, and Kathryn Kerby-Fulton, *Reformist Apocalypticism and "Piers Plowman"* (Cambridge: Cambridge University Press, 1990), 39–41. The Cathars are not mentioned by name in this letter.

73. Hildegard's text is printed in Pitra, 348–51. Although it was not composed as a letter to Elisabeth, Elisabeth seems to have received a copy of the text. In addition to its transmission with other Hildegard letters, it is also found in MSS of Redaction D of Elisabeth's visionary collection.

74. *Visionen*, 74–76.

75. Pitra, 350; *Visionen*, 76.

76. Pitra, 349; *Visionen*, 75.

77. See Walter L. Wakefield and Austin P. Evans, *Heresies of the High Middle Ages*, Records of Civilization: Sources and Studies, vol. 81 (New York: Columbia University Press, 1969), 253, 697, n. 26.

78. PL 197, col. 246–47.

79. "Pastores mei oppressi sunt quasi in gravi somno, et quomodo evigilare eos faciam? . . . Lex enim peribit primum a sacerdotibus et senioribus populi mei, quia venundare inquirunt sacrificia sacramentorum meorum, qui vendunt, vendunt sibi iudicium, et qui emunt, emunt gladium ex utraque parte acutum. . . . Sunt aliqui, qui non intrant in ostium ad ovile meum, sed ascendunt aliunde per aliam viam quasi fures et latrones, fures propter avariciam, latrones, quia perdunt animas sibi commissas. Tegunt enim prava opera eorum, ne videantur ab hominibus. Propterea audacter non contradicunt adversus omnem heresim, quia reprehensibiles sunt in viis eorum" (*Visionen*, 77).

80. Much of the same imagery about pastoral care and simony is also found in Elisabeth's letter to Abbot Reinhard of Reinhausen, *Visionen*, 150–52.

81. "O domina Hildegardis perfice opus domini, sicut usque nunc fecisti, quia posuit te dominus operatricem in vinea sua" (*Visionen*, 74).

82. "Beatus homo, qui metuit dominum universe creature, ut interpellet summum pontificem, ut auferat obprobrium a populo suo, et omnis Israhel salvabitur" (*Visionen*, 75).

83. "Audite verba sacerdotum, . . . in quorum auribus haec verba mea tonabunt, et qui etiam haec verba in nomine meo ad vos dicent" (Pitra, 351). Yet, in her preaching in Cologne, Hildegard was willing to consider the Cathars as instrumental in the eventual reform of the clergy by encouraging princes to rise up and chastise them. See Kerby-Fulton, 39.

84. "Vos autem, qui litterati estis, scrutamini libros de novo testamento, et recordamini verborum eius, qualem fructum inveneritis. Renovamini spiritu sancto et refocillate animas vestras in edificationem ecclesie." (*Visionen*, 76).

85. Raoul Manselli, "Amicizia spirituale ed adzione pastorale nella Germania del sec. XII: Ildegarde di Bingen, Elisabetta ed Eckberto di Schönau contro l'eresia Catara," in *Studi in onore di Alberto Pincherle, Studi e matierali di storia delle religioni* 38 (1867), 312–13.

86. For the date of composition, see Manselli, "Ecberto di Schönau e l'eresia Catara in Germania alla metà del secolo XII," in *Arte e storia: Studi in onore di Leonello Vincenti* (Torino: Giappichelli Editore, 1965), 325. Robert Harrison, who is currently working on a critical edition of the *Sermones*, confirms this date and suggests that the work was not completed until early 1164. I thank him for this information, which was conveyed in a letter.

87. "Et est non parva verecundia nostris, qui litteras sciunt, ut sint muti et elinques in conspectu illorum" (*Sermones contra catharos*, PL 195, col. 13).

88. It is possible that the Cathars in the Rhineland during this period had a theological defense of their own faith that was sophisticated enough to withstand initial attempts of the clergy to debate them with any success. Ekbert implies this (PL 195, col. 13), and his treatise is an attempt to redress this problem. Such a lack

may also have contributed to the failure of earlier investigators, which led to the execution of 1163; see *Chronica Regia Coloniensis*, 114.

89. Emecho, *Vita Eckeberti*, 452. Cf. *Vita Hildegardis*, ed. Peter Dronke in his *Women Writers of the Middle Ages: A Critical Study of Texts from Perpetua (203) to Marguerite Porete (1310)* (Cambridge: Cambridge University Press, 1984), 238. Emecho's narrative suggests that this incident preceded Ekbert's composition of his anti-Cathar treatise, but the more chronologically detailed *Vita* of Hildegard clearly places it after 1167; see Dronke, 163.

90. *Visionen*, 139.

91. "Et quidem nescio quid de hoc opere in vestra regione censebitur; hoc autem scio quod in his nostris partibus non solum ab indoctis, sed ab ipsis episcopis et abbatibus nostris certatim et scribitur et legitur et auditur." Roger's letter is discussed and edited in Ruth J. Dean, "Elizabeth, Abbess of Schönau, and Roger of Ford," *Modern Philology* 41 (1944): 209–20, quoted at 213, n. 18. See also A. G. Rigg, "Roger of Ford's Poem on the Virgin: A Critical Edition," *Cîteaux* 40 (1989): 200–13, esp. n. 2 and ll. 211–28.

92. There are five extant English MSS of Elisabeth's visions, all of which stem from Roger's copy sent to Abbot Baldwin. Roger's autograph is not extant.

93. *Visionen*, 277.

94. Cf. Christopher R. Cheney, *Handbook of Dates for Students of English History* (London: Offices of the Royal Historical Society, 1955), ix.

95. Köster (1965), 39–41, discusses the brief mentions of Elisabeth made in medieval chronicles and theological writings, and many of these passages are printed in *Visionen*, LX–XCI.

96. "Salve fons plenus, rivulus scientie divine, guttas stillans mellifluas deifice doctrine./ Salve vernans arbuscula silve Schonaugiensis, circumdata ramusculis visionum inmensis" (*Visionen*, 346).

97. *Visionen*, 345.

98. For the office, see Roth, *Das Gebetbuch der hl. Elisabeth von Schönau, nach der Originalhandschrift des XII. Jahrhunderts* (Augsburg: Verlag des Literarischen Instituts von Dr. Max Huttler, 1886), 71–72. Several cloisters in the Rhineland acquired relics of Elisabeth in the late fifteenth or early sixteenth century. See Friedrich Wiechert, "Die Reliquien der hl. Elisabeth von Schönau," in *Schönauer Elisabeth Jubiläum 1965*, 63, and Wiechert, "Die Reliquien der Klosterkirche zu Schönau," *Archiv für mittelrheinische Kirchengeschichte* 17 (1965): 271–72.

99. "Sconaugiae S. Elisabeth virginis, monasticae vitae observantiae celebris." Quoted in Köster (1965), 42.

100. "De qua re opusculum quoddam composuit, sed non est in Romana Ecclesia comprobatum" (*Rationale divinorum officiorum*, in PL 202, col. 148).

101. Quoted in Dean, "Elizabeth, Abbess of Schönau, and Roger of Ford," 218.

102. "[S]piritus magis exprimunt energiam et sermonem in sacrarum visionum simplicitate et sinceritate magis repraesentant angelicum." Letter to Adelheid von Ottenstein, in *The Prefatory Epistles of Jacques Lefèvre d'Etaples and Related Texts*, ed. Eugene F. Rice, Jr. (New York: Columbia University Press, 1972), 310. Cf. also Rice, "Jacques Lefèvre d'Etaples and the Medieval Christian Mystics," in

Florilegium Historiale: Essays Presented to Wallace K. Ferguson, ed. J. G. Rowe and W. H. Stockdale (Toronto: University of Toronto Press, 1971), 90–124, and Giles Constable, "Twelfth-Century Spirituality and the Late Middle Ages," *Medieval and Renaissance Studies*, vol. 5, ed. O. B. Hardison (Chapel Hill: University of North Carolina Press, 1969), 27–60.

Chapter 3

1. *Visionen*, 1–2.
2. *Visionen*, 318–19.
3. *Visionen*, 150–52, for Elisabeth's letter to Reinhard.
4. "Omnes, qui lecturi sunt verba libri istius, hoc indubitanter sciant, quoniam sermones angeli dei, . . . quosdam quidem ex toto proferebat latino sermone, quosdam autem omnino teutonica loquela, quosdam vero ex parte latine, et ex parte verbis teutonice lingue pronuntiabat. Ego autem Eckebertus, . . . conscripsi omnia hec, et alia, que de revelationibus eius leguntur ita quidem, ut ubi erant latina verba angeli immutata relinquerem, ubi vero teutonica erant, in latinum transferrem, prout expressius potui, nihil mea presumptione adiungens, nihil favoris humani, nihil terreni commodi querens, testis mihi est deus, cui nuda et aperta sunt omnia" (*Visionen*, 1). Cf. *Visionen*, 49, where Elisabeth's deceased uncle is said to speak to her *miscens verba latina teutonicis*, but no German is given in the text.
5. Cf. Guibert of Gembloux's letter to Hildegard of Bingen asking whether she dictates her visions in Latin or German, which indicates the possibility of such questions about the Latin records of visions, especially visions by ostensibly unlearned women. See Guibert of Gembloux, *Epistolae*, ed. Albert Derolez, CCCM 66 (Turnhout: Brepols, 1988–89), 219, cf. also 222–24. Guibert's letters are discussed in Dronke, *Women Writers*, 167–68.
6. Cf. a smiliar oath by Burchard of Worms in his preface to his *Decretum*, PL 140, col. 502, the truth of which is belied by his extensive tampering with his sources.
7. For the importance of noble background and convent life in the education of women, see Joan M. Ferrante, "The Education of Women in the Middle Ages in Theory, Fact and Fiction," in *Beyond Their Sex: Learned Women from the European Past*, ed. Patricia H. Labalme (New York and London: New York University Press, 1980), 9–42.
8. Gössman, 26.
9. "Psalterium, quod iocundum semper mihi fuerat, quandoque vix uno psalmo perlecto, longe a me proieci. Iterum recogitans ac mecum ammirans, quid mihi accidisset, resumpsi illud, legi" (*Visionen*, 4).
10. Cf. also Emecho's description of her miraculous knowledge, *Visionen*, 355. Emecho probably did not know Elisabeth personally.
11. *Visionen*, 150–51, where she refers to reading a letter she received from Reinhard of Reinhausen.

12. For the various redactions of the visionary collection, see Appendix.

13. For the nuns' recording activities, see *Visionen*, 32–33. For their continued activity even after Ekbert's arrival at the monastery, see p. 65. For Ekbert's work before his arrival, see p. 38. For further evidence that the visions were written down before Ekbert's arrival, see p. 41.

14. The gap in time from the end of *LV1* (August 15, 1154) until the beginning of *LV2* (May 14, 1155), is filled in by the events described in Elisabeth's letter to Hildegard of Bingen regarding the proclamation of the unfulfilled prophecy (August 15, 1154, to March 25, 1155).

15. Significantly, the only place in *LV1* where Elisabeth reports a vision about a deceased acquaintance is one of the rare places in this book where she is directly prompted by Ekbert (*Visionen*, 17).

16. It is not unusual for Elisabeth to talk about Ekbert without naming him; see e.g., *Visionen*, 29.

17. *Visionen*, 52.

18. *Visionen*, 64, 66.

19. Dean, "Elizabeth, Abbess of Schönau, and Roger of Ford," 211. Cf. also the popularity of a fragment of this text that circulated widely in the fourteenth and fifteenth centuries under the rubric *Sermo angeli quo instruxit beatam Elisabeth*, associated wrongly with Elisabeth of Thuringia. See Emil Jakob Spieß, *Ein Zeuge mittelalterlicher Mystik in der Schweiz* (Basle: Buchdruckerei und Verlag Dr. C. Weder Rorschach, 1935), 253–55.

20. *Visionen*, 91.

21. For the date of the *Scivias*, see Newman, *Sister of Wisdom*, 10.

22. *Visionen*, 88; Hildegard, *Scivias*, 7–8.

23. For Honorius, see M.-D. Chenu, "Monks, Canons, and Laymen in Search of the Apostolic Life," in his *Nature, Man, and Society in the Twelfth Century: Essays on New Theological Perspectives in the Latin West*, trans. Jerome Taylor and Lester K. Little (Chicago: University of Chicago Press, 1968), 224. For the identity of Honorius, see V. I. J. Flint, "The Career of Honorius Augustodunensis: Some Fresh Evidence," *Revue Bénédictine* 82 (1972): 63–86, and Flint, "Heinricus of Augsburg and Honorius of Augustodunensis: Are They the Same Person?" *Revue Bénédictine* 92 (1982): 148–58. The possibility of Honorius's German identity and, more importantly, the diffusion of the *Speculum Ecclesie* in southern Germany, suggests an interest in this type of literature in the twelfth-century Rhineland. For the presence of *Speculum* MSS in Germany and Austria, see Flint, "The Chronology of the Works of Honorius Augustodunensis," *Revue Bénédictine* 82 (1972): 215–42. These three articles by Flint are reprinted in her *Ideas in the Medieval West* (London: Variorum Reprints, 1988). For Jacques de Vitry, see Jean Longère, *La Prédication médiévale* (Paris: Etudes Augustiniennes, 1983), 88–89.

24. Newman, *Sister of Wisdom*, 17.

25. *Scivias*, 197, 205–7.

26. For the concern to define social roles, see Bynum, "Did the Twelfth-Century Discover the Individual?" in her *Jesus as Mother: Studies in the Spirituality of the High Middle Ages* (Berkeley: University of California Press, 1982), 88–89. For the articulation of multiple spiritual paths, see Constance Brittain Bouchard, *Spiri-*

tuality and Administration: The Role of the Bishop in Twelfth-Century Auxerre, Speculum Anniversary Monographs, 5 (Cambridge, MA: Medieval Academy of America, 1979), 15, 143.

27. For *Scivias* MSS, see *Scivias*, XXXII–L.

28. "[H]ec verba, que inveneritis in presenti libro, annuntietis Romane ecclesie totique populo, et omni ecclesie dei" (*Visionen*, 122).

29. Roth (1911), 221.

30. The *Nova editio passionis* (= *BHL* 8435, 8436), an attempt to reconcile the new data announced by Elisabeth with the traditional legend, is found in three MSS; two books of revelations by an unknown author (= *BHL* 8433, 8434), an extravagant collection of thousands of new names of the Cologne martyrs, are found in eleven medieval MSS. See Tervarent, vol. I, 28–33, and Levison, 125–26. For the authorship of this latter perplexing text and its possible connection to Schönau, see Karl Koch and Eduard Hegel, *Die Vita des Prämonstratensers Hermann Joseph von Steinfeld: Ein Beitrag zur Hagiographie und zur Frömmigkeitsgeschichte des Hochmittelalters*, Colonia Sacra, Band 3 (Köln: Balduin Pick Verlag, 1958), 105–7. For the debate on whether this text was a serious work or one that parodied the piety of visionary experience, mystical marriage to Christ, belief in miracles, and the veneration of the eleven thousand virgins, see Levison, 127–37, Tervarent, 30–32, and Koch and Hegel, 107.

31. Wilhelm Oehl, *Deutsche Mystikerbriefe des Mittelalters, 1100–1550* (München: Georg Müller, 1931), 114.

32. AASS, Oct. 9, 73–303. For more recent scholarship on the cult of Saint Ursula, see the works of Tervarent and Levison cited in this chapter. Frank Günter Zehnder, *Sankt Ursula: Legende, Verehung, Bilderwelt* (Cologne: Wienand Verlag, 1985), draws on Levison and adds nothing new to the discussion of Elisabeth.

33. Tervarent, vol. 1, 21.

34. Tervarent, vol. 1, 1–7. *Regnante Domino* = *BHL* 8428. Text cited here is from Joseph Klinkenberg, "Studien zur Geschichte der Kölner Märterinnen," *Jahrbücher des Vereins von Alterthumsfreunden im Rheinlande* 93 (1892): 150–63.

35. Klinkenberg, 156.

36. MSS in Levison, 91–96.

37. A condition considered significant by Levison, 97.

38. See, e.g., her description of the maidens' unexpected departure from England, *Visionen*, 126.

39. *Visionen*, 124, 129–30, 132–33.

40. See Chapter 2, n. 59.

41. Brian Stock, *The Implications of Literacy: Written Language and Models of Interpretation in the Eleventh and Twelfth Centuries* (Princeton, NJ: Princeton University Press, 1983).

42. See Stock, 64–71, 244–52. Doubt about relics and saints was not limited to this period. See Klaus Schreiner, "'Discrimen veri ac falsi': Ansätze und Formen der Kritik in her Heiligen- und Reliquenverehrung des Mittelalters," *Archiv für Kulturgeschichte* 48 (1966): 1–53.

43. It is difficult to say whether it was the current pontificate of the British Hadrian IV, or just her continuing tendency to make the martyrs British and give

them family members (Cyriacus is said to have several kinswomen among the British virgins) that led Elisabeth to make the pope come from England.

44. "[R]eclamantibus cunctis, precipue cardinalibus, qui velut deliramentum arbitrabantur, quod quasi post fatuitatem muliercularum declinaret" (*Visionen*, 126).

45. On the artistic legacy of the text, see Köster (1965), 42. For a brief sketch of the fate of Cyriacus, how he was picked up in thirteenth-century chronicles and later debated as a precedent for the resignation of Pope Celestine V, see John J. I. v. Döllinger, *Die Papst-Fabeln des Mittelalters: Ein Beitrag zur Kirchengeschichte* (1863; rpt. Frankfurt: Minerva Verlag, 1962), 45–48.

46. *Chronica*, MGH, SS, vol. 23, 683. See also 843.

47. For a more detailed examination of the theological background of the Assumption, see Chapter 6 below.

48. *Visionen*, 54.

49. Abelard, *Sermo in assumptione beate Mariae*, PL 178, col. 543. For Abelard's views on the assumption, see Hilda Graef, *Mary: A History of Doctrine and Devotion* (London: Sheed and Ward, 1963), vol. 1, 233.

50. For example, Caesarius of Heisterbach cites Elisabeth's vision to corroborate his own tale of a Cistercian monk who learned that Mary was bodily resurrected forty days after her death. See *Dialogus Miraculorum*, ed. Joseph Strange (Cologne: H. Lempertz & Comp., 1851), vol. 2, 46; see also 39. To some degree, the popularity of this text may have been related to its relative restraint—none of the more fantastic episodes in earlier assumption legends are found here.

51. *Visionen*, 153–54. The word *festivitate* does not appear in the one manuscript in which this title is included. Köster accepts Roth's addition of this word. See *Visionen*, 153, n. 2, and Köster (1951), 248. Köster suggests (1952), 104, that this text originated in Austria, apparently on the grounds that one of the two manuscripts that transmit it is from the Cistercian abbey of Zwettl, and the other, whose provenance is unknown, is currently held in the national library in Vienna. An Austrian origin for *De secunda assumptionis* may be corroborated by the observation of September 23 as a commemoration of the feast in some Bavarian dioceses, as well as those of Brandenburg, Mainz, and Frankfort. See Hermann Grotefend, *Zeitrechnung des deutschen Mittelalters und der Neuzeit* (1892–98; rpt. Aalen: Scientia Verlag, 1984), vol. 2, Part 2, 136. But for other evidence that may link it to Belgium and northern France, see Appendix.

52. In *De secunda assumptionis*, Mary is called *theotokon*, and is said to have died *in valle Josaphat*, two details appearing in Pseudo-Jerome but not in *De Resurrectione*. See Albert Ripberger, *Der Pseudo-Hieronymus-Brief IX "Cogitis Me": Ein erster marianischer Traktat des Mittelalters von Paschasius Radbert*, Spigilegium Friburgense, vol. 9 (Freiburg: Universitätsverlag, 1962), 82, 60.

53. The Anglo-Norman poem has not been dated. It is edited in J. P. Strachey, *Poem on the Assumption* (Cambridge: Cambridge University Press, 1924). The Icelandic version was composed between 1226 and 1234. *De secunda assumptionis* was translated into French, and all these vernacular texts survive in single MSS which are listed in Köster (1951), 288–90.

54. Köster (1952), 97. The letters in question are Ep. 21 to Abbot Reinhard of Reinhausen, and a letter to the abbot of Odenheim printed in Philibert Schmitz, "'Visions' inédites de Sainte Élisabeth de Schoenau," *Revue Bénédictine* 47 (1935): 181–83.

55. Ep. 20 to the bishops of Mainz, Cologne and Trier was written on June 19, 1157. Ep. 21 to Abbot Reinhard of Reinhausen was written in the last year of Elisabeth's life. Ep. 4 to Archbishop Hillin of Trier was written shortly after the appointment of Antipope Victor IV in September 1159. Ep. 5, 6, and 17 to Abbot Gerlach of Deutz were written between 1156 and 1160. Ep. 11 to a community of nuns in Cologne and a letter to the abbot of Odenheim were written after the Ursuline affair began in 1156. Ep. 22 to Fulbert of Laach was written after 1155 when Fulbert became abbot.

56. Ep. 14, *Visionen*, 146–48.

57. Wiesbaden, Hessische Landesbibiliothek MS 4 fol. 134r, a late fifteenth-century MS from Schönau, notes this monk to be Ludwig, who later became the abbot of St. Eucharius in Trier. No other evidence for this identification is known, and I thank Dr. Petrus Becker for his response to my queries about Ludwig. Abbot Ludwig of St. Eucharius did visit Hildegard of Bingen and requested letters from her. Ludwig's letter to Hildegard is Ep. 68 in PL 197, col. 287–88, and Hildegard's response is edited in Schrader and Führkötter, 143.

58. "[Q]uatinus aliquando ab ea accipere mereretur epistolam eiusdem gratie, cuius erant cetera, que ab ipsa in spiritu fuerant pronuntiata" (*Visionen*, 139).

59. *Visionen*, 139.

60. The woman addressed in Ep. 14 appears to be the abbess of Dietkirchen, the addressee of Ep. 13, because Ep. 14 refers back to the subject of Ep. 13, and because Bonn, the site of the Dietkirchen convent, is mentioned in Ep. 14 as the home of several people visiting Schönau who brought the greetings of the unnamed addressee. The salutation of Ep. 15, *E. humilis ancilla Christi dilectisssime cognata sue et venerabili magistre G.*, suggests Guda of St. Thomas of Andernach, one of three kinswomen addressed by Ekbert in his *De Obitu*, as the likely recipient. Ep. 16 is addressed simply to *R., dilecto sui*, although later in the letter Elisabeth also addresses *veneranda mater, vos patres*, and *vobis diletissimis in Christo R.H.L.* Roth suggests Reinhard of Reinhausen as the recipient, based apparently on the fact that Reinhard is the recipient of another letter from Elisabeth. Vienna, Österr. Nationalbibliothek Vindob. Pal. MS 488, fol. 166r expands *R.H.L.* to Rudolfo, Lu—, Hermanus. Ruotger, Elisabeth's brother and the provost of Pöhlde, seems a more likely candidate, especially given the very personal, albeit cryptic, content of the letter.

61. See Oehl, 755–56, n. 13, for the practice of writing such condolences.

62. The shorter text is transmitted solely in Vienna, Österr. Nationalbibliothek Vindob. Pal. MS 488; all other manuscripts transmit the expanded version edited by Roth.

63. *Visionen*, 269–70, "Post hec, cum conventus sororum . . . et consensit peticioni earum." A missing page from the Vienna MS precludes confirming any other substantial differences.

64. Cf. Köster (1952), 84. Köster was not aware of the existence of the shorter text found in Vienna, Österr. Nationalbibliothek Vindob. Pal. MS 488.

65. "Benedicta filia tu a domino, quia fructuose inter deum et homines ne-gociata es" (*Visionen*, 264, found only in the long version).

66. See Jaroslav Pelikan, *The Growth of Medieval Theology (600-1300)*, vol. 3 of *The Christian Tradition: A History of the Development of Doctrine* (Chicago: University of Chicago Press, 1978), 165–70, and Graef, 234–40.

67. *Visionen*, 266.

68. *Visionen*, 272. Cf. *Regula Sancti Benedicti*, ed. Adalbert de Vogue and Jean Neufville, printed in *RB 1980: The Rule of Saint Benedict*, ed. Timothy Fry (Collegeville, MN: The Liturgical Press, 1981), ch. 2, 26.

69. *Visionen*, 267 (found only in the long version), 272.

70. These remarks are based on my examination of the 26 MSS listed in the Bibliography, the first stage in my preparation of an edition of Elisabeth's works.

71. See Appendix, n. 1.

72. Köster (1952), 95–97.

73. Because this passage was suppressed in the later redactions, it is not found in *Visionen*. It is printed in AASS, October, vol. 9, 171, ch. 17, and in Roth (1911), 221–22.

74. *Adjuratio conscriptoris*, in Roth (1911), 221.

75. Ekbert's name is not attached to the prayer in any manuscript but his authorship seems probable. Köster (1952), 96–97, cites its similarities to Ekbert's other prayers. To this can be added its dissimilarities with Elisabeth's narratives. The warm address to Jesus is unlike her standard references to Christ as "my Lord." Likewise the reference to Jesus as a pious mother offering her breasts of consolation is not like Elisabeth's typical images of Jesus, which are often images of grand, even threatening power, although cf. *Visionen*, 149. Also, it would be unusual for Elisabeth to compose such a lengthy piece without any direct reference to herself or her experience. The prayer alludes to Elisabeth, but only in an oblique way. Text of prayer is in *Visionen*, VI, n. 1 for p. 40.

76. Roth (1911), 222–23.

77. The letter is found in *Visionen*, 135–38. The unusual form of communicating her revelations, a letter of Ekbert telling what she learned rather than a first-person narrative from Elisabeth herself, may indicate that she was no longer living when the letter was composed. For the influence of this vision, see Theodor Paas, "Ein Steinfelder Altarbild als Zeuge der Potentinus-Legende," *Annalen des Historischen Vereins für den Niederrhein* 102 (1918): 129–39.

78. These two visions are printed in AASS, October, vol. 9, 171q, ch. 18, and 173, note h.

79. E.g., the episode found in *Visionen*, IV-V, n. 4 for p. 28. For its appearance in 2 MSS, see Köster (1952), 96. Also, in Trier, Bistumsarchiv MS 10, fol. 65v, there is a unique witness of an episode in *De Obitu*.

80. "[T]ibi ac domino abbati complacuit, ut scriptis mea verba commendetis" (Paris, Bibliothèque de l'Université MS 790, fol. 59r. Similar readings are found in Avignon, Bibliothèque municipale MS 593, fol. 73v and Oxford, Bodleian Li-

brary MS Bodl. 83, fol. 3.) Cf. "domino abbati conplacuit, ut scriptis verba mea commendentur" (*Visionen*, 2).

81. Giles Constable, "Forgery and Plagiarism in the Middle Ages," *Archiv für Diplomatik, Schriftgeschichte, Siegel- und Wappenkunde* 29 (1983): 3.

82. *Visionen*, 9.

83. *Visionen*, 11.

84. *Visionen*, 3.

85. Tervarent, vol. 1, 39–43, has argued the case for the dispersion of MSS containing any version of the martyrdom account. Köster (1952), 102–3, has applied this argument specifically to the dispersion of MSS transmitting Elisabeth's works.

86. The St. Trond legendary (Liège, Bibliothèque de l'Université MS 210 II) is number 86 in Köster's catalogue (1951), 295. A brief account of how St. Trond acquired the relics is given in Tervarent, vol. 1, 35–36.

87. See Appendix.

88. Alberic of Trois Fontaines, *Chronica*, MGH, SS, vol. 23, 843.

89. Tervarent, vol. 1, 40, notes a Benedictine abbey at Glastonbury as the sole recipient of Cologne relics in England.

90. See the late fifteenth-century library catalogue of this establishment in *Mittelalterliche Bibliothekskataloge Deutschlands und der Schweiz*, vol. 2, ed. Paul Lehmann (Munich: C. H. Beck, 1928), 430–32.

91. Brian Patrick McGuire, "A Lost Clairvaux Exemplum Collection Found: The *Liber Visionum et Miraculorum* Compiled under Prior John of Clairvaux (1171–79)," *Analecta Cisterciensia* 39 (1983): 26–62, cited at 30 and 57.

Chapter 4

1. Cf. Ursula Peters, *Religiöse Erfahrung*, whose analysis of women's mystical and hagiographical texts of the thirteenth and fourteenth centuries raises many issues comparable to those explored in this chapter. One of the major differences between the Schönau texts and those examined by Peters is the lack of any significant hagiographical tendency in Ekbert's motivation to record and disseminate Elisabeth's visions. His concerns are much more focused on the content of the revelations than on portraying Elisabeth as a holy woman or a model of proper monastic conduct.

2. See Peters, "Frauenliteratur im Mittelalter? Überlegungen zur Trobairitzpoesie, zur Frauenmystik und zur feministischen Literaturbetrachtung," *Germanisch-Romanische Monatsschrift*, n.s. 38 (1988): 35–56, for the impossibility of delineating specifically and exclusively female types and themes of literature.

3. "Quoniam igitur omnia, que circa ipsam gesta sunt, ad gloriam dei et ad edificationem fidelium pertinere visa sunt, in presenti libello ex magna parte conscripta sunt iuxta narrationem ipsius, qua uni ex fratribus suis de ordine clericorum, quem pre ceteris familiarem habebat singula exposuit. Cum enim ab inquirentibus multa occultaret, eo quod esset timorata valde et humillima spiritu,

huic diligenter omnia investiganti et memorie ea tradere cupienti germanitatis et dilectionis gratia, et abbatis iussione cuncta familiariter enarrare coacta est" (*Visionen*, 2).

4. *Visionen*, 64.

5. Cf. Stock, p. 455: "For, by and large, the discussion of 'literature,' that is, of the written record, presupposes a clearcut textual tradition, which, in the case of medieval models, is rarely furnished. The final text summarizes and records events, but it omits the stages of oral and written interchange along the way."

6. Cf. the opening of Gregory the Great's *Dialogi de miraculis* where Gregory distinguishes between the stories in which he gives *sensum solummodo* and those in which he gives *verba cum sensu*. Grégoire le Grand, *Dialogues. Texte critique, notes, et traduction*, ed. Adalbert de Vogue, trans. Paul Antin. SC, No. 251, 260, 265 (Paris: Les Editions du Cerf, 1980), vol. 2, 16, 18.

7. "[E]a quoque, que post prioris libri consummationem dominus in ancilla sua operari dignatus est, secundum narrationem oris eius premissis annectantur" (*Visionen*, 40).

8. "Ego autem Eckebertus, germanus ancille dei mirificentia dei ad cenobium Sconaugiense de Bunna attractus, et primum quidem monachus, deinde autem gratia dei ad abbatiam vocatus, conscripsi omnia hec, et alia, que de revelationibus eius leguntur ita quidem, ut ubi erant latina verba angeli immutata relinquerem, ubi vero teutonica erant, in latinum transferrem, prout expressius potui, nihil mea presumptione adiungens, nihil favoris humani, nihil terreni commodi querens, testis mihi est deus, cui nuda et aperta sunt omnia" (*Visionen*, 1).

9. *Visionen*, 318.

10. "Qui universa magnalia, que dominus noster cum ipsa operatus est, diligenter perscrutans, ea que fidelium utilitati congruere videbat, conscripsit, ea vero, que legentibus non prodesse sciebat, omnino reticuit" (ed. Widmann in *Neues Archiv* 11 [1886]: 448–49).

11. Köster (1965), 24–25.

12. *Visionen*, 38.

13. For example: "alia quedam ipsi revelassem, que scriptis committi nolueram" (*Visionen*, 71).

14. *Visionen*, 3.

15. *Visionen*, 22.

16. *Visionen*, 26–27.

17. *Visionen*, 71.

18. Roth (1911), 221. On authorial concern for scribal accuracy, see Lynn Staley Johnson, "The Trope of the Scribe and the Question of Literary Authority in the Works of Julian of Norwich and Margery Kempe," *Speculum* 66 (1991): 820–38.

19. *Visionen*, 318.

20. *Visionen*, 265.

21. See *Visionen*, 42, 268.

22. *Visionen*, 58.

23. Hildegard of Bingen, *Epistolarium: Pars Prima I—XC*, ed. L. Van Acker,

CCCM 91 (Turnhout: Brepols, 1991), 102–3. Odo's letter is discussed in Dronke, *Women Writers*, 149.

24. See A. J. Minnis, *Medieval Theory of Authorship: Scholastic Literary Attitudes in the Later Middle Ages* (London: Scolar Press, 1984), 46–58.

25. *Visionen*, 62–63. Jean Leclercq discusses this vision in the context of twelfth-century monastic admiration of Origen. See *The Love of Learning and the Desire for God: A Study of Monastic Culture*, 2d ed., trans. Catharine Misrahi (New York: Fordham University Press, 1974), 118–22.

26. "Adhuc loquente ad me angelo sermones istos de pastoribus ecclesie, visum est quibusdam oportunum, ut interrogarem de his, in quibus erroris sui occasionem accipiunt dubii quidam. Interrogavi igitur non quasi in fide hesitans, sed quasi cupiens fidem nostram ex angelica auctoritate firmari ac dicebam: Nunquid domine in ecclesiasticis sacramentis parem habent virtutem officia eorum pontificum, qui sinistre et non secundum deum ad pontificatum suum introierunt, et eorum, quorum bonus introitus est? Qui respondens ait: Multi, dum talia profunde scrutantur, magis depravantur, quam emendentur, et talia dominus revelaret, si non eo liberius peccarent illi, ad quos pertinent ista. His dictis confestim ablatus est ab oculis meis" (*Visionen*, 114, reading *pertinent* rather than *pentinent*, following Douai, Bibliothèque Municipale MS 865, fol. 149r; Paris, Bibliothèque de l'Université MS 790, fol. 87v; Vienna, Österr. Nationalbibliothek Vindob. Pal. MS 488, fol. 141r).

27. *Visionen*, 53.

28. "Quod inquiris, nondum scire potes, futurum tamen est, ut per te hoc reveletur" (*Visionen*, 53).

29. *Visionen*, 54.

30. *Visionen*, 63–65.

31. *Visionen*, 68–69.

32. *Visionen*, 67–68.

33. *Visionen*, 64.

34. See, e.g., *Visionen*, 64, 66.

35. Dinzelbacher sees this development of allegoresis as one of several characteristics which mark a significant change in the tradition of visionary literature during the twelfth century. However, his citation of LV3, Ch. 31, as an example of this particular kind of interplay between vision and exegesis is misleading, for this lengthy allegorical interpretation is solely the product of Ekbert's exegesis. See *Vision und Visionsliteratur im Mittelalter* (Stuttgart: Anton Hiersemann, 1981), 178–79.

36. *Visionen*, 103, 119.

37. Roth, *Visionen*, CIX–CX; Köster (1965), 28. This opinion is in fact a mitigation of a more extreme view. Two eighteenth-century French historical surveys refer to certain scholars (who remain unnamed in both texts) who suspect that Ekbert composed the revelations and published them under Elisabeth's name. See the citations from *Histoire de Lorraine*, t. IV, and Fulbert, *Bibliothèque générale des ecrivains de l'order de saint Benoit* excerpted in *Visionen*, 189–90. Another eighteenth-century historian, Eusebius Amort, considered the possibility that Ekbert was the author of the visions. Amort is primarily concerned with *Revelatio*, al-

though he says that his conclusions are equally applicable to the entire visionary corpus. He finally rejects the possibility of Ekbert's authorship because the revelations were so famous in Elisabeth's day. See Amort, *De revelationibus, visionibus et apparitionibus privatis* (Augustae Vindelicorum, 1744), 180ff. Quoted in AASS, October, vol. 9, 81ff.

38. See, e.g., Jean Verdon, "Les moniales dans la France de l'Ouest aux XIe et XIIe siècles: Etude d'histoire sociale," *Cahiers de civilisation médiévale, X^e–XIIe siècles* 19 (1976): 248–55.

39. For example, Countess Beatrice; see *Visionen*, 49–50.

40. See D. L. d'Avray and M. Tausche, "Marriage Sermons in *Ad Status* Collections of the Central Middle Ages," *Archives d'histoire doctrinale et littéraire du Moyen Age* 47 for 1980 (1981): 71–119.

41. *Visionen*, 103.

42. PL 195, col. 34. Ekbert's proof texts are 1 Cor. 7:39–40 and 1 Tim. 5:14.

43. PL 195, col. 35. For a brief discussion of Ekbert's view of marriage, see Jean Leclercq, *Monks on Marriage: A Twelfth-Century View* (New York: Seabury Press, 1982), 8–9.

44. "Ubi tale coniugium esse potest, gratum est domino. Sed rarum est valde, ut ita contingat. . . . Alioquin nimis contraheretur numerus populi dei" (*Visionen*, 104).

45. Roth, *Visionen*, CIX–CX; Köster (1965), 28.

46. "Velox pes eorum, et discurrunt in tumultu, ut evellant et absorbeant carnalia plebis mee, cui spiritalia non ministrant, qui digitum movere pigri sunt ad eruendum ab iniquitate animas meas, pro quibus mortem gustavi" (*Visionen*, 112).

47. "Non est, qui insudet purgandis ab iniquitate animabus subditorum, quas mercatus est Christus anima sua, sed purgandis a lucello loculis eorum inminent cuncti" (*Visionen*, 314).

48. The condemnation of the clergy's exploitation of their congregations to support their own luxury can be traced back to the eleventh-century reform movements. See, e.g., Karl F. Morrison, "The Gregorian Reform," in *Christian Spirituality: Origins to the Twelfth Century*, ed. Bernard McGinn, John Meyendorf, and Jean Leclercq (New York: Crossroad Publishing Company, 1987), 192.

49. "Ecce enim fetere fecistis sanctificationem vestram in conspectu populi mei, et versa est in abhominationem mihi" (*Visionen*, 112). "Os eorum patens est, lingua eorum versatilis et acuta ad vindemiandum vineam meam, in qua non laboraverunt" (p. 112). "Vigilate et custodite vigilias noctis super gregem meum, sicut boni emulatores, ne forte superveniat grex caprarum, quod sunt spiritus maligni, a quibus disperguntur greges ovium mearum" (p. 114).

50. "[I]n rupibus sive in ruribus ad ocium electis, structuras lapidum, modice utilitatis, aut concupiscibiles formas celiis ac penicillis curiose laboratas" (*Visionen*, 312).

51. "[P]otentis patriarche, quem nec opulentia terrena nec allocutio divina sue immemorem conditionis fecit" (*Visionen*, 313). Cf. Gen. 12:27.

52. "[I]n penuria necessitatum" (*Visionen*, 113).

53. *Visionen*, p. 313.

54. *Visionen*, 119–22.

55. "[I]terum se mihi presentavit, et allocuta sum eum dicens: Nunquid domine mi secure affirmare poterimus, omnes hos sermones ex te processisse? Hec idcirco dicebam, quia ex parte verba ista protulerat, ita ut tamen faciem eius non viderem, ex parte vero per os meum in spiritu fuerant pronuntiata. Ille igitur cum magna severitate me intuens ait: Crede ex toto corde tuo, verba hec, que descripta sunt, de ore meo processerunt" (*Visionen*, 95).

Chapter 5

1. For the New Testament examples, see the disciples who prophesied at Ephesus (Acts 19:6), the four prophesying daughters of Philip of Caesarea (Acts 21:8–9), the prophecy of Agabus (Acts 21:11), the prophets at the church of Antioch (Acts 13:1; 15:32), Peter's vision *in excessu mentis* at Joppa (Acts 11:5), and Paul's references to prophecy (1 Thes. 5:19–20; 1 Cor. 14).

2. James L. Ash, Jr., "The Decline of Ecstatic Prophecy in the Early Church," *Theological Studies* 37 (1976): 227–52.

3. Paul Alphandéry, "La Glossalalie dans le prophétisme médiéval latin," *Revue de l'histoire des religions* 103 (1931): 417–36.

4. "[G]ratia interpretandi, id est exponendi verba divina," Peter Abelard, *Commentaria in epistolam Pauli ad Romanos*, ed. E. M. Buytaert, CCCM 11 (Turnholt: Brepols, 1969), 275. See also William of St. Thierry, for whom prophecy was identified with *discretio*, understanding the secrets of Scripture. *Expositio in epistola ad Romanos*, PL 180, col. 673, cited in Morton W. Bloomfield, "Joachim of Flora: A Critical Survey of his Canon, Teachings, Sources, Biography and Influence," *Traditio* 13 (1957): 262. For the development of this idea of prophecy, see R. X. Redmond, "Prophecy, Theology of," *New Catholic Encyclopedia* (New York: McGraw-Hill Book Company, 1967), vol. 11, 861–66.

5. Wilhelm Kamlah, *Apokalypse und Geschichtstheologie: Die mittlelalterliche Auslegung der Apokalypse vor Joachim von Fiore*, Historische Studien, Heft 285 (Berlin: Dr. Emil Ebering, 1935), 121–22. The identification of prophecy with exegesis is common to religious traditions in which written prophecy becomes enshrined in scriptural canons, and this development can be seen in medieval Judaism and Islam as well as Christianity. See Gerald T. Sheppard and William E. Herbrechtsmeier, "Prophecy: An Overview," *The Encyclopedia of Religion*, ed. Mircea Eliade (New York: Macmillan, 1987), vol. 12, 8–14.

6. Marjorie Reeves, *The Influence of Prophecy in the Later Middle Ages: A Study in Joachimism* (Oxford: Clarendon Press, 1969), 3–27.

7. Robert E. Lerner, "Medieval Prophecy and Religious Dissent," *Past and Present* 72 (1976): 3–24.

8. John J. von Döllinger links a noticeable increase in attributions of prophecy to "the great ecclesiastical and political movement in the second half of the eleventh century," citing Peter Damian's prophecy of the death of the anti-pope Honorius II, Gregory VII's prediction of the death of Henry III, and Bernard of Clairvaux's preaching of the Second Crusade. Döllinger, *Prophecies and the Pro-*

phetic Spirit in the Christian Era: An Historical Essay, trans. Alfred Plummer (London: Rivertons, 1873), 68–69. For Gregory VII, see also, A. Stacpoole, "Hugh of Cluny and the Hildebrandine Miracle Tradition," *Revue Bénédictine* 77 (1967): 341–63.

9. Otto of Freising, *Gesta Friderici I Imperatoris*, MGH, SS, vol. 20, 370–71; *The Deeds of Frederick Barbarossa*, trans. Charles Christopher Mierow, Records of Civilization, Sources and Studies, no. 49 (New York: Columbia University Press, 1953), 70–71.

10. It seems likely that Bernard's preaching, widely noted for its eloquence, owed some of its forcefulness to his animated delivery. To at least one critic, however, Bernard's style was too extreme. Peter Abelard equated what others saw as the divine impulse in Bernard's *habitus corporis* with frenzy, an attribute often associated with ecstatic prophecy or even possession. See Paul Alphandéry, "De quelque faits de prophétism dans les sectes latines antérieures au Joachisme," *Revue de l'histoire des religions* 52 (1905): 193–94.

11. MGH, SS, vol. 20, 372; *The Deeds of Frederick Barbarossa*, 74.

12. MGH, SS, vol. 20, 370, 372; *The Deeds of Frederick Barbarossa*, 70, 74. For a general discussion of the role of *prophetae* in the crusades, see Norman Cohn, *The Pursuit of the Millennium*, 2d ed. (New York: Harper and Row Publishers, 1961), 40–52.

13. *De consideratione ad Eugenium Papam*, in *Sancti Bernardi Opera*, vol. 3, II, 3; *Five Books on Consideration: Advice to a Pope*, trans. John D. Anderson and Elizabeth T. Kennan, Cistercian Fathers Series, no. 37 (Kalamazoo, MI: Cistercian Publications, 1976), 49.

14. Eugene III makes a different use of the Moses example when rationalizing the pitiful end of the Crusade in a letter to Conrad III. Not needing to justify any personal claim to a direct divine chain of command as Bernard did, Eugene can use the example of the Hebrews' hardship in Egypt to illustrate how God uses earthly oppression to encourage people to withdraw from the love of this world (JL 9334; MGH, SS, vol. 20).

15. MGH, SS, vol. 20, 387; *The Deeds of Frederick Barbarossa*, 106.

16. "Aliquando vero prophetiae spiritus prophetis deest, nec semper eorum mentibus praesto est . . . " (Gregory the Great, *Homélies sur Ezéchiel. Texte latin, introduction, traduction et notes*, ed. Charles Morel, SC, no. 327 [Paris: Les Editions du Cerf, 1986], I, 15, p. 70). The same opinion is found in Gregory's *Dialogi de Miraculis*, II, 2.

17. C. 1 q. 1 c.79. See Döllinger, *Prophecies and the Prophetic Spirit*, 61–62: In the universities, "it was universally taught that the prophetic gift was in itself no sign of peculiar piety or holiness of life, that indeed even wicked men could receive the gift from God; and appeal was thereupon made to the words of Scripture respecting Caiaphas." Citing Caiaphas as an example of one prophesying without being holy goes back at least to Augustine. See *De Genesi ad litteram*, PL 34, col. 472. Augustine also credits Satan with inspiring true prophecy as part of his technique for luring victims into his snares. See *De Genesi ad litteram*, col. 464–65.

18. Despite the theoretical severance between prophecy and sanctity, the two were still often associated, particularly in hagiographical accounts. For the general

connection between prophecy and virtue, see Simone Roisin, *L'hagiographie cister-cienne dans le diocèse de Liège au XIIIe siècle*, Université de Louvain, Recueil de travaux d'histoire et de philologie, 3. sér., fasc. 27 (Louvain: Bibliothèque de l'U-niversité, 1947), 190–92. By the fourteenth century, when canonization inquests had become standardized, a final chapter was frequently added to the *vitae*, in which information about visions, revelations, and prophecies was given. See Vauchez, 592.

19. MGH, SS, vol. 20, 373.

20. Hildegard, *Epistolarium*, 3–4. Cf. the similar passages in *Scivias*, 3, 8.

21. Hildegard, *Epistolarium*, 6–7.

22. For these and other biograpical details, see Newman, *Sister of Wis-dom*, 8–9.

23. "Hec ad audienciam Moguntine ecclesie allata cum essent et discussa, omnes ex deo esse dixerunt, et ex prophecia quam olim prophete prophetaverant." This and other autobiographical fragments from Hildegard's *Vita* are newly edited in Dronke, *Women Writers*, 232. The complete *Vita* by Gottfried of St. Disibod and Dieter of Echternach is in PL 197, 91–130.

24. "In eadem visione scripta prophetarum, ewangeliorum, et aliorum sanc-torum, et quorumdam philosophorum, sine ulla humana doctrina intellexi, ac que-dam ex illis exposui, cum vix noticiam litterarum haberem, sicut indocta mulier me docuerat. Sed et cantum cum melodia in laude dei et sanctorum absque doctrina ullius hominis protuli, et cantavi, cum nunquam vel neumam vel cantum aliquem didicissem" (Dronke, *Women Writers*, 232, cf. 145).

25. *Homélies sur Ezéchiel* I, 1, 50–52. This point is confirmed in Gregory's *Dialogi de miraculis* where some of his stories about holy people endowed with the spirit of prophecy are not concerned with the prediction of future events but with knowlege of hidden events of the present and past. See, e.g., II, 11–16; III, 5.

26. For other parts of Hildegard's work that do evince a concern to announce the course of the imminent future, see Kerby-Fulton, 26–75.

27. At this point, most studies about Hildegard refer to the Trier synod held by Eugene in 1147/48, e.g., Führkötter and Schrader, 108; Dronke, *Women Writers*, 148–49; Newman, *Sister of Wisdom*, 9. There is, however, no conclusive evidence for the occurrence of such a synod. See JL 9188. The events described in the *Vita* probably transpired on a much smaller scale than a papal synod.

28. *Sanctae Hildegardis Vita*, PL 197, col. 95. Neither Eugene's letter to Hilde-gard nor the letters he is said to have written to Abbot Kuno and the monks at St. Disibod are extant. The letter of Eugene to Hildegard that is transmitted in Wies-baden, Hessische Landesbibliothek 2, fol. 328r, and printed as Ep. 1 in PL 197, col. 145, is spurious. See *Germania Pontificia*, vol. IV, part IV, ed. Hermannus Jakobs (Göttingen: Vandenhoeck et Ruprecht, 1978), 241–43, and Schrader and Führköt-ter, 111–22. The absence of any letters recording these events does not necessarily mean that the events described in the *Vita* did not take place. A later letter of Hildegard to Eugene on her completion of the *Scivias* refers to the *Scivias* as a text he would know. See Hildegard, *Epistolarium*, 7. Also, the very rapid spread of Hildegard's reputation after these events, a reputation of one having a special au-thority to write her visions, can be seen in letters addressed to her during this

period (see, e.g., Haverkamp, 118–19), and in chronicles and hagiographical texts (see, e.g., Herbert Grundmann, "Zur Vita S. Gerlaci Eremeticae," *Deutsches Archiv für Erforschung des Mittelalters* 18 [1962]: 539–54; rpt. in Grundmann, *Ausgewählte Aufsätze*, vol. 1 [Stuttgart: Anton Hierseman, 1976], 187–94. I would like to thank Robert Lerner for this notice.)

29. Dronke, *Women Writers*, 148–49.

30. MGH, SS, vol. 20, 381–82. More details about the career of Eudo are found in William of Newburg, *Historia rerum anglicarum*, ed. Richard Howlett, Rolls Series 82, vol. 1, 60–64. Otto's emphasis on Eudo's ignorance differs from that of William, who repeatedly describes him as being under demonic sway and granted magical power by the devil.

31. For Hildegard's self-consciousness as a prophet in the tradition of the Old Testament, see Newman, *Sister of Wisdom*, 25–36, and Kerby-Fulton, 64–75. For discussion of other examples of visionary experience defended in terms of God's continuing direct revelation to particular individuals, see Carol Zaleski, *Otherworld Journeys: Accounts of Near-Death Experience in Medieval and Modern Times* (New York: Oxford University Press, 1987), 81–85, and C. J. Holdsworth, "Visions and Visionaries in the Middle Ages," *History* 48 (1963): 144–45.

32. Vauchez, *La Sainteté en Occident*, 445–46. See also Bynum, *Holy Feast and Holy Fast*, 26. Not all references to the prophetic spirit were made of women. For examples of men, see e.g., Richard Kieckhefer, *Unquiet Souls: Fourteenth-Century Saints and Their Religious Milieu* (Chicago: University of Chicago Press, 1984), 161–65. In the early Christian male fascination with female seers known as the Sibyls, there was also an association between women and access to revelation, but here the men (e.g., Lactantius [died c. 320]) were dealing with texts and not women themselves when they referred to these prophets. See *Apocalyptic Spirituality*, trans. Bernard McGinn (New York: Paulist Press, 1979), 21–22.

33. "[P]rophetias spernunt: quia spirituales quosque, quasi insanos vel idiotas despiciunt; et prophetias sive Sanctorum revelationes, tamquam phantasmata vel somniorum illusiones reputant" (*Vita Mariae Oigniacensis*, AASS, June, vol. 5, 549).

34. For Aristotle's physiological evidence for the intellectual and moral inferiority of women and its influence on medieval thought, see Vern L. Bullough, "Medieval Medical and Scientific Views of Women," *Viator* 4 (1973): 487–90, and Prudence Allen, *The Concept of Woman: The Aristotelian Revolution, 750 BC to AD 1250* (Montreal: Eden Press, 1985), 108–9.

35. Bynum, "Women Mystics in the Thirteenth Century: The Case of the Nuns of Helfta," in her *Jesus as Mother*, 251–52, n. 292, and the literature cited therein.

36. *Visionen*, 11, 13, 14, 16, 18, 34, 35; cf. 21, 41.

37. For the date of composition of this section of 4 Esdras, see N. Turner, "Esdras, Books of," *The Interpreter's Dictionary of the Bible*, ed. George Arthur Buttrick (Nashville, TN: Abingdon Press, 1962).

38. *Visionen*, 16–17, 27, 30, 92.

39. *Visionen*, 56–60.

40. *Visionen*, 19, 29, 34–35.

41. *Visionen*, 12.

42. *Visionen*, 20–21, cf. 78–87.

43. Theodore Bogdanos, "'The Shepherd of Hermas' and the Development of Medieval Visionary Allegory," *Viator* 8 (1977): 34.

44. *Visionen*, 59–60; cf. Bogdanos, 38–40.

45. For Gregory's important role in the tradition of medieval otherworld visions, see Zaleski, 28–31, et passim. For a collection of otherworld literature, see *Visions of Heaven and Hell Before Dante*, ed. Eileen Gardiner (New York: Italica Press, 1989).

46. Gregory the Great, *Dialogues*, trans. Odo John Zimmerman (New York: Fathers of the Church, Inc., 1959), 251; *Dialogi*, IV, 43.

47. *Dialogues*, 84; *Dialogi*, II, 16. Gregory also acknowledges that sometimes people can make predictions "through a subtle power of their own"; thus not all extraordinary knowledge is due to spiritual union, 219; *Dialogi*, IV, 27.

48. *Dialogues*, 219; *Dialogi*, IV, 27.

49. For *oculus mentis*, see *Visionen*, 7, 23. The phrase is also found in *Dialogi*, IV, 7.

50. *Visionen*, 31; cf., *Dialogues*, 196–203; *Dialogi*, IV, 5–11.

51. "Et ecce angelus domini veniens extulit me in sublime, ita ut omnes fines terre conspicerem" (*Visionen*, 37; cf. *Dialogues*, 105; *Dialogi*, II, 35).

52. *Dialogues*, 237–41; *Dialogi*, IV, 37. Cf. *Visionen*, 17, 47, 48–49, 66–67.

53. *Self and Society in Medieval France: The Memoirs of Abbot Guibert of Nogent (1065–c. 1125)*, ed. John F. Benton (New York: Harper Torchbooks, 1970), 92–97.

54. Zaleski, 92.

55. *Visionen*, 11, 12, 15, 16, 27, 34–35.

56. Zaleski, 93.

57. For conversion as the typical denouement of otherworld journey narratives, see Zaleski, 77–79; cf. Gregory the Great, who acknowledges that some people are unwilling to avoid hell even after having a vision of it and its torments, *Dialogi*, IV, 37.

58. Adumbrating the move to more personal hagiographical/biographical accounts are Eadmer's *Vita* of Anselm of Canterbury and the anonymous life of Christina of Markyate. See respectively R. W. Southern, *St. Anselm and His Biographer: A Study of Monastic Life and Thought, 1059-c.1130* (Cambridge: Cambridge University Press, 1963), 329–36, and Robert Hanning, *The Individual in Twelfth-Century Romance* (New Haven, CT: Yale University Press, 1977), 35–50.

59. Dinzelbacher, 33–36, et passim.

60. Dinzelbacher, 37–38.

61. Dinzelbacher, 184–99.

62. Dinzelbacher, 194–95.

63. Dinzelbacher, 208.

64. Dinzelbacher, 226–28. The preponderance of male visionaries in the otherworld journey narratives can be seen at a glance in the chronological tables of these visions given on 13–23, or in Zaleski, 206–9.

65. Bynum, "Women's Stories, Women's Symbols: A Critique of Victor Turner's Theory of Liminality," in *Anthropology and the Study of Religion*, ed. Robert

L. Moore and Frank E. Reynolds (Chicago: Center for the Scientific Study of Religion, 1984), 108.

66. For this development in the use and influence of written documents, see Stock, 30–87.

67. "[A] die, quo sub regulari institutione cepi vivere, usque ad hanc horam ita confirmata est super me manus domini" (*Visionen*, 3).

68. *Visionen*, 15, 16.

69. "Frequenter enim et quasi ex consuetudine in diebus dominicis aliisque festivitatibus circa horas, in quibus maxime fidelium fervet devotio, cecidit super eam passio quedam precordiorum, et anxiata est vehementer tandemque velut exanimis requievit, ita ut nullus aliquando in ea halitus aut vitalis motus sentiri potuisset. Post longum vero excessum resumpto paulatim spiritu, subito verba quedam divinissima latino sermone proferebat" (*Visionen*, 1–2).

70. The unusual style and content of this passage indicate Ekbert's hand at work. Furthermore, the explicit association of Elisabeth with "holy people" is highly uncharacteristic of her own expressions and is much more congruent with Ekbert's apologetic attempts to explain her experience by comparing her to other noteworthy recipients of divine revelation. See, e.g., his comparison of her to prophetic women of the Old Testament, *Visionen*, 40.

71. "Hoc, quod dico, in temetipsa frequenter experta es. Contingit aliquando in sanctis hominibus, ut spiritus eorum qui sensus carnales vivificat ad sentiendum ea, que extrinsecus posita sunt, tanto impetu ad ea, que spiritualia sunt, introrsus rapiatur, ut carnem absque sensu et motu relinquat, et tunc discernere non valet homo, utrum in corpore an extra corpus spiritus eius sit. Tali modo raptus fuerat Paulus, cum usque ad tercium celum in spiritu ascendit" (*Visionen*, 64).

72. *Visionen*, 2, 12–23.

73. *Visionen*, 264.

74. "[E]langui toto corpore, et formicare ceperunt primo summitates manuum et pedum meorum, et tota denique caro mea, et erupit undique sudor de me. Factumque est cor meum quasi ferro scinderetur in duas partes" (*Visionen*, 11).

75. *Visionen*, 31, 32, 35.

76. *Visionen*, 32. Cf. *Sanctae Hildegardis Vita*, PL 197, col. 96.

77. *Visionen*, 3, 5.

78. *Visionen*, 3. Here Elisabeth notes that at the early stage of this physical affliction, the sisters in her community applied medications for her ailment before she realized the futility of such an effort. The only other reference to resorting to "human medicine" for Elisabeth is Ekbert's remark in *De Obitu* that during her final illness he hurried to Mainz "to consult doctors and procure medicines" ("consulere medicos et comparare medicinas," *Visionen*, 269).

79. Vienna, Österr. Nationalbibliothek Vindob. Pal. MS 488, fol. 66r; Avignon, Bibliothèque municipale MS 593, fol. 87v; Paris, Bibliothèque de l'Université MS 790, fol. 67v. Cf. *Visionen*, 21, which is full of printer's errors.

80. Ernst Benz, *Die Vision: Erfahrungsformen und Bilderwelt* (Stuttgart: Ernst Klett Verlag, 1969), 20.

81. *Visionen*, 35.

82. *Visionen*, 44.

83. *Visionen*, 28, 12.

84. "[C]anonice scripture testimonia, aliaque divinarum laudum verba" (*Visionen*, 2).

85. *Visionen*, 27.

86. Despite this emphasis on loss of control, neither she nor Ekbert ever describe her spontaneous divine outpourings in terms that suggest glossolalia. Cf. Alphandéry, "La Glossolalie dans le prophetism médiéval latin," 426, who asserts that Elisabeth had habitual experiences of glossolalia. This observation appears to be based on an equation of glossolalia with ecstasy, which in my reading of the visionary records seems not to be borne out.

87. See, e.g., *Visionen*, 3, 24, 32–33, 38.

88. *Visionen*, 31.

89. *Visionen*, 30.

90. "Et reclinans me in sinum magistre iterum veni in extasim. Et vidi eadem, que videram. Iterumque ad me rediens, hec verba arripui, Adiuva me domine deus meus, et cetera. Et adieci, Gratia dei sum id quod sum, et cetera. Dicunt etiam me dixisse, Ne magnitudo revelationum extollat me, et non amplius." Paris, Bibliothèque de l'Université MS 790, fol. 67v. Similar readings are found in Avignon, Bibliothèque municipale MS 593, fol. 87v and Oxford, Bodleian Library MS Bodl. 83, fol. 21r. The later redactions used by Roth omit *Et adieci: Gratia . . . et cetera.* (*Visionen*, 14).

91. *Visionen*, 27–28.

92. See, e.g., *Visionen*, 7, 45, III.

93. See Rudolph Arbesmann, "Fasting and Prophecy in Pagan and Christian Antiquity," *Traditio* 7 (1949–51): 59.

94. In his survey of medieval visionary literature, Dinzelbacher maintains a distinction between vision and apparition (pp. 37–38), which I am not following here. His category of vision roughly corresponds to what Elisabeth describes as *raptus* (discussed below). The fact that her descriptions do not fit cleanly into his categorization of vision/apparition is seen in his remarks about Elisabeth as a good example of a mixed form of apparition and vision.

95. Cf. *Visionen*, 9, where she reports directing *oculos carnis* toward a vision, and then not being able to see it.

96. *Visionen*, 10–11, 23.

97. For *mentis excessus*, cf. Acts 11:5. For Elisabeth's interchangeable use of these phrases, see, for example *Visionen*, 20, 27.

98. See, e.g., *Visionen*, 9: "in extasim veni, moxque respiravi." Although there is no description of a particular vision occurring between entering this ecstasy and reviving from it, this ecstasy is described in the context of a series of ongoing visions, and it is difficult to know if Elisabeth was trying to distinguish this ecstasy from the visions she was having at that time.

99. *Visionen*, 10, 16.

100. See, e.g., *Visionen*, 13, 23.

101. "[V]eniens in extasim quievi" (*Visionen*, 16); "ad quietem extasis deveni" (p. 18).

102. "[V]eni in extasim sine dolore" (*Visionen*, 16).

103. "Mane autem hora tercia cum multa fatigatione veni in extasim, in qua permansi usque circa horam sextam" (*Visionen*, 24).

104. "[C]um paululum respirassem" (*Visionen*, 25); "post pusillum expergiscens, antequam plene ad me ipsam redirem" (p. 31).

105. "Post hec tota nocte illa, sive dormirem, sive vigilarem, videbam, qualiter impii illi dominum blasphemabant verberando, conspuendo, colaphis et alapis cedendo. Et quidem in extasim non veni, set totus sensus meus illic erat, et ad nihil aliud poteram intendere, ita ut pene insensata viderer" (*Visionen*, 24).

106. Elisabeth's description of ecstasy does not conform to ecstatic conditions defined in one of the few texts that treat this topic. According to Augustine's *De Genesi ad litteram*, ecstasy occurs when the mind focuses on a spiritual image to the exclusion of seeing any other object that is present to the physical eye (PL 34, col. 263). Elisabeth does sometimes describe a state comparable to Augustine's definition, e.g., her characterization of herself as *insensata* while seeing the humiliation of Jesus. More frequently, however, she describes an ecstatic vision which incorporates her physical vision. For example, during Mass she goes into ecstasy and sees a dove place small flames over the heads of each of the nuns as they go to the altar to receive communion (*Visionen*, 26.) Here her physical vision of the nuns participating in Mass is not cut off by her ecstasy, but instead is enhanced by it.

107. *Visionen*, 14, 26, 25.

108. "In vigilia omnium sanctorum ad vesperam diu in agone laboravi, et dum vehementi dolore coartarer, signum crucifixi domini pectori meo fortiter astrinxi, et tandem veniens in extasim quievi. Tunc insolito more visum est mihi, quasi raperetur spiritus meus in sublime, et vidi ostium apertum in celo, et tantam sanctorum multitudinem, quantam numquam ante videram" (*Visionen*, 16).

109. The novelty cannot be that she saw the open door, which Ekbert took as the defining characteristic of her early visions, because before this point she had already narrated four other such visions. See *Visionen*, 11, 13, 14, 15.

110. *Visionen*, 17.

111. "[V]isum est mihi, quasi abstraheretur spiritus meus a corpore, ac sublevaretur in altum" (*Visionen*, 21); "Venit angelus domini ad me, et rapuit spiritum meum a corpore meo, et subito veni cum illo, et duxit me in altum" (p. 27); "Rursus ad miserabile corpus reducta sum" (pp. 35–36).

112. "[V]isum est mihi quasi" (*Visionen*, 16, 21); "visum sum mihi" (p. 17); "sensi autem quasi" (p. 18).

113. "[P]uerum amabilem valde, indutum veste alba et precinctum" (*Visionen*, 17). Cf. Mark 16:5.

114. "Visum est mihi quasi raperetur spiritus meus" (*Visionen*, 16); "Angelus domini . . . rapuit spiritum meum a corpore meo" (p. 27). The words *sustulit* (pp. 28, 46), *extulit* (pp. 35, 37), *transtulit* (pp. 42, 47, 48, 50), and *assumpsit* (pp. 49, 56) are also used to describe the angel's action.

115. *Visionen*, 28–30 et passim.

116. *Visionen*, 29, 36.

117. *Visionen*, 32, 38.

178 Notes to Pages 88–93

118. *Visionen*, 47–48.

119. Elisabeth's visions of God refer only to seeing "gloriam maiestatis immense" (*Visionen*, 11) or to seeing "in medio throni sedentem, cuius facies terribilis erat" (p. 27). There are several examples where she describes visions of the risen Christ and of the Holy Spirit in the form of a dove, but these are not, strictly speaking, visions of God.

120. Cf. *Visionen*, 13, for another example of a purely aural experience.

121. *Visionen*, 18.

122. "Cibum et potum pre tedio sumere non potui nisi tenuissime et ibam deficiens et tabescens toto corpore" (*Visionen*, 4); "ad prandium accessissem, pre nimia vexatione vix cibum attigi" (p. 7); "incidi in lectum toto corpore languens, ita ut pene nichil refectionis corpori meo possem adhibere" (p. 21).

123. *Visionen*, 264–65.

124. See, for example, Barbara W. Lex, "The Neurobiology of Ritual Trance," in *The Spectrum of Ritual: A Biogenetic Analysis*, ed. Eugene G. D'Aquili et al. (New York: Columbia University Press, 1979), 117–51, and Robert E. Ornstein, "Two Sides of the Brain," in *Understanding Mysticism*, ed. Richard Woods (Garden City, NY: Doubleday and Company, Inc., 1980), 270–85.

125. *Visionen*, 4.

126. *Visionen*, 5–7.

127. *Visionen*, 5–10 et passim.

128. It is noteworthy that even with Elisabeth's relatively frequent claims to speak spontaneously God's words, she never describes herself as possessed by the Spirit, despite the important precedent of the prophet Ezekiel, whose words, "Et ingressus est in me spiritus" (Ezekiel 2:2), would have been well known to Elisabeth.

129. "Et post pusillum venit angelus domini, et erexit me velociter, et statuit me supra pedes meos dicens: O homo surge et sta supra pedes tuos, et loquar tecum, et noli timere, quia ego tecum sum omnibus diebus vite tue. Viriliter age et confortetur cor tuum, et sustine dominum. Et dices prevaricatoribus terre: Sicut olim gentes crucifixerunt me, sic cottidie crucifigor inter illos, qui prevaricati sunt me in cordibus suis" (*Visionen*, 32).

130. "Domine, nescio loqui, et tarda sum ad loquendum" (*Visionen*, 33).

131. "Aperi os tuum, et ego dicam, et qui audit te, audit et me" (*Visionen*, 33).

132. "Sufficit tibi gratia mea" (*Visionen*, 33).

133. "Et tu fili hominis dices ad eos, qui habitant in terra. Audite populi! Deus deorum locutus est" (*Visionen*, 38).

134. "Viriliter age et confortetur cor tuum, et sustine temptationes huius mundi" (*Visionen*, 146).

135. *Visionen*, 33.

136. *Visionen*, 21–22.

137. "[C]lero et monialibus non bona gradientibus via" (*Visionen*, 29).

138. *Visionen*, 32–33.

139. "Quare abscondis aurum in luto? Hoc est verbum dei, quod missum est per os tuum in terram, non ut abscondatur, sed ut manifestetur ad laudem et gloriam domini nostri, et ad salvationem populi sui" (*Visionen*, 38).

140. *Visionen*, 38.

141. *Visionen*, 43–47.

142. *Visionen*, 42.

143. "Misit dominus manum suam et tetigit os meum et implevit illud spiritu sapientie et intellectus" (*Visionen*, 44). Cf. Jer. 1:9; Isa. 6:7; Eccli. 15:5.

144. "[P]ropter incredulitatem multorum, et ad confirmationem fidei" (*Visionen*, 48).

145. "[P]auci vero sunt, qui eum sequi cupiunt, a quo nomen acceperunt" (*Visionen*, 48).

146. Elisabeth's sense of her role in salvation history can be compared to a similar aspect found in what Ernst Benz has categorized as "prophetic visions," despite the fact that Elisabeth's visions are not what Benz would consider prophetic visions because they are not generally concerned with the future of the church. See Benz, 131–36.

147. "[C]um essem in spiritu, duxerat me quasi in pratum quoddam, in quo fixum erat tentorium, et introivimus illuc. Et ostendit mihi congeriem magnam librorum illic repositorum et ait: Vides libros istos? Omnes adhuc ante diem iudicii dictandi sunt. Elevans autem unum ex eis dixit: Hic est liber viarum dei, qui per te revelandus est, quando visitaveris sororem Hildigardim, et audieris eam. Et ita quidem impleri cepit, continuo cum ab ea redissem" (*Visionen*, 91).

148. Newman, *Sister of Wisdom*, 38.

149. "Beatus qui legerit et audierit verba libri huius quia vera sunt" (*Visionen*, 95). Cf. also p. 77, for another expression of blessing to the reader of Elisabeth's message.

150. Roth (1911), 221.

151. *Visionen*, 122.

152. "Ante multa tempora ad hoc ipsum preelegit te deus, ut ea, que hactenus de nobis incognita fuerunt, per te faceret manifesta" (*Visionen*, 125). A similar incident occurs on p. 129.

153. For this sense of divine predestination, see also *Visionen*, 47.

154. For Elisabeth's fear of being judged an *inventrix novitatum* in connection with her revelations about the Assumption of Mary, see *Visionen*, 54. In her letter to Hildegard explaining her experience, Elisabeth acknowledges that she is concerned lest she appear to be an *auctrix novitatum* (*Visionen*, 71).

155. Klinkenberg, 161–63.

156. "Quedam parva scintilla emissa de sede magne maiestatis, et vox tonans in cor cuiusdam vermiculi hominis dicit. H. archiepiscopo Treverensi. Admonet te, qui erat et qui est et qui venturus est" (*Visionen*, 140).

157. *Visionen*, 140–41, 143–45.

158. *Visionen*, 140.

159. *Visionen*, 146.

160. *Visionen*, 151.

161. "Non enim cohibetur murmuratione eorum, qui magnos se estimantes et que videntur infirmiora spernentes, divitias bonitatis eius in illa subsannare non formidant. . . . Hoc illos scandalizat, quod in his diebus plurimum in sexu fragili misericordiam suam dominus magnificare dignatur. Sed cur in mentem non venit,

quoniam simile factum est in diebus patrum nostrorum, quando viris socordie deditis, spiritu dei replete sunt mulieres sancte, ut prophetarent, populum dei strennue gubernarent, sive etiam de hostibus Israel gloriose triumpharent, quemadmodum Olda, Debora, Judith, Jahel, et huiusmodi?" (*Visionen*, 40).

162. Cf. Ekbert's other use of an image of strong women in contrast with weak men to emphasize the mystery of God's grace: his unconventional exegesis of Gen. 2, which is found in his allegorical interpretation of one of Elisabeth's visions (*Visionen*, 87). Cf. Newman, *Sister of Wisdom*, 40–41, and Gössman, 42, who refer to this passage as part of Elisbaeth's vision rather than Ekbert's interpretation.

163. *Visionen*, 2–3.

164. *Visionen*, 7–8, 11.

165. "Quoniam igitur omnia, que circa ipsam gesta sunt, ad gloriam dei et ad edificationem fidelium pertinere visa sunt" (*Visionen*, 2).

166. See, e.g., *Visionen*, 39.

167. *Visionen*, 12.

168. On the "radical disjunction between knowledge and belief," see John Van Engen, "The Christian Middle Ages as an Historiographical Problem," *American Historical Review* 91 (1986): 545.

169. *Visionen*, 38.

Chapter 6

1. See "Allerheiligenbild," in *Lexikon der Christlichen Ikonographie*, ed. Engelbert Kirschbaum (Rome: Herder, 1968–), vol. 1, 101.

2. *Visionen*, 12.

3. "Vidi . . . in medio throni sedentem, cuius facies terribilis erat" (*Visionen*, 27).

4. *Visionen*, 48.

5. "Deinde post modicum tempus ceperunt fratres officium diei celebrare, et cum processissent usque ad lectionem passionis, cepi agonizare et artari supra omnem modum, ita ut nulli hominum possim eloqui. Certe frater mi, si universa caro mea per partes discerperetur, videtur mihi, quod levius ferrem. Tandem autem in extasim veniens vidi iterum dominum in cruce, iamque in illa hora emisit spiritum" (*Visionen*, 24).

6. R. W. Southern, *The Making of the Middle Ages* (New Haven, CT: Yale University Press, 1953), 231–38; Colin Morris, *The Discovery of the Individual, 1050–1200* (New York: Harper and Row, 1972), 139–44.

7. *Visionen*, 15, 16, 44; cf. 45.

8. *Visionen*, 23, 37.

9. *Visionen*, 23.

10. *Visionen*, 26.

11. *Visionen*, 31–32.

12. *Visionen*, 36.

13. *Visionen*, 50.

14. *Visionen*, 5–6, 9, 26, 36, 38.

15. For example: "aspexi pixidem et cogitabam intra me de dignitate sacramenti illius, et subito cor meum dissolutum est, ita ut vix me continerem ab extasi" (*Visionen*, 16).

16. *Visionen*, 10, 22–26, 30.

17. *Visionen*, 60–61.

18. "[U]t tanto congruentius etiam ad significandam beatam matrem eius visio posset aptari" (*Visionen*, 62).

19. For this association within the exegetical tradition and the particularly influential work of Ambrose and Augustine, see Marie-Thérèse d'Alverney, "Comment les theologiens et les philosophes voient la femme," *Cahiers de civilisation médiévale X–XIIe siècles* 20 (1977): 108–9. In the thirteenth century, this exegetical basis for associating femaleness with body (and thereby with sensuality and intellectual inferiority as well) was complemented by the newly available Aristotelian physiological work in which conception was articulated as male semen actively imparting form on shapeless, female matter. See Charles T. Wood, "The Doctors' Dilemma: Sin, Salvation, and the Menstrual Cycle in Medieval Thought," *Speculum* 56 (1981): 715, and Bullough, 487–89. For the impact of this view of women and the connection between Mary and Christ's humanity, see Caroline Walker Bynum, "Women Mystics and Eucharistic Devotion in the Thirteenth Century," *Women's Studies* 11 (1984): 204. A striking example of this connection is Hildegard of Bingen, *Ordo Virtutum*, lines 235–41, ed. Peter Dronke, in his *Poetic Individuality in the Middle Ages: New Departures in Poetry, 1000–1150* (Oxford: Clarendon Press, 1970), 191.

20. Cf. Lewis, 79–80.

21. There is one other place in the visionary texts where Elisabeth offers an image which distinguishes the humanity and divinity of Christ. In a series of visions that appears to come from the same period as the virgin in the sun vision, Elisabeth describes a city which she later understands to be a figure of Christ (*figura domini salvatoris*). The city is surrounded by a gold wall that is "the sign of his precious humanity" ("signum preciose humanitatis eius"). Standing within the wall is a magnificent, high tower that represents the majesty of divinity (*Visionen*, 56–57). Any gender associations in this vision remain unstated. Cf. Hildegard, *Scivias*, 492, a vision of a column that represents the humanity of Christ.

22. Bynum, "Women Mystics and Eucharistic Devotion," 179–214.

23. *Visionen*, 11–12, 15, 21–22, 27.

24. *Visionen*, 27.

25. "Vidi autem in illo excessu meo celos apertos, et dominum Jesum cum infinitis milibus sanctorum. . . . Et non erat ei species neque decor, sed tanquam recenter crucifixus fuisset, sic miserandus apparuit. Cunque demonstrasset universo mundo crucem, in qua pependerat, et vulnera passionis sue quasi recenti cruore madentia, clamabat voce magna ac nimium terribili dicens: Talia propter te sustinui, tu vero, quid pro me sustinuisti?" (*Visionen*, 21).

26. "Serve dei, quid retribues salvatori tuo" (*Visionen*, 98).

27. *Visionen*, 98.

28. See B. D. Napier, "Prophet," *The Interpreter's Dictionary of the Bible*, vol. 3, 912.

29. *Visionen*, 61.

30. "[S]i sui incessabili oratione iram domini non contineret, totus iam mundus pro abundantia iniquitatis sue in perditionem abisset" (*Visionen*, 62).

31. "[V]idi similitudinem regalis femine" (*Visionen*, 5); "vidi dominam meam stantem secus altare in veste qualis est casula sacerdotalis" (p. 6).

32. *Visionen*, 6.

33. *Visionen*, 7.

34. *Visionen*, 53.

35. Quoted in Pelikan, 173.

36. Ripberger, 57–113.

37. Martin Jugie, *La Mort et l'assomption de la sainte vierge: Etude historico-doctrinale* (Vatican: Bibliotheca Apostolica Vaticana, 1944), 276. A similar ambiguity in the nature of *assumptio* is found in art where it is often difficult to distinguish a representation of the ascent of Mary's soul into heaven after her death from an image of the resurrection of her body. The earliest image that can be confidently described as the latter is found in a twelfth-century sacramentary from St. Martin's in Tours. In the late twelfth century, the Assumption motif became conflated with another iconographical theme—the coronation of Mary. See Christa Schaffer, *Koimesis, Der Heimgang Mariens: Das Entschlafungsbild in seiner Abhängigkeit von Legende und Theologie*, Studia Patristica et Liturgica, 15 (Regensburg: Kommissionsverlag Friedrich Pustet, 1985), 107–31.

38. Graef, *Mary*, vol. 1, 222–23.

39. Aelred of Rievaulx, *De Institutione inclusarum*, in *Opera Omnia*, 1, ed. A. Hoste and C. H. Talbot, CCCM 1 (Turnhout: Brepols, 1971), 664.

40. *Visionen*, 54–55.

41. *Visionen*, 54.

42. *Visionen*, 54.

43. Roth, "Seelbuch des ehem. Nonnenklosters Schönau in Nassau, Benedictinerordens," *Studien und Mitteilungen aus dem Benedictiner- und Cistercienser-Orden* 4 (1883): 371. But in a calendar dating from 1462, there is no mention made of the observance (*Visionen*, 168).

44. *Visionen*, 154.

45. Grotefend, vol. 2, pp. 17, 48, 116, 150, 160, 163. The sixteenth-century Pseudo-Bedan martyrology of Cologne also makes reference to this feast (PL 94, col. 1051). On Pseudo-Bede, see Henri Quentin, *Les Martyrologes historiques du Moyen Age: Etude sur la Formation du Martyrologe Romain* (Paris, 1908; rpt. Aalen: Scientia Verlag, 1969), 4 and 468. n. 1.

46. See, e.g., *Visionen*, 44.

47. *Visionen*, 123, 135.

48. Klinkenberg, 163.

49. *Visionen*, 21–22.

50. "[T]anta precordiorum tortura me arripi, ut morti proximam me existimarem" (*Visionen*, 3); "gravissima cordis tortione arrepta sum, ita ut morituram me estimarem" (p. 12); "amplius anxiari cepi quam antea, ita ut mori me estima-

rent" (p. 23); "me febris valida apprehendit, et desideravi unctionis sacramentum" (p. 31); "ita aggravatus est languor meus, ut venirent ad stratum meum sorores ac dicerent letanium super me" (p. 32); "indubitanter morituram me existimabam" (p. 37).

51. Jacques Le Goff, *The Birth of Purgatory*, trans. Arthur Goldhammer (Chicago: University of Chicago Press, 1984), 154–68, et passim.

52. These remarks are not addressed to LeGoff's overarching scheme, in which he forged a link between the "birth of purgatory" and the three-tiered economic stratification of twelfth-century society. I am concerned here only with his characterization of the development of a religious idea. For other views of how traditional the idea of purgatory was before the 1170s, see A. Ja. Gurevich, "Popular and Scholarly Medieval Cultural Traditions: Notes in the Margin of Jacques Le-Goff's Book," *Journal of Medieval History* 9 (1983): 71–90; Brian Patrick McGuire, "Purgatory, the Communion of Saints, and Medieval Change," *Viator* 20 (1989): 61–84.

53. For *purgatorium*, see *Visionen*, 66. Once LeGoff determined that the word was not used before 1170, he dismissed occurrences of the term in earlier writers as later scribal substitutions. None of the three MSS that transmit this vision of Elisabeth is earlier than 1170, so none would escape LeGoff's razor.

54. "Locus autem, qui medius videbatur inter hoc edificium et vallem predictam, spinis asperrimis et quasi ambustis totus videbatur occupatus. Cumque hec aspicerem ecce copiosa multitudo candide plebis de valle consurgens, per medium invii illius dumeti cum magna festinatione, [et multo conatu ad edificium predictum], tendere visa est, tandemque perveniens introivit. Quidam autem ex eis extra sentes viam elegerunt, et absque labore pervenerunt. Factus est autem hic transitus pluribus vicibus et per intervalla" (*Visionen*, 17). The phrase in brackets does not appear in Vienna, Österr. Nationalbibliothek Vindob. Pal. MS 488, fol. 63r.

55. *Visionen*, 88–89.

56. E.g., *Visionen*, 43, 48, 50; cf. 56–60, where the image shifts from *edificium* to *urbs* or *civitas*.

57. *Visionen*, 47, 101.

58. "[G]rave tormentum in ore habentem, atque ita eum torqueri dicebat propter verba indisciplinata, que habebat in consuetudine" (*Visionen*, 49).

59. *Visionen*, 49. Later under Ekbert's guidance, when Elisabeth is considering the role of guardian angels, she will announce that twice a year souls in purgatorial torment receive consolation: on the feast of Saint Michael (September 29) and on the day of the dead (November 2) (*Visionen*, 70). The notion of a weekly, Sunday respite in hell and its association with Saint Michael can be found in various Latin redactions of the *Visio Sancti Pauli*, dating from the ninth to the eleventh century. See Theodore Silverstein, *Visio Sancti Pauli: The History of the Apocalypse in Latin Together with Nine Texts* (London: Christophers, 1935), 9–10, 79–81.

60. One soul requires the celebration of thirty masses (*Visionen*, 49), which suggests the so-called "Gregorian masses"—masses on thirty consecutive days, which became a very popular form of suffrage by the high Middle Ages. See Daniel Callam, "Purgatory, Western Concept of," *Dictionary of the Middle Ages*, vol. 10, p. 216. Cf. Gregory the Great, *Dialogi*, IV, 57.

61. Elisabeth herself distinguished between the Eucharist and the Mass. The most explicit example is found in a record of her visions which took place when the celebration of the Mass was suspended at Schönau. Although Mass was not celebrated, the nuns received communion from a pyx. Elisabeth reports that while the pyx was on the altar, a ray of light shone down from heaven upon it, a white dove flew down from heaven and sat beside it on the altar, and "the angel of the Lord, as if a witness to our devotion, came and stood by the altar until all of us in order had received communion" ("Venit et angelus domini, et quasi devotionis nostre testis, astitit secus altare, quousque omnes per ordinem communicavimus" *Visionen*, 35).

62. "[U]t ad honorem dei pro nostra et omnium fidelium defunctorum liberatione sacrificium divinum offerret" (*Visionen*, 43).

63. "[I]pse devota mente convenientes corporalem afflictionem communiter pro eis susceperunt et diviso inter se psalterio cum omni diligentia dominum pro earum liberatione deprecate sunt" (*Visionen*, 43).

64. *Visionen*, 46.

65. Cf. McGuire, "Purgatory, the Communion of Saints, and Medieval Change," 68, who considers the development of the traditions of purgatory and the communion of saints to have offered a greater optimism to men and women about shaping their own lives.

66. "Quicquid mihi preter illum panem vite et calicem salutis exhibetur, talem michi virtutem prestat, qualis datur homini famelico, si absque pane et vino aliis reficitur alimentis" (*Visionen*, 49).

67. *Visionen*, 28.

68. Ekbert also devoted one of his thirteen anti-Cathar sermons (written in 1163–64), to affirming the existence of purgatorial punishments in response to the Cathar assertion that at the hour of death souls pass immediately into eternal blessedness or damnation (PL 195, col. 15, 55–69).

69. LeGoff, 134–35, 146–47.

70. LeGoff is not primarily interested in the effects this theological development might have had on women's spirituality, but Elisabeth's visions present a concrete example of such a situation. In a different context, LeGoff cites the very interesting story of the mother of Guibert of Nogent without noting a significant point. To free her husband from the purgative torments he was enduring after death, Guibert's mother undertook certain trials in her own life. For his sin of begetting an illegitimate child, she adopted and raised a troublesome, orphaned baby. There is no ecclesiastical component to her plan for liberating her husband—no Masses, no alms given to the church. It is not surprising that this type of offering which emphasized her female role as mother is found in a text that significantly predated the emergence of the scholastically articulated concept of purgatory.

71. Cf. Jo Ann McNamara, "The Need to Give: Suffering and Female Sanctity in the Middle Ages," in *Images of Sainthood in Medieval Europe*, ed. Renate Blumenfeld-Kosinski and Timea Szell (Ithaca, NY: Cornell University Press, 1991), 199–221.

72. *Visionen*, 36–37.

73. *Visionen*, 42–43.

74. "Anime mee fideliter et cum seria mente curam gerite, neque aliquid negligatis ex his, que pertinent ad debitum meum, pro eo, quod estimetis, non indigere me suffragiis orationum vestrarum. Hoc autem dico, quia sepe, qui religiosi videntur, negligi solent, dum hi, qui eorum bonam conversationem cognoverunt, cogitant, non eos magnopere indigere adiutorio ipsorum" (*Visionen*, 268). Cf. her similar concern about young children in purgatory who will not be prayed for because of their ostensible innocence (*Visionen*, 121–22).

75. For the popularity of this motif in twelfth-century secular as well as religious texts, see Southern, *The Making of the Middle Ages*, 222.

76. See, e.g., *Visionen*, 47.

77. For the importance in later medieval preaching of this threefold distinction found in Gregory's *Regulae pastoralis liber*, see Longère, 32–33. Cf. the variation on this threefold scheme which Gregory VII uses in service of arguing for clerical celibacy in his letter to Otto of Constance, JL 4970. See *The Epistolae Vagantes of Pope Gregory VII*, ed. H. E. J. Cowdrey (Oxford: Clarendon Press, 1972), 18–22.

78. *Visionen*, 94.

79. "[I]n omnibus viis veritatis contemplandus est deus" (*Visionen*, 90).

80. "Propter hoc ecce contemptum patitur religio, et fides scissuram" (*Visionen*, 93).

81. "Caput ecclesie elanguit, et membra illius mortua sunt, quoniam sedes apostolica obsessa est superbia, et colitur avaricia, et repleta est iniquitate et impietate et scandalizant oves meas, et errare eas faciunt, quas custodire et regere debuerunt" (*Visionen*, 113).

82. *Visionen*, 74.

83. *Visionen*, 113.

84. "[U]t hec verba, que inveneritis in presenti libro, annuntietis Romane ecclesie totique populo, et omni ecclesie dei" (*Visionen*, 122).

85. "Iterum admonet te idem dominus dicens: Redde rationem, quia defraudasti michi margaritas electas, et gemmas preciosas, que tibi misse fuerant de magne maiestatis potentia, proiecisti post tergum tuum, et noluisti obedire mihi. Nonne tu scis, quia dixi: Abscondisti hec a sapientibus et prudentibus et revelasti ea parvulis? Recipe et revolve volumen et invenies, que dixi, et facta sunt. Sedes apostolica obsessa est superbia, et colitur avaricia, et cetera. Quod si non indicabis eis, que tibi revelata sunt, et ipsi in peccatis suis moriuntur, iudicium dei portabis" (*Visionen*, 140).

86. "Et notum sit tibi, quod, qui electus est a Cesare, ipse acceptabilior est ante me" (*Visionen*, 140). For Hillin's support of Victor and his subsequent support of Alexander III after Victor's death in 1164, see Hilpisch, 9–21.

87. I. S. Robinson, *Authority and Resistance in the Investiture Contest: The Polemical Literature of the Late Eleventh Century* (Manchester: Manchester University Press, 1978), 169–75.

88. Munz, 125–26, 188–93.

89. See, e.g., Roth, *Visionen*, XCIX–C.

90. "Ecce enim effusa est contentio super principes principalis ecclesie, que

omnium mater est, et sciderunt unitatem summi sacerdocii, ruperunt vinculum pacis ecclesiastice, ita ut invicem mordeant, invicem se interficiant, anathemathizando alterutrum. Est tamen incertum, que duarum partium percutiat in gladio Petri, cum nec possit in partes dividi, nec indivisus sibi adversari" (*Visionen*, 315).

91. For the widespread opinion of Rainald's responsibility, see Munz, 213.

92. Cf. Munz, 289.

93. For the double election and Frederick Barbarossa's subsequent support of Victor IV, see Munz, 205–19.

94. For this first papal declaration against the Cathars, see Robert Somerville, *Pope Alexander III and the Council of Tours (1163): A Study of Ecclesiastical Politics and Institutions* (Berkeley: University of California Press, 1977), 50–53.

95. *Visionen*, 111–17.

96. For the significance of the papal mantle, see Robert L. Benson, *The Bishop-Elect: A Study in Medieval Ecclesiastical Office* (Princeton, NJ: Princeton University Press, 1968), 150–56.

97. *Visionen*, 95–96.

98. *Visionen*, 122.

99. "[Q]uia sciebat eum ab infancia delicate educatum; . . . ne rigorem regule nostre in ieiuniis et vigiliis et in abstinenciis possit sustinere" (*Vita Eckeberti*, 450).

100. *Visionen*, 119. Cf. *Regula Sancti Benedicti*, ch. 66, p. 136.

101. Cf. *Regula Benedicti*, ch. 64, p. 130.

102. *Visionen*, 119.

103. Henrietta Leyser, *Hermits and the New Monasticism: A Study of Religious Communities in Western Europe, 1000–1150* (New York: St. Martin's Press, 1984), 18–22, 87–96.

104. On the misperceptions surrounding the "new hermits," see Leyser, 78–86.

105. "[A]d nihilum utilis, nisi ad suffocandos partus" (*Visionen*, 102).

106. For Hildegard's critique of the effeminate age, see Newman, *Sister of Wisdom*, 238–49.

107. "Pronus est per se omnis caro in malum" (*Visionen*, 122).

108. *Visionen*, 92–93.

109. *Cenum*, following Douai, Bibl. Municipale MS 865, fol. 142v; Paris, Bibl. de l'Université MS 790, fol. 81r; Fulda, Hessische Landesbibliothek MS Aa96, fol. 157rb; Cf. *scenum* in *Visionen*, 108.

110. *Visionen*, 121–22.

111. John F. Benton, "Consciousness of Self and Perceptions of Individuality," in Benson and Constable, eds., *Renaissance and Renewal in the Twelfth Century*, 271–74.

112. *Visionen*, 109–10. Cf., e.g., Aelred of Rievaulx, *De Institutione inclusarum*, 656; Peter Abelard, *Institutio seu Regula Sanctimonialium*, ed. T. P. McLaughlin, *Medieval Studies* 18 (1956): 243. See Clarissa W. Atkinson, "'Precious Balsam in a Fragile Glass': The Ideology of Virginity in the Later Middle Ages," *Journal of Family History* 8 (1983): 131–43, for a range of physical and moral definitions of virginity.

113. John Bugge, *Virginitas: An Essay in the History of a Medieval Ideal*, Archives internationales d'histoire des idées: Series Minor, 17 (The Hague: Martinus Nijhoff, 1975), esp. 30–58. Cf. Bynum, *Holy Feast and Holy Fast*, 1.

114. "Horum [i.e., continentium] etenim proprium est a curis et sollicitudinibus vite presentis mentem abstrahere, et sola, que domini sunt, cogitare, ut sint sancti corpore et spiritu" (*Visionen*, 90).

115. *Visionen*, 143.

116. Cf. Giles Constable, "Opposition to Pilgrimage in the Middle Ages," *Studia Gratiana* 19 (1976), rpt. in Constable, *Religious Life and Thought (11th-12th Centuries)* (London: Variorum Reprints, 1979).

117. Robert E. Lerner, *The Powers of Prophecy: The Cedar of Lebanon Vision from the Mongol Onslaught to the Dawn of the Enlightenment* (Berkeley: University of California Press, 1983), 196.

Conclusion

1. "[Q]uerebat audire consilium eius, quia sciebat, eam esse magne sapientie mulierem" (*Visionen*, 132).

2. "Illa autem divina virtute inspirata, et intelligens, verbum exisse a domino" (*Visionen*, 132).

3. "Eius itaque consiliis totus ille sacer exercitus virginum collectus et ordinatus est, et erat ductrix omnium in cunctis viis peregrinationis earum per consiliorum suorum gubernationem et ad ultimum martirium cum eis passa est" (Vienna, Österr. Nationalbibliothek Vindob. Pal. MS 488, fol. 153v. Similar readings are found in Fulda, Hessische Landesbibliothek MS Aa 96, fol. 145ra and Douai, Bibliothèque Municipale MS 865, fol. 161r–161v. Cf. *Visionen*, 132, and St. Omer, Bibliothèque Municipale MS 710, fol. 116rb–116va.)

4. "[E]rat de fideli radice Aaron, et habebat spiritum domini habundanter" (*Visionen*, 132).

5. Cf. Constable, "Forgery and Plagiarism in the Middle Ages," 9.

6. In the first vision of the *Scivias* (p. 8), Hildegard reports she has been divinely commissioned to announce her revelation because others are tepid and dull in preaching God's justice.

Appendix

1. Cf. Köster (1952), 93. The last event recorded in these texts is March 25, 1159. Köster suggests 1160. The first outside evidence for the existence of a collection is Ekbert's letter to Reinhard of Reinhausen (1164/65, before Elisabeth's death), in which he directs Reinhard to the abbey of Pöhlde if he is interested in seeking a copy of Elisabeth's works.

2. For Ekbert's vision at the monastery at Deutz, see Roth (1911), 222–23.

3. Redaction B includes the entire British transmission of Elisabeth's

visions, all of which derive from the original MS sent by Roger of Ford to his abbot Baldwin.

4. The year of Ekbert's death is 1184.

5. Pitra, 348–51.

6. In the prologue to the collection which appears only in this redaction, Ekbert describes himself as abbot of Schönau, thus dating this redaction to 1166 or thereafter.

7. Köster (1952), 94.

8. MSS 4, 6a, and 6b in Köster (1951), 252–54.

9. It appears that the author of *De secunda assumptione*, the versified abridgment of Elisabeth's *De Resurrectione* knew the text as it appeared in this special transmission which did not include *LVD*. The author of *De secunda assumptione* dates the visions about Mary not in relation to the composition of the *LVD*, as *De resurrectione Marie* does in its fullest version (i.e., the version of Redaction A where these references have not been omitted as they were in the St. Omer MS), but rather dates it in relation to *Revelatio*. Thus the author of *De secunda assumptione* refers to Elisabeth seeing visions about Mary and about Ursula, but shows no awareness of the *LVD*, the longest of the visionary texts. Also, *De secunda assumptione* describes the Marian visions occurring after the Ursuline visions. The only reason for concluding that the Marian visions followed the Ursuline visions would be that in a MS the text of *De Resurrectione* came after *Revelatio*, an arrangement that never occurs in the standard version of Redaction A, but occurs in two of the three MSS of Redaction F. The likelihood that the author of *De secunda assumptione* used a MS of this special transmission whose circulation was limited to northern France and Belgium may modify Köster's suggestion that the versified abridgment originated in Austria.

10. *Visionen*, 272.

11. *Visionen*, 272.

12. This MS has most recently been discussed in Franz Unterkircher, "Zwei Vers-Viten des 13 Jhs. (Hl. Ursula und Hl. Euphrosyne) in der Wiener Handschrift Cod. 488," *Analecta Bollandiana* 88 (1970): 301–16.

13. The description of H$_{II}$ is given in Köster (1951), 124. The contents of the MS are listed as *Vita Christi ancille Marie de Oegenes; Item visiones ste. Elizabeth*. Vienna, Österr. Nationalbibliothek Vindob. Pal. MS 488 is comprised of the *Vita* of Mary of Oignies, a poem about the Cologne martyrdom, and the visions of Elisabeth. The date of the Eberbach catalogue is 1502, and Vienna MS 488 was not acquired by the Bibliotheca Palatina in Vienna until 1575–1608.

14. The Cistercian monastery at Eberbach was less than twenty kilometers from Schönau, which makes it a not unlikely site for a manuscript of Redaction E, which had such limited circulation outside of Schönau. Also, the cloister at Eberbach received relics from the Cologne excavation of the Ursuline martyrdom, and some monasteries and churches that possessed such relics also acquired books which recounted some version of the Ursula legend, such as Elisabeth's *Revelatio*. More conclusive evidence may be discovered when a transmission history is worked out for the *Vita Marie Oigniacensis*.

15. Köster (1952), 90–91.

16. Köster (1952), 103, n. 91. The abbey of Odenheim received relics from the Cologne site, and Abbot Burchard wrote to Elisabeth seeking background information on the lives of his new patrons. But there is no MS of Elisabeth's visions associated with Odenheim. Elisabeth's response to Burchard is preserved in a collection of Ursuline materials from the Benedictine abbey of St. Magnus in Füssen and printed in Schmitz, 181–83.

Bibliography

MANUSCRIPTS CONSULTED

MANUSCRIPTS TRANSMITTING ELISABETH'S WORKS

Avignon, Bibliothèque municipale MS 593.
Cologne, Stadtarchiv MS GB 8° 60.
Cologne, Stadtarchiv MS GB f° 86.
Cologne, Stadtarchiv MS GB 4°214.
Cologne, Stadtarchiv MS W133.
Cologne, Stadtarchiv MS W164 A.
Douai, Bibliothèque municipale MS 865.
Fulda, Hessische Landesbibliothek MS Aa96.
Halle (Saale), Universitäts- und Landesbibliothek Sachsen-Anhalt MS Yc 4°6.
Munich, Bayerische Staatsbibliothek MS CLM 324.
Munich, Bayerische Staatsbibliothek MS CLM 2610.
Munich, Bayerische Staatsbibliothek MS CLM 4405.
Munich, Bayerische Staatsbibliothek MS CLM 4723.
Munich, Bayerische Staatsbibliothek MS CLM 18626.
Munich, Bayerische Staatsbibliothek MS CLM 22253.
Oxford, Bodleian Library MS Bodl. 83.
Paris, Bibliothèque de l'Université MS 790.
St. Omer, Bibliothèque municipale MS 710.
Trier, Bistumsarchiv MS 10.
Trier, Stadtbibliothek MS 718/273 4°.
Trier, Stadtbibliothek MS 771/1350 8°.
Trier, Stadtbibliothek MS 1143/445 8°.
Trier, Stadtbibliothek MS 1173/475 8°.
Vienna, Österreichische Nationalbibliothek Vindob. Pal. MS 488.
Wiesbaden, Hessische Landesbibliothek MS 4.

OTHER MANUSCRIPTS

Trier Stadtbibliothek MS 646/869 8° (text of Hildegard of Bingen attributed to
    Elisabeth of Schönau).
Trier, Stadtbibliothek MS 229/1397 8° (sermons of Ekbert of Schönau).

PRIMARY SOURCES

Abelard, Peter. *Commentaria in epistolam Pauli ad Romanos*. In *Opera Theologica*, vol. 1. Edited by E. M. Buytaert. CCCM 11. Turnholt: Brepols, 1969.

———. *Institutio seu regula sanctimonialium*. Edited by T. P. McLaughlin. *Medieval Studies* 18 (1956): 241–92.

———. *Sermo in assumptione beate Mariae*. PL 178, col. 539–47.

Aelred of Rievaulx. *De Institutione inclusarum*. In *Opera Omnia*, vol. 1. Edited by A. Hoste and C. H. Talbot. CCCM 1. Turnhout: Brepols, 1971.

Alberic of Trois Fontaines. *Chronica*. Edited by P. Scheffer-Boischorst. MGH, SS, 23, 674–950. 1874.

Annales Palidenses. Edited by G. H. Pertz. MGH, SS, 16, 48–96. 1859.

Annalista Saxo. Edited by G. H. Waitz. MGH, SS, 6, 550–777. 1844.

Apocalyptic Spirituality: Treatises and Letters of Lactantius, Adso of Montier-en-Der, Joachim of Fiore, the Franciscan Spirituals, Savonarola. Translated by Bernard McGinn. New York: Paulist Press, 1979.

Augustine. *De Genesi ad litteram*. PL 34, col. 220–485.

Bernard of Clairvaux. *Five Books on Consideration: Advice to a Pope*. Translated by John D. Anderson and Elizabeth T. Kennan. Cistercian Fathers Series, no. 37. Kalamazoo, MI: Cistercian Publications, 1976.

———. *On the Song of Songs*. Translated by Killian Walsh and Irene Edmonds. Cistercian Fathers Series, nos. 4, 7, 31, 40. Kalamazoo, MI: Cistercian Publications, 1971–80.

———. *Sancti Bernardi Opera*. Vols. 1–2. Edited by J. Leclercq, C. H. Talbot, and H. M. Rochais. Rome: Editiones Cistercienses, 1957–58.

Caesarius of Heisterbach. *Dialogus miraculorum*. 2 vols. Edited by Joseph Strange. Cologne: H. Lempertz & Comp., 1851.

Chronica Regia Coloniensis. Edited by George Waitz. Scriptores Rerum Germanicarum in Usum Scholarum, vol. 18. Hanover: Bibliopolium Hahianionum, 1880.

De SS. Ursula et Sociabus. AASS. October 9, 73–303.

Ekbert of Schönau. *Sermones contra catharos*. PL 195, col. 11–102.

Emecho of Schönau. *Vita Eckeberti*. Edited by S. Widmann. *Neues Archiv der Gesellschaft für ältere deutsche Geschichtskunde* 11 (1886): 447–54.

The Epistolae Vagantes of Pope Gregory VII. Edited and translated by H. E. J. Cowdrey. Oxford: Clarendon Press, 1972.

Gregory the Great. *Dialogues*. Translated by Odo John Zimmerman. New York: Fathers of the Church, Inc., 1959.

———. *Dialogues. Texte critique, notes, et traduction*. Edited by Adalbert de Vogue. Translated by Paul Antin. SC 251, 260, 265. Paris: Les Editions du Cerf, 1980.

———. *Homélies sur Ezéchiel. Texte latin, introduction, traduction et notes*. Edited by Charles Morel. SC 327. Paris: Les Editions du Cerf, 1986.

Guibert of Gembloux. *Epistolae*. 2 vols. Edited by Albert Derolez. CCCM 66. Turnholt: Brepols, 1988–89.

Günther, Wilhelm. *Codex Diplomaticus Rheno-Mosellanus*. Vol. I. Coblenz: B. Heriot, 1822.

Hermannus quondam Judaeus: Opusculum de conversione sua. Edited by Gerlinde Niemeyer. MGH, Geistesgeschichte, 4. 1963.

Hildegard of Bingen. *Analecta Sanctae Hildegardis.* Edited by J.-B. Pitra. Analecta Sacra, vol. 8. Monte Cassino, 1882. Reprint. Farnborough: Gregg Press Limited, 1966.

———. *Briefwechsel.* Translated by Adelgundis Führkötter. Salzburg: Muller, 1965.

———. *Epistolarium: Pars Prima I–XC.* Edited by Lieven Van Acker. CCCM 91. Turnholt: Brepols, 1991.

———. *Opera.* PL 197.

———. *Scivias.* Edited by Adelgundis Führkötter and Angela Carlevaris. CCCM 43. Turnholt: Brepols, 1978.

———. *Symphonia: A Critical Edition of the "Symphonia armonie celestium revelationum."* Edited and translated by Barbara Newman. Ithaca, NY: Cornell University Press, 1988.

Jacques de Vitry. *Vita Mariae Oigniacensis.* AASS. June 5, 542–72.

Libellus de diversis ordinibus et professionibus qui sunt in aecclesia. Edited and translated by G. Constable and B. Smith. Oxford: Clarendon Press, 1972.

Medieval Women Writers. Edited by Katharina M. Wilson. Athens: University of Georgia Press, 1984.

Medieval Women's Visionary Literature. Edited by Elizabeth Alvilda Petroff. New York: Oxford University Press, 1986.

Mittelalterliche Bibliothekskataloge Deutschlands und der Schweiz. Vol. 2. Edited by Paul Lehmann. Munich: C. H. Beck, 1928.

Oliger, P. Livarius. "Revelationes B. Elisabeth: Disquisitio critica una cum textibus latino et catalaunensi." *Antonianum* 1 (1926): 24–83.

Otto of Freising. *The Deeds of Frederick Barbarossa.* Translated by Charles Christopher Mierow. Records of Civilization, Sources and Studies, no. 49. New York: Columbia University Press, 1953.

———. *Gesta Friderici I Imperatoris.* Edited by R. Wilmans. MGH, SS, 20, 347–493. 1868.

Poem on the Assumption. Edited by J. P. Strachey. *Poem on the Day of Judgment.* Edited by H. J. Chaytor. *Divisiones Mundi.* Edited by O. H. Prior. Cambridge: Cambridge University Press, 1924.

The Prefatory Epistles of Jacques Lefèvre d'Etaples and Related Texts. Edited by Eugene F. Rice, Jr. New York: Columbia University Press, 1972.

Regula Sancti Benedicti. Edited by Adalbert de Vogue and Jean Neufville. In *RB 1980: The Rule of Saint Benedict.* Edited by Timothy Fry. Collegeville, MN: The Liturgical Press, 1981.

Rigg, A. G. "Roger of Ford's Poem on the Virgin: A Critical Edition," *Cîteaux* 40 (1989): 200–13.

Roth, F. W. E. "Aus einer Handschrift der Schriften der heil. Elisabeth von Schönau." *Neues Archiv der Gesellschaft für ältere deutsche Geschichteskunde* 36 (1911): 219–25.

———. *Das Gebetbuch der hl. Elisabeth von Schönau, nach der Originalhandschrift des XII. Jahrhunderts.* Augsburg: Verlag des Literarischen Instituts von Dr. Max Huttler, 1886.

————. "Seelbuch des ehem. Nonnenklosters Schönau in Nassau, Benedictinerordens." *Studien und Mitteilungen aus dem Benedictiner- und Cistercienser-Orden* 4 (1883): 357–76.

Roth, F. W. E., ed. *Die Visionen der hl. Elisabeth und die Schriften der Aebte Ekbert und Emecho von Schönau.* Brünn: Verlag der Studien aus dem Benedictiner- und Cistercienser-Orden, 1884.

Schmitz, Ph. "'Visions' inédites de Sainte Elisabeth de Schoenau." *Revue Bénédictine* 47 (1935): 181–83.

Self and Society in Medieval France: The Memoirs of Abbot Guibert of Nogent (1064?-c. 1125). Edited by John F. Benton. New York: Harper Torchbooks, 1970.

Thioderic of Deutz. *Opuscula.* Edited by O. Holder-Egger. MGH, SS, 14, 652–664. 1883.

Tisset, Pierre. *Procès de condamnation de Jeanne d'Arc.* Paris: Libraire C. Klincksieck, 1960.

Visions of Heaven and Hell Before Dante. Edited by Eileen Gardiner. New York: Italica Press, 1989.

William of Newburg. *Historia rerum anglicarum.* Edited by Richard Howlett. Rolls Series 82, 1.

SECONDARY SOURCES

Allen, Prudence. *The Concept of Woman: The Aristotelian Revolution, 750 BC to AD 1250.* Montreal: Eden Press, 1985.

Alphandéry, Paul. "De quelque faits de prophétism dans les sectes latines antérieures au Joachisme." *Revue de l'histoire des religions* 52 (1905): 193–94.

————. "La Glossolalie dans le prophetism médiéval latin." *Revue de l'historie des religions* 103 (1931): 417–36.

————. "Prophètes et ministère prophetique dans le moyen âge latin." *Revue de l'histoire des religions* 52 (1905): 187–218.

Amort, Eusebius. *De revelationibus, visionibus et apparitionibus privatis.* 1744. Reprint. AASS. October 9, 82–85.

Arbesmann, Rudolph. "Fasting and Prophecy in Pagan and Christian Antiquity." *Traditio* 7 (1949–51): 1–72.

Ash, James L., Jr. "The Decline of Ecstatic Prophecy in the Early Church." *Theological Studies* 37 (1976): 227–52.

Atkinson, Clarissa. "'Precious Balsam in a Fragile Glass': The Ideology of Virginity in the Later Middle Ages." *Journal of Family History* 8 (1983): 131–43.

Backmund, Norbert. *Monasticon Praemonstratense.* 3 vols. Straubing: Cl. Attenkofersche Buchdruckerei, 1949–56.

Barrow, Julia. "Education and the Recruitment of Cathedral Canons in England and Germany 1100–1225." *Viator* 20 (1989): 117–38.

Becker, Petrus. "Die Abstreihe von St. Eucharius in Trier (Die ersten 160 Jahren)." *Kurtrierisches Jahrbuch* 3 (1971): 24–37.

————. "Die Hirsauische Erneuerung des St. Euchariusklosters in Trier." *Studia Anselmiana* 85 (1982): 185–206.

Benson, Robert L. *The Bishop-Elect: A Study in Medieval Ecclesiastical Office*. Princeton, NJ: Princeton University Press, 1968.

Benson, Robert L., and Giles Constable, eds. *Renaissance and Renewal in the Twelfth Century*. Cambridge, MA: Harvard University Press, 1982.

Benton, John F. "A Reconsideration of the Authenticity of the Correspondence of Abelard and Heloise." In *Petrus Abaelardus: Person, Werk und Wirkung*, edited by Rudolf Thomas, 41–52. Trierer Theologisches Studien, 38. Trier: Paulinus-Verlag, 1980.

Benz, Ernst. *Die Vision: Erfahrungsformen und Bilderwelt*. Stuttgart: Ernst Klett Verlag, 1969.

Berliner, Rudolf. "God is Love." *Gazette des Beaux-Arts* 42 (1953): 9–26.

Bernards, Matthäus. *Speculum Virginum: Geistigkeit und Seelenleben der Frau im Hochmittelalter*. Beihefte zum Archiv für Kulturgeschichte, Heft 16. 2d ed. Vienna: Böhlau Verlag, 1982.

Bernhardi, Wilhelm. *Lothar von Supplinburg*. 1879. Reprint. Berlin: Duncker und Humbolt, 1975.

Bibliotheca Hagiographica Latina Antiquae et Mediae Aetatis. 2 vols. Brussels: n.p., 1898–1911.

Bloomfield, Morton W. "Joachim of Flora: A Critical Survey of his Canon, Teachings, Sources, Biography and Influence." *Traditio* 13 (1957): 249–311.

Bogdanos, Theodore. "'The Shepherd of Hermas' and the Development of Medieval Visionary Allegory." *Viator* 8 (1977): 33–46.

Bouchard, Constance Brittain. *Spirituality and Administration: The Role of the Bishop in Twelfth-Century Auxerre*. Speculum Anniversary Monographs, 5. Cambridge, MA: Medieval Academy of America, 1979.

Bugge, John. *Virginitas: An Essay in the History of a Medieval Ideal*. Archives internationales d'histoire des idées: Series Minor 17. The Hague: Martinus Nijhoff, 1975.

Bullough, Vern L. "Medieval Medical and Scientific Views of Women." *Viator* 4 (1973): 485–501.

Bynum, Caroline Walker. *Holy Feast and Holy Fast: The Religious Significance of Food to Medieval Women*. Berkeley: University of California Press, 1987.

———. *Jesus as Mother: Studies in the Spirituality of the High Middle Ages*. Berkeley: University of California Press, 1982.

———. "Women Mystics and Eucharistic Devotion in the Thirteenth Century." *Women's Studies* 11 (1984): 179–214.

———. "Women's Stories, Women's Symbols: A Critique of Victor Turner's Theory of Liminality." In *Anthropology and the Study of Religion*, edited by Robert L. Moore and Frank E. Reynolds, 105–125. Chicago: Center for the Scientific Study of Religion, 1984.

Callam, Daniel. "Purgatory, Western Concept of." *Dictionary of the Middle Ages*, edited by Joseph R. Strayer. New York: Charles Scribner's Sons, 1982.

Cheney, Christopher R. *Handbook of Dates for Students of English History*. London: Offices of the Royal Historical Society, 1955.

Chenu, M.-D. *Nature, Man, and Society in the Twelfth Century: Essays on New Theo-*

logical Perspectives in the Latin West. Translated by Jerome Taylor and Lester K. Little. Chicago: University of Chicago Press, 1968.

Chodorow, Stanley. *Christian Political Theory and Church Politics in the Mid-Twelfth Century: The Ecclesiology of Gratian's Decretum*. Berkeley: University of California Press, 1972.

Cizewski, Wanda. "Adam of the Little Bridge." *Dictionary of the Middle Ages*, edited by Joseph R. Strayer. New York: Charles Scribner's Sons, 1982.

Cohn, Norman. *The Pursuit of the Millennium*. 2d ed. New York: Harper and Row Publishers, 1961.

Constable, Giles. "Forgery and Plagiarism in the Middle Ages." *Archiv für Diplomatik, Schriftgeschichte, Siegel- und Wappenkunde* 29 (1983): 1–41.

———. "Opposition to Pilgrimage in the Middle Ages," *Studia Gratiana* 19 (1976). Reprint. Constable, *Religious Life and Thought (11th–12th Centuries)*. London: Variorum Reprints, 1979.

———. "Renewal and Reform in Religious Life." In *Renaissance and Renewal in the Twelfth Century*, edited by Robert L. Benson and Giles Constable, 37–67. Cambridge, MA: Harvard University Press, 1982.

———. "Twelfth-Century Spirituality and the Late Middle Ages." *Medieval and Renaissance Studies*, Vol. 5, edited by O. B. Hardison, 27–60. Chapel Hill: University of North Carolina Press, 1969.

d'Alverny, Marie-Thérèse. "Comment les théologiens et les philosophes voient la femme." *Cahiers de civilisation médiévale X–XIIe siècles* 20 (1977): 105–29.

d'Avray, D. L., and M. Tausche. "Marriage Sermons in *Ad Status* Collections of the Central Middle Ages." *Archives d'histoire doctrinale et littéraire du Moyen Age* 47 for 1980 (1981): 71–119.

Dean, Ruth J. "Elizabeth, Abbess of Schönau, and Roger of Ford." *Modern Philology* 41 (1944): 209–20.

———. "Manuscripts of St. Elizabeth of Schönau in England." *Modern Language Review* 32 (1937): 62–71.

de Fontette, Micheline. *Les Religieuses à l'âge classique du droit canon: Recherches sur les structures juridiques des branches féminines des ordres*. Paris: Librairie Philosophique J. Vrin, 1967.

Deikman, Arthur. "De-automatization and the Mystic Experience." *Psychiatry* 29 (1966): 324–38.

Dinzelbacher, Peter. *Vision und Visionsliteratur im Mittelalter*. Monographien zur Geschichte des Mittelalters, 23. Stuttgart: Anton Hiersemann, 1981.

Dinzelbacher, Peter, and Dieter R. Bauer, eds. *Frauenmystik im Mittelalter*. Ostfildern: Schwabenverlag, 1985.

———, eds. *Religiöse Frauenbewegung und mystische Frömmigkeit im Mittelalter*. Cologne and Vienna: Böhlau Verlag, 1988.

Döllinger, John J. von. *Die Papst-Fabeln des Mittelalters: Ein Beitrag zur Kirchengeschichte*. 1863. Reprint. Frankfurt: Minerva Verlag, 1962.

———. *Prophecies and the Prophetic Spirit in the Christian Era: An Historical Essay*. Translated by Alfred Plummer. London: Rivertons, 1873.

Dronke, Peter. *Poetic Individuality in the Middle Ages: New Departures in Poetry, 1000–1150*. Oxford: Clarendon Press, 1970.

———. *Women Writers of the Middle Ages: A Critical Study of Texts from Perpetua (d. 203) to Marguerite Porete (d. 1310)*. Cambridge: Cambridge University Press, 1984.

Ehlers, Joachim. "Deutsche Scholaren in Frankreich während des 12. Jahrhunderts." In *Schulen und Studium in Sozialen Wandel des Hohen und Späten Mittelalters*, edited by Johannes Fried, 97–120. Vorträge und Forschungen, 30. Sigmaringen: Jan Thorbecke Verlag, 1986.

Elkins, Sharon K. *Holy Women of Twelfth-Century England*. Chapel Hill: University of North Carolina Press, 1988.

Ennen, Edith. *Frauen im Mittelalter*. Munich: Verlag C. H. Beck, 1984.

Farmer, Hugh. "The Vision of Orm." *Analecta Bollandiana* 75 (1957): 72–82.

Ferrante, Joan M. "The Education of Women in the Middle Ages in Theory, Fact and Fiction." In *Beyond Their Sex: Learned Women from the European Past*, edited by Patricia H. Labalme, 9–42. New York and London: New York University Press, 1980.

Flanagan, Sabina. *Hildegard of Bingen, 1098–1179: A Visionary Life*. London: Routledge, 1989.

Flint, Valerie I. J. *Ideas in the Medieval West*. Variorum Collected Studies Series. London: Variorum Reprints, 1988.

From the High Middle Ages to the Eve of the Reformation. Vol. 4 of *History of the Church*, edited by Hubert Jedin and John Dolan. Translated by Anselm Biggs. New York: Crossroad, 1986.

Germania Pontificia, Vol. IV, Part IV, edited by Hermannus Jakobs. Göttingen: Vandenhoeck et Ruprecht, 1978.

Goodich, Michael. "The Contours of Female Piety in Later Medieval Hagiography." *Church History* 50 (1981): 20–32.

Gössmann, Elisabeth. "Das Menschenbild der Hildegard von Bingen und Elisabeth von Schönau vor dem Hintergrund der frühscholastischen Anthropologie." In *Frauenmystik im Mittelalter*, edited by Peter Dinzelbacher and Dieter R. Bauer, 24–47. Ostfildern: Schwabenverlag, 1985.

Graef, Hilda. *Mary: A History of Doctrine and Devotion*. London: Sheed and Ward, 1963.

Grotefend, Hermann. *Zeitrechnung des deutschen Mittelalters und der Neuzeit*. 1892–98. Reprint. Aalen: Scientia Verlag, 1984.

Grundmann, Herbert. "Zur Vita S. Gerlaci Eremitae." *Deutsches Archiv für Erforschung des Mittelalters* 18 (1962): 539–54. Reprint. Grundmann, *Ausgewählte Aufsätze*, Vol. 1, 181–200. Schriften der Monumenta Germaniae Historica, Band 25.1. Stuttgart: Anton Hiersemann, 1976.

Gurevich, A. Ja. "Popular and Scholarly Medieval Cultural Traditions: Notes in the Margin of Jacques LeGoff's Book." *Journal of Medieval History* 9 (1983): 71–90.

Hamburger, Jeffrey M. "The Visual and the Visionary: The Image in Late Medieval Monastic Devotions." *Viator* 20 (1989): 161–82.

Hanning, Robert. *The Individual in Twelfth-Century Romance*. New Haven, CT: Yale University Press, 1977.

Haverkamp, Alfred. "Tenxwind von Andernach und Hildegard von Bingen: Zwei

'Weltanschauungen' in der Mitte des 12. Jahrhunderts." In *Institutionen, Kultur und Gesellschaft im Mittelalter: Festschrift für Josef Fleckenstein zu seinem 65 Geburtstag*, edited by Lutz Fenske, Werner Rösner, and Thomas Zotz, 515–48. Sigmaringen: Jan Thornbecke Verlag, 1984.

Hilpisch, Stephen. "Erzbischof Hillin von Trier, 1152–69." *Archiv für mittelrheinische Kirchengeschichte* 7 (1955): 9–21.

Holdsworth, C. J. "Visions and Visionaries in the Middle Ages." *History* 48 (1963): 141–53.

Holweck, Frederick G. "Assumption." In *The Catholic Encyclopedia*, edited by Charles G. Herbermann, et al. New York: Robert Appleton Company, 1907.

———. *Fasti Mariani, sive Calendarium Festorum Sanctae Mariae Virginis Deiparae.* Freiburg: Herder, 1892.

Jaffé, Phillippus. *Regesta Pontificum Romanorum ab condita ecclesia ad annum post christum natum MCXCVIII.* 2d ed., Vol. 2, edited by S. Loewenfeld. Graz: Akademische Druck- und Verlag, 1956.

Johnson, Lynn Staley. "The Trope of the Scribe and the Question of Literary Authority in the Works of Julian of Norwich and Margery Kempe." *Speculum* 66 (1991): 820–38.

Johnson, Penelope D. *Equal in Monastic Profession: Religious Women in Medieval France.* Chicago, IL: The University of Chicago Press, 1991.

Jugie, Martin. *La Mort et l'assomption de la sainte vierge: Etude historico-doctrinale.* Vatican: Bibliotheca Apostolica Vaticana, 1944.

Kamlah, Wilhelm. *Apokalypse und Geschichtstheologie: Die mittlelalterliche Auslegung der Apokalyse vor Joachim von Fiore.* Historische Studien, Heft 285. Berlin: Dr. Emil Ebering, 1935.

Kennan, Elizabeth. "The 'De Consideratione' of St. Bernard of Clairvaux and the Papacy in the Mid-Twelfth Century: A Review of Scholarship." *Traditio* 23 (1967): 73–115.

Kerby-Fulton, Kathryn. *Reformist Apocalypticism and "Piers Plowman."* Cambridge Studies in Medieval Literature, vol. 7. Cambridge: Cambridge University Press, 1990.

Kerby-Fulton, Kathryn, and Dyan Elliott. "Self-Image and the Visionary Role in Two Letters from the Correspondence of Elizabeth of Schönau and Hildegard of Bingen." *Vox Benedictina* 2 (1985): 204–23.

Keuffer, Max. *Beschreibendes Verzeichnis der Handschriften der Stadtbibliothek zu Trier.* 10 vols. Trier: Kommissionsverlag der Fr. Lintz'schen Buchhandlung, 1856–1902.

Kieckhefer, Richard. *Unquiet Souls: Fourteenth-Century Saints and Their Religious Milieu.* Chicago, IL: University of Chicago Press, 1984.

Klinkenberg, Joseph. "Studien zur Geschichte der Kölner Märterinnen." *Jahrbücher des Vereins von Alterthumsfreunden im Rheinlande* 93 (1892): 150–63.

Knipping, Richard. *Die Regesten des Erzbischöfe von Köln im Mittelalter.* Vol. 2. Bonn: P. Hanstein's Verlag, 1901.

Koch, Karl, and Eduard Hegel. *Die Vita des Prämonstratensers Hermann Joseph von Steinfeld: Ein Betrag zur Hagiographie und zur Frömmigkeitsgeschichte des Hochmittelalters.* Colonia Sacra, Band 3. Köln: Balduin Pick Verlag, 1958.

Köster, Kurt. "Ekbert von Schönau." *Die deutscher Literatur des Mittelalters: Verfasserlexikon*. 2d ed. Berlin: Walter de Gruyter, 1980.

———. "Elisabeth von Schönau: Werk und Wirkung im Spiegel der mittelalterlichen handschriftlichen Überlieferung." *Archiv für mittelrheinische Kirchengeschichte* 3 (1951): 243–315.

———. "Das visionäre Werk Elisabeths von Schönau: Studien zu Entstehung, Überlieferung und Wirkung in der mittelalterlichen Welt." *Archiv für mittelrheinische Kirchengeschichte* 4 (1952): 79–119.

Kottje, Raymund. "Klosterbibliotheken und monastische Kultur in der zweiten Hälfte des 11. Jahrhunderts." *Zeitschrift für Kirchengeschichte* 80, 2 (1969): 145–62.

Krämer, Sigrid. *Handschriftenerbe des deutschen Mittelalters*. Mittelalterliche Bibliothekskataloge Deutschlands und der Schweiz, Ergänzungsband 1. Munich: C. H. Beck'sche Verlagsbuchhandlung, 1989.

Küsters, Urban. *Der verschlossene Garten: Volkssprachliche Hohelied-Auslegung und monastische Lebensform im 12. Jahrhundert*. Studia humaniora: Düsseldorfer Studien zu Mittelalter und Renaissance, Band 2. Düsseldorf: Droste Verlag, 1985.

Lawrence, C. H. *Medieval Monasticism: Forms of Religious Life in Western Europe*. 2d ed. London: Longman, 1989.

Leclercq, Jean. *The Love of Learning and the Desire for God: A Study of Monastic Culture*. 2d ed. Translated by Catharine Misrahi. New York: Fordham University Press, 1974.

———. *Monks on Marriage: A Twelfth-Century View*. New York: Seabury Press, 1982.

LeGoff, Jacques. *The Birth of Purgatory*. Translated by Arthur Goldhammer. Chicago, IL: University of Chicago Press, 1984.

Lerner, Robert E. "Medieval Prophecy and Religious Dissent." *Past and Present* 72 (1976): 3–24.

———. *The Powers of Prophecy: The Cedar of Lebanon Vision from the Mongol Onslaught to the Dawn of the Enlightenment*. Berkeley: University of California Press, 1983.

Levison, Wilhelm. "Das Werden der Ursula-Legende." *Bonner Jahrbücher* 132 (1927): 1–164.

Lewis, Gertrud Jaron. "Christus als Frau: Eine Vision Elisabeths von Schönau." *Jahrbuch für Internationale Germanistik* 15 (1983): 70–80.

Lex, Barbara W. "The Neurobiology of Ritual Trance." In *The Spectrum of Ritual: A Biogenetic Analysis*, edited by Eugene G. D'Aquili et al., 117–51. New York: Columbia University Press, 1979.

Lexikon der Christlichen Ikonographie, edited by Engelbert Kirschbaum. Rome: Herder, 1968–.

Leyser, Henrietta. *Hermits and the New Monasticism: A Study of Religious Communities in Western Europe 1000–1150*. New York: St. Martin's Press, 1984.

Little, Lester K. "Intellectual Training and Attitudes toward Reform, 1075–1150." In *Pierre Abélard, Pierre le Vénérable: Les Courants philosophiques, littéraires et artistiques en Occident au milieu du XIIe siècle*, 235–54. Colloques Internationaux du Centre National de la Recherche Scientifique, No. 546. Paris: Editions du Centre National de la Recherche Scientifique, 1975.

Longère, Jean. *La Prédication médiévale*. Paris: Etudes Augustiniennes, 1983.

Loos, Josef. "Hildegard von Bingen und Elisabeth von Schönau." In *Hildegard von Bingen, 1179–1979: Festschrift zum 800. Todestag der Heiligen*, edited by Anton Ph. Brück, 263–72. Mainz: Selbstverlag der Gesellschaft für Mittelrheinische Kirchengeschichte, 1979.

Manselli, Raoul. "Amicizia spirituale ed adzione pastorale nella Germania del sec. XII: Ildegarde di Bingen, Elisabetta ed Eckberto di Schönau contro l'eresia Catara." In *Studi in onore di Alberto Pincherle, Studi e matierali di storia delle religioni* 38 (1967): 302–13.

————. "Ecberto di Schönau e l'eresia Catara in Germania alla metà del secolo XII." In *Arte e storia: Studi in onore di Leonello Vincenti*, 311–48. Torino: Giappichelli Editore, 1965.

Marx, J. *Handschriftenverzeichnis der Seminar-Bibliothek zu Trier*. Veröffentlichungen der Gesellschaft für Trierische Geschichte und Denkmalpflege, 4. Trier: Verlag der Fr. Lintzschen Buchhandlung, 1912.

Marx, Jakob. *Geschichte des Erzstifts Trier als Kurfürstenten und Erzdiözese von den ältesten Zeiten bis zum Jahre 1816*. 1860. Reprint. Aalen: Scientia Verlag, 1970.

McDonnell, Ernest W. *The Beguines and the Beghards in Medieval Culture*. New Brunswick, NJ: Rutgers University Press, 1954.

————. "The *Vita Apostolica*: Diversity or Dissent." *Church History* 24 (1955): 15–31.

McGinn, Bernard. "Apocalypticism in the Middle Ages: An Historiographical Sketch." *Medieval Studies* 37 (1975): 252–86.

————. *Visions of the End: Apocalyptic Traditions in the Middle Ages*. Records of Civilization: Sources and Studies, vol. 96. New York: Columbia University Press, 1979.

McGinn, Bernard, John Meyendorff, and Jean LeClercq, eds. *Christian Spirituality: Origins to the Twelfth Century*. World Spirituality: An Encyclopedic History of the Religious Quest, vol. 16. New York: Crossroad Publishing Company, 1987.

McGuire, Brian Patrick. "A Lost Clairvaux Exemplum Collection Found: The *Liber Visionum et Miraculorum* Compiled under Prior John of Clairvaux (1171–79)." *Analecta Cisterciensia* 39 (1983): 26–62.

————. "Purgatory, the Communion of Saints, and Medieval Change." *Viator* 20 (1989): 61–84.

McLaughlin, Eleanor Commo. "Equality of Souls, Inequality of Sexes: Women in Medieval Theology." In *Religion and Sexism: Images of Women in the Jewish and Christian Traditions*, edited by Rosemary Radford Ruether, 213–66. New York: Simon and Schuster, 1974.

McNamara, Jo Ann. "The Need to Give: Suffering and Female Sanctity in the Middle Ages." In *Images of Sainthood in Medieval Europe*, edited by Renate Blumenfeld-Kosinski and Timea Szell, 199–221. Ithaca, NY: Cornell University Press, 1991.

McNamara, Jo Ann, and Suzanne F. Wemple. "Sanctity and Power: The Dual Pursuit of Medieval Women." In *Becoming Visible: Women in European His-*

tory, edited by R. Bridenthal and C. Koonz, 90–118. Boston, MA: Houghton Mifflin Company, 1977.

Milz, Joseph. *Studien zur mittelalterlichen Wirtschafts- und Verfassungsgeschichte der Abtei Deutz*. Veröffentlichungen des Kölnischen Geschichtsvereins e.V. 30. Köln: Verlag der Buchhandlung H. Wamper GMBH, 1970.

Minnis, A. J. *Medieval Theory of Authorship: Scholastic Literary Attitudes in the Later Middle Ages*. London: Scolar Press, 1984.

Montebaur, Josef. *Studien zur Geschichte der Bibliothek der Abtei St. Eucharius-Matthias zu Trier*. Römische Quartalschrift für christliche Altertumskunde und für Kirchengeschichte, 26. Freiburg: Herder and Co. G.M.B.H. Verlagsbuchhandlung, 1931.

Moore, R. I. *The Origins of European Dissent*. New York: St. Martin's Press, 1977.

Morris, Colin. *The Discovery of the Individual, 1050–1200*. New York: Harper and Row, 1972.

Munz, Peter. *Frederick Barbarossa: A Study in Medieval Politics*. Ithaca, NY: Cornell University Press, 1969.

Napier, B. D. "Prophet." *The Interpreter's Dictionary of the Bible*, edited by George Arthur Buttrick. Nashville, TN: Abingdon Press, 1962.

Nebe, A. "Die heilige Elisabeth und Egbert von Schönau." *Annalen des Vereins für Nassauische Alterthumskunde und Geschichtsforschung* 8 (1866): 157–292.

Newman, Barbara. "Hildegard of Bingen: Visions and Validation." *Church History* 54 (1985): 163–75.

———. *Sister of Wisdom: St. Hildegard's Theology of the Feminine*. Berkeley: University of California Press, 1987.

Nichols, John A., and Lillian Thomas Shank, eds. *Medieval Religious Women*. 2 vols. Kalamazoo, MI: Cistercian Publications, 1984–87.

Oehl, Wilhelm. *Deutsche Mystikerbriefe des Mittelalters, 1100–1550*. München: Georg Müller, 1931.

Omont, H. "Bibliothèque Nationale MS. nouv. acq. lat. 760." *Notices et extraits des manuscrits de la Bibliothèque Nationale* 38 (1903): 341–96.

Ornstein, Robert E. "Two Sides of the Brain." In *Understanding Mysticism*, edited by Richard Woods, 270–85. Garden City, NY: Doubleday and Company, Inc., 1980.

Paas, Theodor. "Ein Steinfelder Altarbild als Zeuge der Potentinus-Legende." *Annalen des Historischen Vereins für den Niederrhein* 102 (1918): 129–39.

Patch, Howard Rollin. *The Other World According to Descriptions in Medieval Literature*. Cambridge, MA: Harvard University Press, 1950.

Pelikan, Jaroslav. *The Growth of Medieval Theology (600–1300)*. Vol. 3 of *The Christian Tradition: A History of the Development of Doctrine*. Chicago, IL: University of Chicago Press, 1978.

Peters, Ursula. "Frauenliteratur im Mittelalter? Überlegungen zur Trobairitzpoesie, zur Frauenmystik und zur feministischen Literaturbetrachtung." *Germanisch-Romanische Monatsschrift*, n.s. 38 (1988): 35–56.

———. *Religiöse Erfahrung als literarisches Faktum: Zur Vorgeschichte und Genese frauenmystischer Texte des 13. und 14. Jahrhunderts*. Hermaea Germanistische Forschungen, Neue Folge, Band 56. Tübingen: Max Niemeyer Verlag, 1988.

Principe, Walter H. "Monastic, Episcopal and Apologetic Theology of the Papacy, 1150–1250." In *The Religious Roles of the Papacy: Ideals and Realities, 1150–1300*, edited by Christopher Ryan, 117–80. Papers in Mediaeval Studies 8. Toronto: Pontifical Institute of Mediaeval Studies, 1989.

Quentin, Henri. *Les Martyrologes historiques du Moyen Age: Etude sur la Formation du Martyrologe Romain*. Paris, 1908. Reprint. Aalen: Scientia Verlag, 1969.

Redmond, R. X. "Prophecy, Theology of." *New Catholic Encyclopedia*. New York: McGraw-Hill Book Company, 1967.

Reeves, Marjorie. *The Influence of Prophecy in the Later Middle Ages: A Study in Joachimism*. Oxford: Clarendon Press, 1969.

Religious Dissent in the Middle Ages. Edited by Jeffrey B. Russell. New York: John Wiley and Sons, 1971.

Rice, Eugene F., Jr. "Jacques Lefèvre d'Etaples and the Medieval Christian Mystics." In *Florilegium Historiale: Essays Presented to Wallace K. Ferguson*, edited by J. G. Rowe and W. H. Stockdale, 90–124. Toronto: University of Toronto Press, 1971.

Ripberger, Albert. *Der Pseudo-Hieronymus-Brief IX "Cogitis Me": Ein erster marianischer Traktat des Mittelalters von Paschasius Radbert*. Spigilegium Friburgense, vol. 9. Freiburg: Universitätsverlag, 1962.

Rissel, Hiltrud. "Hildegard von Bingen an Elisabeth von St. Thomas an der Kyll: Die heilige Hildegard und die frühesten deutschen Zisterzienserinnen," *Cîteaux* 41 (1990): 5–44.

Robinson, I. S. *Authority and Resistance in the Investiture Contest: The Polemical Literature of the Late Eleventh Century*. Manchester: Manchester University Press, 1978.

Roisin, Simone. "L'efflorescence cistercienne et le courant féminin de piété au XIIIe siècle." *Revue d'histoire ecclésiastique* 39 (1943): 342–78.

———. *L'hagiographie cistercienne dans le diocèse de Liège au XIIIe siècle*. Université de Louvain, Recueil de travaux d'histoire et de philologie, 3. Sér., Fasc. 27. Louvain: Bibliothèque de l'Université, 1947.

Roth, F. W. E. "Die Handschriften der ehemaligen Benedictiner- und Cistercienserklöster Nassaus in der k. Landesbibliothek zu Wiesbaden." *Studien und Mitteilungen aus dem Benedictiner- und Cistercienser-Orden* 6. 2 (1886): 172–80.

Russell, Jeffrey Burton. *Dissent and Reform in the Early Middle Ages*. Berkeley: University of California Press, 1965.

Schaffer, Christa. *Koimesis, Der Heimgang Mariens: Das Entschlafungsbild in seiner Abhängigkeit von Legende und Theologie*. Studia Patristica et Liturgica, 15. Regensburg: Kommissionsverlag Friedrich Pustet, 1985.

Schönauer Elisabeth Jubiläum 1965: Festschrift anlässlich des achthundertjährigen Todestages der heiligen Elisabeth von Schönau. Prämonstratenser-Chorherrenstift Tepl in Kloster Schönau. Limburg: Pallottiner Druckerei, 1965.

Schrader, Marianna. "Hildegarde de Bingen." *Dictionnaire de spiritualité, ascétique et mystique*. Paris: Beauchesne, 1932–.

Schrader, Marianna, and Adelgundis Führkötter. *Die Echtheit des Schrifttums der heiligen Hildegard von Bingen: Quellenkritische Untersuchungen*. Beihefte zum Archiv für Kulturgeschichte, Heft 6. Köln-Graz: Böhlau Verlag, 1956.

Schreiner, Klaus. "'Discrimen veri ac falsi': Ansätze und Formen der Kritik in her Heiligen- und Reliquenverehrung des Mittelalters." *Archiv für Kulturgeschichte* 48 (1966): 1–53.

Schulenburg, Jane Tibbetts. "Sexism and the Celestial Gynaeceum—from 500-1200." *Journal of Medieval History* 4 (1978): 117–33.

Sheppard, Gerald T., and William E. Herbrechtsmeier. "Prophecy: An Overview." *The Encyclopedia of Religion*, edited by Mircea Eliade. New York: Macmillan, 1987.

Silverstein, Theodore. *Visio Sancti Pauli: The History of the Apocalypse in Latin Together with Nine Texts*. London: Christophers, 1935.

Somerville, Robert. *Pope Alexander III and the Council of Tours (1163): A Study of Ecclesiastical Politics and Institutions in the Twelfth Century*. Berkeley: University of California Press, 1977.

Southern, R. W. *The Making of the Middle Ages*. New Haven, CT: Yale University Press, 1953.

———. *St. Anselm and His Biographer: A Study of Monastic Life and Thought, 1059–c.1130*. Cambridge: Cambridge University Press, 1963.

Spieß, Emil Jakob. *Ein Zeuge mittelalterlicher Mystik in der Schweiz*. Basle: Buchdruckerei und Verlag Dr. C. Weder Rorschach, 1935.

Stacpoole, A. "Hugh of Cluny and the Hildebrandine Miracle Tradition." *Revue Bénédictine* 77 (1967): 341–63.

Stock, Brian. *The Implications of Literacy: Written Language and Models of Interpretation in the Eleventh and Twelfth Centuries*. Princeton, NJ: Princeton University Press, 1983.

Strait, Paul. *Cologne in the Twelfth Century*. Gainesville: University Presses of Florida, 1974.

Stroll, Mary. *The Jewish Pope: Ideology and Politics in the Papal Schism of 1130*. Leiden: E. J. Brill, 1987.

Tervarent, Guy de. *La Légende de Sainte Ursule dans la littérature et l'art du moyen âge*. 2 vols. Paris: Les Editions G. Van Oest, 1931.

Thouzellier, Ch. "Heresie et Croisade au XIIe siècle." *Revue d'histoire ecclésiastique* 49 (1954): 855–72.

Turner, N. "Esdras, Books of." *The Interpreter's Dictionary of the Bible*, edited by George Arthur Buttrick. Nashville, TN: Abingdon Press, 1962.

Unterkircher, Franz. "Zwei Vers-Viten des 13 Jhs. (Hl. Ursula und Hl. Euphrosyne) in der Wiener Handschrift Cod. 488." *Analecta Bollandiana* 88: 3–4 (1970): 301–16.

Van Acker, L. "Der Briefwechsel zwischen Elisabeth von Schönau und Hildegard von Bingen." *Instrumenta Patristica* 23 (1991): 409–17.

Van Engen, John H. "The Christian Middle Ages as an Historiographical Problem." *American Historical Review* 91 (1986): 519–52.

———. "The 'Crisis of Cenobitism' Reconsidered: Benedictine Monasticism in the Years 1050–1150." *Speculum* 61 (1986): 269–304.

———. *Rupert of Deutz*. Berkeley: University of California Press, 1983.

Vauchez, André. *La sainteté en Occident aux derniers siècles du moyen âge d'après les procès de canonisation et les documents hagiographiques*. Bibliothèque des Ecoles

Français d'Athènes et de Rome, vol. 241. Rome: Ecole Française de Rome, 1981.

Vennebusch, Joachim, *Die Theologischen Handschriften der Stadtarchiv Köln*. 4 vols. Mittheilungen aus dem Stadtarchiv von Köln. Köln: Böhlau-Verlag, 1976–86.

Verdon, Jean. "Les moniales dans la France de l'Ouest aux XIe et XIIe siècles: Etude d'histoire sociale." *Cahiers de civilisation médiévale: Xe–XIIe siècles* 19 (1976): 247–64.

Wakefield, Walter L., and Austin P. Evans. *Heresies of the High Middle Ages*. Records of Civilization: Sources and Studies, vol. 81. New York: Columbia University Press, 1969.

Wattenbach, Wilhelm, and Franz-Josef Schmale. *Deutschlands Geschichtsquellen im Mittelalter: Vom Tode Kaiser Heinrichs V. bis zum Ende des Interregnum*. Darmstadt: Wissenschaftliche Buchgesellschaft, 1976.

Wiechert, Friedrich. "Die Reliquien der Klosterkirche zu Schönau." *Archiv für mittelrheinische Kirchengeschichte* 17 (1965): 262–72.

Weiers, Hans Josef. *Studien zur Geschichte des Bistums Münster im Mittelalter*. Kölner Schriften zu Geschichte und Kultur, Band 8. Köln: DME-Verlag, 1984.

Wemple, Suzanne. Review of *Frauen im Mittelalter*, by Edith Ennen. *Speculum* 61 (1986): 924.

White, Haydon V. "The Gregorian Ideal and Saint Bernard of Clairvaux." *Journal of the History of Ideas* 21 (1960): 321–48.

Wood, Charles T. "The Doctors' Dilemma: Sin, Salvation, and the Menstrual Cycle in Medieval Thought." *Speculum* 56 (1981): 710–27.

Zaleski, Carol. *Otherworld Journeys: Accounts of Near-Death Experience in Medieval and Modern Times*. New York: Oxford University Press, 1987.

Zedler, Gottfried. *Die Handschriften des Nassauischen Landesbibliothek zu Wiesbaden*. Zentralblatt für Bibliothekswesen, Beiheft 63. Leipzig: Otto Harrassowitz, 1931.

Zehnder, Frank Günter. *Sankt Ursula: Legende, Verehung, Bilderwelt*. Cologne: Wienand Verlag, 1985.

Index

University of Pennsylvania Press
MIDDLE AGES SERIES
EDWARD PETERS, *General Editor*

Books in the series that are out of print are marked with an asterisk.

F. R. P. Akehurst, trans. *The* Coutumes de Beauvaisis *of Philippe de Beaumanoir.* 1992

Peter L. Allen. *The Art of Love: Amatory Fiction from Ovid to the* Romance of the Rose. 1992

David Anderson. *Before the Knight's Tale: Imitation of Classical Epic in Boccaccio's* Teseida. 1988

Benjamin Arnold. *Count and Bishop in Medieval Germany: A Study of Regional Power, 1100–1350.* 1991

Mark C. Bartusis. *The Late Byzantine Army: Arms and Society, 1204–1453.* 1992

J. M. W. Bean. *From Lord to Patron: Lordship in Late Medieval England.* 1990

Uta-Renate Blumenthal. *The Investiture Controversy: Church and Monarchy from the Ninth to the Twelfth Century.* 1988

Daniel Bornstein, trans. *Dino Compagni's Chronicle of Florence.* 1986

Betsy Bowden. *Chaucer Aloud: The Varieties of Textual Interpretation.* 1987

James William Brodman. *Ransoming Captives in Crusader Spain: The Order of Merced on the Christian-Islamic Frontier.* 1986

Kevin Brownlee and Sylvia Huot, eds. *Rethinking the* Romance of the Rose: *Text, Image, Reception.* 1992

Otto Brunner (Howard Kaminsky and James Van Horn Melton, eds. and trans.). Land *and Lordship: Structures of Governance in Medieval Austria.* 1992

Robert I. Burns, S.J., ed. *Emperor of Culture: Alfonso X the Learned of Castile and His Thirteenth-Century Renaissance.* 1990

David Burr. *Olivi and Franciscan Poverty: The Origins of the* Usus Pauper *Controversy.* 1989

Thomas Cable. *The English Alliterative Tradition.* 1991

Leonard Cantor, ed. *The English Medieval Landscape.* 1982*

Anthony K. Cassell and Victoria Kirkham, eds. and trans. *Diana's Hunt. Caccia di Diana. Boccaccio's First Fiction.* 1991

Brigitte Cazelles. *The Lady as Saint: A Collection of French Hagiographic Romances of the Thirteenth Century.* 1991

Willene B. Clark and Meradith T. McMunn, eds. *Beasts and Birds of the Middle Ages: The Bestiary and Its Legacy.* 1989

G. G. Coulton. *From St. Francis to Dante: Translations from the Chronicle of the Franciscan Salimbene (1221–1288).* 1972*

Richard C. Dales. *The Scientific Achievement of the Middle Ages.* 1973

Charles T. Davis. *Dante's Italy and Other Essays*. 1984

George T. Dennis, trans. *Maurice's Strategikon: Handbook of Byzantine Military Strategy*. 1984*

Katherine Fischer Drew, trans. *The Burgundian Code: The Book of Constitutions or Law of Gundobad and Additional Enactments*. 1972

Katherine Fischer Drew, trans. *The Laws of the Salian Franks*. 1991

Katherine Fischer Drew, trans. *The Lombard Laws*. 1973

Nancy Edwards. *The Archaeology of Early Medieval Ireland*. 1990

Margaret J. Ehrhart. *The Judgment of the Trojan Prince Paris in Medieval Literature*. 1987

Richard K. Emmerson and Ronald B. Herzman. *The Apocalyptic Imagination in Medieval Literature*. 1992

R. D. Fulk. *A History of Old English Meter*. 1992

Patrick J. Geary. *Aristocracy in Provence: The Rhône Basin at the Dawn of the Carolingian Age*. 1985

Julius Goebel, Jr. *Felony and Misdemeanor: A Study in the History of Criminal Law*. 1976*

Peter Heath. *Allegory and Philosophy in Avicenna (Ibn Sînâ), With a Translation of the Book of the Prophet Muḥammad's Ascent to Heaven*. 1992

Avril Henry, ed. *The Mirour of Mans Saluacioune: A Middle English Translation of Speculum Humanae Salvationis*. 1987

J. N. Hillgarth, ed. *Christianity and Paganism, 350–750: The Conversion of Western Europe*. 1986

Richard C. Hoffmann. *Land, Liberties, and Lordship in a Late Medieval Countryside: Agrarian Structures and Change in the Duchy of Wrocław*. 1990

Robert Hollander. *Boccaccio's Last Fiction: "Il Corbaccio."* 1988

Edward B. Irving, Jr. *Rereading* Beowulf. 1989

C. Stephen Jaeger. *The Origins of Courtliness: Civilizing Trends and the Formation of Courtly Ideals, 939–1210*. 1985

William Chester Jordan. *The French Monarchy and the Jews: From Philip Augustus to the Last Capetians*. 1989

William Chester Jordan. *From Servitude to Freedom: Manumission in the Sénonais in the Thirteenth Century*. 1986

Ellen E. Kittell. *From* Ad Hoc *to Routine: A Case Study in Medieval Bureaucracy*. 1991

Alan C. Kors and Edward Peters, eds. *Witchcraft in Europe, 1100–1700: A Documentary History*. 1972

Barbara M. Kreutz. *Before the Normans: Southern Italy in the Ninth and Tenth Centuries*. 1992

Jeanne Krochalis and Edward Peters, ed. and trans. *The World of Piers Plowman*. 1975

E. Ann Matter. *The Voice of My Beloved: The Song of Songs in Western Medieval Christianity*. 1990

María Rosa Menocal. *The Arabic Role in Medieval Literary History*. 1987

A. J. Minnis. *Medieval Theory of Authorship*. 1988

Lawrence Nees. *A Tainted Mantle: Hercules and the Classical Tradition at the Carolingian Court*. 1991

Lynn H. Nelson, trans. *The Chronicle of San Juan de la Peña: A Fourteenth-Century Official History of the Crown of Aragon*. 1991

Charlotte A. Newman. *The Anglo-Norman Nobility in the Reign of Henry I: The Second Generation*. 1988

Thomas F. X. Noble. *The Republic of St. Peter: The Birth of the Papal State, 680–825*. 1984

Joseph F. O'Callaghan. *The Cortes of Castile-León, 1188–1350*. 1989

William D. Paden, ed. *The Voice of the Trobairitz: Perspectives on the Women Troubadours*. 1989

Kenneth Pennington. *Pope and Bishops: The Papal Monarchy in the Twelfth and Thirteenth Centuries*. 1984*

Edward Peters. *The Magician, the Witch, and the Law*. 1982

Edward Peters, ed. *Christian Society and the Crusades, 1198–1229*. Sources in Translation, including The Capture of Damietta by Oliver of Paderborn. 1971

Edward Peters, ed. *The First Crusade: The Chronicle of Fulcher of Chartres and Other Source Materials*. 1971

Edward Peters, ed. *Heresy and Authority in Medieval Europe*. 1980

Edward Peters, ed. *Monks, Bishops, and Pagans: Christian Culture in Gaul and Italy, 500–700*. 1975*

Clifford Peterson. *Saint Erkenwald*. 1977*

James M. Powell. *Albertanus of Brescia: The Pursuit of Happiness in the Early Thirteenth Century*. 1992

James M. Powell. *Anatomy of a Crusade, 1213–1221*. 1986

Donald E. Queller. *The Fourth Crusade: The Conquest of Constantinople, 1201–1204*. 1977*

Joel T. Rosenthal. *Patriarchy and Families of Privilege in Fifteenth-Century England*. 1991

Michael Resler, trans. *EREC by Hartmann von Aue*. 1987

Pierre Riché (Jo Ann McNamara, trans.). *Daily Life in the World of Charlemagne*. 1978

Jonathan Riley-Smith. *The First Crusade and the Idea of Crusading*. 1986

Barbara H. Rosenwein. *Rhinoceros Bound: Cluny in the Tenth Century*. 1982

Steven D. Sargent, ed. and trans. *On the Threshold of Exact Science: Selected Writings of Anneliese Maier on Late Medieval Natural Philosophy*. 1982

Robert Somerville and Kenneth Pennington, eds. *Law, Church, and Society: Essays in Honor of Stephan Kuttner*. 1977*

Sarah Stanbury. *Seeing the Gawain-Poet: Description and the Act of Perception*. 1992

Susan Mosher Stuard. *A State of Deference: Ragusa/Dubrovnik in the Medieval Centuries*. 1992

Susan Mosher Stuard, ed. *Women in Medieval History and Historiography*. 1987

Susan Mosher Stuard, ed. *Women in Medieval Society*. 1976

Jonathan Sumption. *The Hundred Years War: Trial by Battle*. 1992

Ronald E. Surtz. *The Guitar of God: Gender, Power, and Authority in the Visionary World of Mother Juana de la Cruz (1481–1534)*. 1990

Patricia Terry, trans. *Poems of the Elder Edda*. 1990

Frank Tobin. *Meister Eckhart: Thought and Language*. 1986

Ralph V. Turner. *Men Raised from the Dust: Administrative Service and Upward Mobility in Angevin England*. 1988

Harry Turtledove, trans. *The Chronicle of Theophanes: An English Translation of* anni mundi *6095–6305 (A.D. 602–813)*. 1982

Mary F. Wack. *Lovesickness in the Middle Ages: The* Viaticum *and Its Commentaries*. 1990

Benedicta Ward. *Miracles and the Medieval Mind: Theory, Record, and Event, 1000–1215*. 1982

Suzanne Fonay Wemple. *Women in Frankish Society: Marriage and the Cloister, 500–900*. 1981

This book has been set in Linotron Galliard. Galliard was designed for Mergenthaler in 1978 by Matthew Carter. Galliard retains many of the features of a sixteenth-century typeface cut by Robert Granjon but has some modifications that give it a more contemporary look.

Printed on acid-free paper.